Studies in Mobilities, Literature, and Culture

Series Editors
Marian Aguiar
Department of English
Carnegie Mellon University
Pittsburgh, PA, USA

Charlotte Mathieson
University of Surrey
Guildford, UK

Lynne Pearce
Department of English & Creative Writing
Lancaster University
Lancaster, UK

This series represents an exciting new publishing opportunity for scholars working at the intersection of literary, cultural, and mobilities research. The editors welcome proposals that engage with movement of all kinds – ranging from the global and transnational to the local and the everyday. The series is particularly concerned with examining the material means and structures of movement, as well as the infrastructures that surround such movement, with a focus on transport, travel, postcolonialism, and/ or embodiment. While we expect many titles from literary scholars who draw upon research originating in cultural geography and/or sociology in order to gain valuable new insights into literary and cultural texts, proposals are equally welcome from scholars working in the social sciences who make use of literary and cultural texts in their theorizing. The series invites monographs that engage with textual materials of all kinds – i.e., film, photography, digital media, and the visual arts, as well as fiction, poetry, and other literary forms – and projects engaging with non-western literatures and cultures are especially welcome.

More information about this series at
http://www.palgrave.com/gp/series/15385

Emma Short

Mobility and the Hotel in Modern Literature

Passing Through

Emma Short
Durham University
Durham, UK

Studies in Mobilities, Literature, and Culture
ISBN 978-3-030-22128-7   ISBN 978-3-030-22129-4   (eBook)
https://doi.org/10.1007/978-3-030-22129-4

This Palgrave Macmillan imprint is published by the registered company Springer Nature
Switzerland AG
The registered company address is: Gewerbestrasse 11, 6330 Cham, Switzerland

For Dylan

ACKNOWLEDGEMENTS

Firstly, I would like to thank Dr Stacy Gillis for her supervision of my original doctoral work on the hotel, and for the unfailing support, guidance, and friendship she has given so unquestioningly since then. Particularly heartfelt thanks go also to Dr Katherine Cooper for reading and providing consistently insightful feedback on chapter drafts, and for cheering me on.

I am also very grateful to the School of English Literature, Language and Linguistics at Newcastle University for their support, and I thank in particular Dr Ruth Connolly for her invaluable comments and encouragement. I would also like to thank my anonymous reader for their incredibly helpful support and guidance, and the series editors and my editors at Palgrave for their support and patience throughout this project. I am also grateful to the Arts and Humanities Research Council for funding the PhD research that formed the initial basis of this work. For the laughter and pep talks, I would like to thank Hannah Jane Walker, and I am forever grateful to Susan and Michael Ryan for all their kindness, help, and support. For their unfailing love and belief in me, and for everything they have done to help, I thank Bill Short, Jane O'Hare, Margaret O'Hare, Tim Bowles, and my brothers Ben, Thom, and Dom. Finally, I want to thank Mark for propping me up when I needed it most, and Dylan, for keeping me company.

CONTENTS

CHAPTER 1

Introduction: Modern Mobilities in the Hotel

Among the proliferation of spaces of mobility in nineteenth- and early-twentieth-century literature, the hotel stands out as one of the most complex, contradictory, and compelling. Characterised by impermanence in the constant coming and going of its guests and yet underpinned by the routine and order of the work of the hotel staff, it is a space that at once exemplifies the flux and chaos of modernity in the early twentieth century, as well as the rationalisation of space that was taking place during the same period. It encapsulates what Tim Cresswell refers to as the 'tension between a spatializing ordering principle seen by many to be central to modernity, and sense of fluidity and mobility emphasized by others' (2006, p. 16). From the Ormond Hotel in James Joyce's *Ulysses* (1922) to the eponymous Grand Babylon Hotel in Arnold Bennett's 1902 novel, the hotel features heavily across the literatures of this period and offers crucial insight into the shifting tensions and ideologies of modernity. This book, the first account of the hotel in British fiction, interrogates this tension through a consideration of the diverse ways in which the hotel functions in early-twentieth-century literature. The hotel offers itself as the ideal literary setting, enabling authors to bring disparate characters together, and often acting as a microcosm of society as a whole. All of this is thanks to the mobility by which the hotel is necessarily characterised and defined.

In order to fully interrogate the relationship between the hotel and mobility, or indeed, to understand the hotel as a space of mobility, it is first necessary to clarify what we mean when we refer to mobility. For while the

© The Author(s) 2019
E. Short, *Mobility and the Hotel in Modern Literature*,
Studies in Mobilities, Literature, and Culture,
https://doi.org/10.1007/978-3-030-22129-4_1

1

two terms are often conflated or used seemingly interchangeably, it is crucial to recognise that mobility does not simply equate to movement. Indeed, mobility is more than movement—as Cresswell argues, movement might well be better understood as 'abstracted mobility (mobility abstracted from contexts of power)' (2006, p. 2). Where movement represents the basic act of getting from one destination to another, mobility is always implicated in relations and practices of power. Mobility is, as Cresswell summarises, 'socially produced motion' (2006, p. 3). Following Cresswell, mobility is defined by Emma Bond as 'movement that carries meaning' (2018, p. 4), and similarly, by Peter Adey, as 'movement imbued with meaning' (2010, p. 33). Adey's use of the word 'imbued' here, however, suggests a definition that is attuned to the complexity of the connection between mobility and meaning, implying as it does a *context* in which meaning is conferred upon movement. This is key, as according to Adey, 'the way [mobility] is given meaning is dependent upon the context in which it occurs and who decides upon the significance it is given' (2010, p. 37). The immediate context of the mobilities discussed in this book is, of course, the hotel, but just as important, if not more so, is the wider context of modernity, or more specifically, of British society and culture in the nineteenth and early twentieth centuries.

The hotel encourages, enables, and engenders a reconsideration of mobilities in western modernity, of how and why they are produced, and by whom or by what they come to be imbued with meaning. Mobilities have, of course, always existed, but they arguably come into sharper focus in that period of flux and flow in the nineteenth and early twentieth centuries that is widely defined as modernity. As Cresswell argues, 'mobility is central to what it is to be modern', and indeed the links between mobility and modernity are manifold. They are to be found, for example, in that aforementioned 'tension between a spatialized ordering principle [...] and sense of fluidity and mobility' that frequently underpins understandings of modernity (2006, p. 16). On a more fundamental level, these connections can be detected in the relationship to time and space that is so intrinsic to both mobility and modernity. In his seminal work on modernity, Marshall Berman defines it, for example, as 'a mode of vital experience—experience', first and foremost, 'of space and time' (2010 [1982], p. 15). Building upon Berman's understanding of modernity, David Harvey argues that it is a period that can be further characterised by the development of 'time-space compression', a phenomenon of capitalist societies that involves a 'speed-up in the pace of life, while so overcoming spatial barriers that the world sometimes seems to collapse inwards upon us' (1990, p. 240). And mobility is, of course, central to these debates. As Cresswell maintains, '[m]oving people and objects are agents in the production of time and space', and he points out that this understanding of time-space compression is '[p]erhaps the most well-known formulation of this [...]—the effective shrinking of the globe by ever-increasing mobility at speed enabled by innovations in transportation and communications technology' (2006, p. 4). With the growth of the hotel so deeply bound up in the development of new technologies of transport such as the railway, this space is located at the nexus of these changing perceptions of time and space in this period.

The hotel is, then, a truly modern space. The inherent transience of the hotel existence encapsulates the spirit of Zygmunt Bauman's definition of modernity as 'an obsessive march forwards', a march which 'must go on because any place of arrival is but a temporary station' (1991, p. 10). By its very nature, the hotel is just such a 'temporary station', and again, Bauman's interpretation of modernity is saturated with notions of mobility, with the image of modernity's 'march forwards' conjuring up a decidedly bodily mobility at that. Mobility is always, as Bond argues, necessarily 'an embodied mode of movement, [...] one that is imbued with a range of meanings for both the mobile subject and for the people and places that are encountered through that movement' (2018, pp. 2–3). The body is that which enables our mobility—it is, as Elizabeth Grosz points out, 'the very condition of our access to and conception of space' (1994, p. 91)—but, equally, it is also that which is 'brought into being' through mobility (Merleau-Ponty 2002 [1948], p. 117). For Maurice Merleau-Ponty, mobility engenders an unparalleled knowledge and awareness of one's body, and he argues:

> By considering the body in movement, we can see better how it inhabits space (and, moreover, time) because movement is not limited to submitting passively to space and time, it actively assumes them, it takes them up in their basic significance which is obscured in the commonplace of established situations. (2002 [1948], p. 117)

The mobile body, the way in which the body moves through space (and time), thus lies at the heart of phenomenological approaches to embodiment that form the theoretical backbone of this book.

To consider the hotel as a space of mobility is to consider first and foremost the ways in which embodied subjects move through that space. It is through the body that we, as subjects, locate ourselves in and interact with the space surrounding us. Indeed, the very materiality of the body dictates that we cannot avoid interacting, at least in some way, with our location. Sara Ahmed locates the body as '[t]he starting point for orientation [...] the point from which the world unfolds' (2006, p. 8). Edward Casey argues similarly that 'to be embodied is *ipso facto* to assume a particular perspective and position; it is to have not just a point of view but a *place* in which we are situated' (2000, p. 182). Crucially, the places through which we move have a significant effect on us as embodied subjects. As Ahmed suggests, 'bodies do not dwell in spaces that are exterior but rather are shaped by their dwellings and take shape by dwelling' (2006, p. 8). Grosz's theory of corporeal inscription might enable a fuller understanding of the nature of these effects, and what lies behind them. Maintaining that the surface of the body is constantly inscribed and re-inscribed by, among other things clothes, diet, make-up and surroundings, Grosz suggests that it is 'through exercise and habitual patterns of movement, through negotiating its environment whether this be rural or urban [...] [that] the body is more or less marked, constituted as appropriate, or, as the case may be, an inappropriate body for its cultural requirements' (1994, p. 142). We are, in other words, constructed and re-constructed by our environments, by the spaces through which we move; the navigation of uneven rural terrain results, for example, in the strengthening of certain muscles, while the negotiation of flat, urban streets produces a markedly different body. Such effects are not just evident at a purely muscular level—in cities, the body engages with and is influenced by countless cultural elements in a wide range of media. As Grosz acknowledges, the city has become 'the place where the body is representationally reexplored, transformed, contested, reinscribed' (1995, p. 108). Shifting the discussion indoors to the domestic environment, Iris Marion Young observes that the interior of one's home, and the distribution of one's possessions throughout, inscribes the body in a similar way, suggesting that it is not merely the presence of personal belongings in the home, 'but their arrangement in space in a way that supports the body habits and routines of those who dwell there' (2005, p. 139). For Young, subjectivity is constructed and sustained by the unique individual pathways created in the home. Through arguments such as these, the importance of space and place in the construction and constitution of the embodied subject is made strikingly apparent.

It is, however, important to recognise here the mutually constitutive nature of the relationship between the body and space, and to thereby acknowledge the ways in which bodies themselves continually construct and reinscribe the environments they inhabit. Commenting on the capacity of the walker to challenge and physically alter the landscape of the city, Michel de Certeau suggests that

> if it is true that a spatial order organizes an ensemble of possibilities (e.g., by a place in which one can move) and interdictions (e.g., by a wall that prevents one from going further), then the walker actualizes some of these possibilities. In that way, he makes them exist as well as emerge. But he also moves them about and he invents others, since the crossing, drifting away, or improvisation of walking privilege, transform or abandon spatial elements. (1984, p. 98)

In highlighting the radical potential inherent in the act of walking, de Certeau here rescues the embodied subject from the role of passive entity or blank surface inscribed and constructed by the space around her or him, instead affording the subject an active and vital role in the constant reimaginings of that space. Considering the continual expansion of cities, Grosz too notes the way in which 'the body [...] transforms, reinscribes the urban landscape according to its changing (demographic) needs, extending the limits of the city ever towards the countryside that borders it' (1995, pp. 108–9). The space of the home undergoes a similar process of continual revisioning and reconstruction by the bodies that inhabit it, and, as Casey points out, often comes to 'resemble our own material bodies in certain quite basic respects'. Casey adds that this 'resemblance, moreover, is two-way. A dwelling where we reside comes to exist in our own image, but *we*, the residents, also take on certain of *its* properties. *How we are*, our bodily being, reflects how we reside in built places' (1993, p. 120; emphasis in original). These comments return the discussion once more to the reciprocal relationship between the body and space, the way in which both are continuously and unavoidably altered and transformed by each other through mobility.

The bodily mobility theorised in these debates tends, however, to be located either in the public space of the urban or rural landscape, or in the private space of the home. Yet, the hotel does not sit easily in either of these categories. Neither public nor private, but rather a hybrid of both, the hotel exists somewhere in between the space of the city and that of the home, and those theorising the hotel space often highlight its inherent liminality. In his critical analysis of the hotel lobby, for example, Douglas Tallack posits the space as 'a semi-public gateway to private places' (1998, p. 6). Yet, while he is right in locating the lobby as a 'semi-public' space, Tallack's sweeping definition of the interior spaces of the hotel—including the lounge, dining room, and bedrooms—as 'private' fails to capture their true quality. These spaces are not private in the same sense—or, to put it more accurately, to the same extent—that a lounge, dining room or bedroom in a home is private. Nor is it the case, however, that all spaces within the hotel are semi-public in exactly the same way as the lobby. Rather, we might instead conceive of a spectrum of semi-public to semi-private space, along which each location within the hotel can be placed. Spaces such as the hotel dining room, for example, are slightly more public than that of the lounge—due to the increased presence of waiting staff and higher likelihood that non-guests will also be dining there—but slightly less public than the space of the lobby. What does it mean, then, to conceive of mobility in such a space? As I demonstrate throughout this book, the hotel functions as a space of mobility on a number of levels. Firstly, it is a space that is brought into being and reified by the movement of people from one place to another, and is typically (though not always) a point on a journey or a destination in itself. Mobility is also, however, inherent in the hotel at an architectural level. The spaces within the hotel are dictated by and arranged according to the movements of its guests and the staff who serve them. It is therefore a space that is both produced and continually constituted by bodily mobilities.

'This Improbable Place': Locating the Hotel in British Literature and Culture

Though it is often conflated with other types of temporary accommodation such as the boarding house, the pension, the inn, or the motel, the hotel is, as I maintain throughout this book, a very specific and distinct type of space. The boarding house, for example, while seemingly similar in its impermanence, is more closely related to the domestic environment than the hotel, a fact borne out in the amount of time people generally lodge within them. As Terri Mulholland notes, early-twentieth-century 'guides to hotel and boarding house management generally differentiate boarders from guests at a hotel on the length of stay', with 'boarders' tending to stay longer than guests in hotels (2017, p. 6). Admittedly, these rules are, as Mulholland notes, 'fairly flexible', and it is entirely possible for boarders to only stay for a matter of days, and for the sojourns of hotel guests to last indefinitely. Indeed, there are numerous literary examples of guests effectively taking up residence in the hotel, such as Major Brutt in Elizabeth Bowen's *The Death of the Heart* (1938), Rhys's Sasha Jansen in *Good Morning, Midnight* (1939) and, later, the eponymous heroine of Elizabeth Taylor's *Mrs Palfrey at the Claremont* (1971). Yet fictional representations of the boarding house, such as those found throughout the work of Rhys, Katherine Mansfield, Dorothy Richardson, and Storm Jameson, characterise this space through descriptions of idiosyncratic furniture and décor, and through the overt presence of the landlady. The links between the boarding house and domesticity are thereby reaffirmed, as it is revealed to be someone's home into which guests are welcomed for a fee, rather than the markedly more impersonal space of the hotel.

Impersonality and anonymity, then, might well be understood as two defining characteristics of the hotel that distinguish it from the more homely boarding house, and indeed from the pension which, in its tendency to be family run, is more closely aligned with the latter than the former. This homeliness is exemplified by the Pension Bertolini in E.M. Forster's *A Room with a View* (1908), in which the 'Cockney Signora' (who, in her first appearance in the novel, is accompanied by her son and daughter, and thereby firmly located as a familial, maternal figure) has 'attempted to rival the solid comfort of a Bloomsbury boarding-house' through her choice of décor and furnishings (1990 [1908], pp. 6, 15). While the layout of the public rooms of the hotel may well, as I discuss elsewhere in this book, echo that of the home in its demarcation of spaces for dining and leisure, the hotel is otherwise decisively distanced from the domestic. As Joanna Walsh points out, 'a hotel, restless, cannot be a home, not even a home away from home; far from it. […] a hotel sets itself apart from home and, in doing so, proves rather than denies home's existence' (2015, p. 13). In its impersonality, anonymity, and perhaps above all in the transience and mobility by which it is characterised, the hotel is a space which is distinctly not home, and which thereby compels a reconsideration in so many hotel narratives of home, and of what it means to belong.

Yet, while it can be distinguished from the home, and from the more domestically aligned spaces of the boarding house and pension, the hotel nevertheless resists straightforward definitions and/or categorisations. Attempts to adequately define the hotel have typically fallen somewhat short. In their *Official Hotel Directory* of 1900, for example, the Hotel and Restaurant Protection Association offered a definition that was at once vague and oddly specific, describing hotels as 'establishments offering sleeping accommodation, of a minimum for eight guests in towns of over 100,000 inhabitants, and for four guests in any locality whatsoever'.[1] Etymologically, the parameters of this space were originally bound up with questions of class, the word hotel deriving from the French, *hôtel*, roughly translated as 'mansion'. As Derek Taylor and David Bush note, 'French innkeepers had been permitted to use the diminutive "*hôtellerie*" to describe their business, but were not allowed to use "*hôtel*" before the French Revolution' (1974, p. 4). It was only during and after the Revolution that many servants of the aristocracy, finding themselves unemployed, became innkeepers and used the term '*hôtel*' to distinguish themselves from the more lowly inns. In this sense, hotels were therefore, at least initially, always associated with the wealthy and elite, an association which persisted up until at least their initial emergence in Britain in the late eighteenth century when, as A.K. Sandoval-Strausz notes, '*hotel* became a specific architectural category' (2007, p. 7). The first 'architecturally distinct hotels' were, according to Sandoval-Strausz, built in 'provincial spa towns like Bath and Tunbridge Wells', locations that

> had long been served by alehouses and inns, relatively small establishments built on the same scale as dwellings. Hotels were much grander structures that included not only bedchambers and dining areas but also ballrooms, dancing halls, and assembly rooms. The first purpose-built English hotels were intended not to facilitate mobility but to foster exclusivity. (2007, p. 7)[2]

The arrangement of rooms within the hotel further reflects this association with wealth and privilege. Observing the division of space within the wealthy home in the nineteenth century, Leonora Davidoff notes a tendency

---

[1] *The Official Hotel Directory of the British Isles*, 60, July (1900), p. 3.

[2] An 1847 article in *Chambers's Edinburgh Journal*, however, reveals that the number of 'purpose-built' hotels to which Sandoval-Strausz refers here remained limited until at least the mid-nineteenth century, with the author noting that 'a hotel in any part of Great Britain is a mansion fitted up very much like a private house. People live in it apart from each other, as they would do in a lodging establishment; and for this seclusion, and the special way in which they are served, they usually pay at an extravagant rate. The consequence of this extravagance is, that people go to hotels as little as they possibly can, instead of resorting to them freely'. See: "English and Foreign Hotels", *Chamber's Edinburgh Journal*, 192, September (1847): 153–155 (p. 153).

to organise rooms according to gender and class, often including a 'lady's boudoir, [...] gentleman's smoking-room or study, mixed-sex public drawing-rooms and the back passages or basements inhabited by servants' (1995, p. 6). As noted above, this same demarcation of rooms and spaces most often found within wealthy homes tends to be replicated almost entirely in the hotel. The hotel—and particularly the grand hotel (the more expensive the hotel, the greater the number and variety of public rooms)—is laid out in accordance with the wealthy home or mansion.[3] Thus, at least in their earliest conception, hotels were distinguished from other temporary accommodations according to their size and grandeur, and, consequently, by the wealth of the guests they were designed to attract.

Across the Atlantic, size and grandeur were certainly key factors for the early pioneers of the nascent hotel industry. As in Britain, the first American hotels were driven by a desire for exclusivity. The manager of the City Hotel in New York (generally acknowledged to be the first purpose-built American hotel) made, Molly Berger notes, 'conscious efforts to court a fashionable clientele' through advertisements claiming to offer 'irresistible attractions to gentlemen of taste' (2011, p. 15).[4] These efforts, Berger maintains, 'indicated a demand for exclusive accommodations that provided—in contrast to the city's numerous inns and taverns—a superior level of service and comfort' (2011, p. 15). In America, the notion of the 'first-class' hotel emerged, Berger notes, as early as the 1820s, and such establishments were established according to the principles of luxury, opulence, convenience, and size, as '[f]or hotels—like many things in America—bigger meant better' (2011, p. 20). The American hotel has been the focus of the majority of the recent critical commentary on hotels, commentary which is prone to making bold claims about its primacy and innovation in hospitality. Sandoval-Strausz, for example, argues that

by the middle of the nineteenth century, travelers from Europe, the United States, and Latin America were all in agreement not only that American hotels were fundamentally different from similar institutions elsewhere in the world, but also that they were setting the standard for hotels everywhere. (2007, p. 9)

---

[3] For a more in-depth discussion of the division of public rooms within the hotel, see Chap. 4 of this book.

[4] The advertisement referred to here by Berger is cited in: Meryle Evans, "Knickerbocker Hotels and Restaurants, 1800–1850", *New York Historical Quarterly*, 36 (1952): 382–383.

The distinction between English and American hotels was indeed openly acknowledged by British writers and journalists in the nineteenth century. An 1853 article in *Reynolds's Miscellany*, for example, praises New York hotels, with the author noting that they 'are a remarkable feature, and excite the astonishment of a wanderer from Europe by their enormous size' (1853, p. 102). Not only were they superior in terms of their size, but, the author writes, American hotels 'are far more comfortable and better conducted than in Europe' (1853, p. 102). Writing in 1861, George Augustus Sala remarks that 'the New York hotel has not even the faintest resemblance to Mivart's, Long's, the Hummums, the Tavistock, or Wood's', all renowned London hotels, which he characterises as 'costly, cozy, secretive place[s], with fat, velvet-footed waiters' (1861, p. 345). Recognising the exclusivity of such establishments, Sala maintains that the 'vast caravanserai' (1861, p. 345) that is the American hotel 'is for the many, and not for the few', and maintains that the 'American system of hotels encourages travelling' (1861, p. 356). In his recognition of an 'American System' of hotels, Sala here joins a number of nineteenth-century commentators who, as Berger observes, expressed a 'deep dissatisfaction' with the lack of a fixed rate for services in English hotels, which led to a trend for tipping hotel staff that many saw as little more than overt greed (2011, p. 114). Writing in 1855, Albert Smith referred to this practice as 'the spirit of Extortion brooding over most hotels', and decried 'the nuisance [...] of having to pay "what you please" to servants, without a fixed charge to the bill' (1858 [1855], pp. 18–9). American hotels, on the other hand, generally operated on a fixed-rate system, whereby charges were included in one's bill. It was this system that Sala regarded as far more democratic than that which existed in England, and which has led subsequent critics like Caroline Field Levander and Matthew Pratt Guterl to link the rise of the hotel in the United States to 'American beliefs about liberal democracy and the consent of the governed' (2015, p. 7). Sandoval-Strausz takes even further the notion that the hotel embodies the values enshrined in the American constitution, maintaining that 'the hotel was the physical manifestation of a distinctly American vision of mobility, civil society, democracy, and, ultimately, space' (2007, p. 9). Yet, while it is true to an extent that American hotels often led the way in developments in billing, technology, and comfort that came to be the standard internationally, such claims that the hotel is an inherently American institution are nevertheless somewhat overstated, and drastically overlook the significance of British (and indeed European) hotels.

With a few exceptions (in the form, for example, of Henry James's *The Ambassadors* (1903) and the early novels of Jean Rhys), this book focuses primarily either on representations of the hotel in the work of British and Anglo-Irish authors (whether these hotels be located at home or abroad), or on literary depictions of the hotel in Britain and Ireland. This particular emphasis is in part for the sake of brevity, as to extend the scope of this book beyond this focus would require at least another volume. But it is also an attempt to redress the lacuna of critical commentary on the British and Irish hotel, and/or on British and Anglo-Irish perspectives of the hotel. There are, as the nineteenth-century commentators cited above suggest, clear distinctions to be made between British and American hotels, and consequent divergences in the ways in which they function in the work of authors of the respective nationalities. While the American hotel may well, as Levander, Guterl, and Sandoval-Strausz maintain, be imbued with American liberal values, the circumstances from which the British hotel emerged were the industrial and technological developments that took place in Britain in the nineteenth century. More specifically, the history of the hotel in Britain is inextricably bound up with the history of the British rail network.

The first modern public railway in Britain, the Liverpool and Manchester Railway, opened on 15 September 1830. A mere seven years later, the Crewe Arms Hotel opened next to Crewe Station, the world's first hotel to cater specifically to rail travellers (Biddle 1997, p. 212). This was soon followed in 1839 by the first hotels built by a railway company, the Victoria and Euston Hotels built at Euston Station in London by the London and Birmingham Railway Company. These hotels, as Gordon Biddle observes, 'began a long period of building or acquisition of hotels by or for railways that lasted into the twentieth century' (1997, p. 212). While progress was relatively slow at first, with a handful of railway hotels opening over the next fifteen years in locations such as Derby (1841), Gateshead (1844), Newhaven (1847), and Hull (1851), the opening of the Great Western Royal Hotel at Paddington Station on 9 June 1854 might well be regarded as a watershed moment in hotel history. With 103 bedrooms and fifteen sitting rooms, the Great Western Hotel was not only, as Oliver Carter notes, 'the finest in London' (1990, p. 9), but, was also, Biddle points out, 'the largest in the country', and thereby 'immediately set a new standard in comfort and marked the beginning of large palace-type hotels' (1997, p. 212). From this point on, the development of the hotel industry in Britain rapidly gathered momentum, fuelled even further by the Limited

Liability Act of 1855 and the Companies Act of 1862, which together gave rise to the joint-stock limited-liability company. Prior to this legislation, as Biddle highlights, 'the railways were the only organizations with the capital resources to build hotels' (1997, p. 212).[5] Nevertheless, even after these changes, railway hotels remained at the forefront of developments in the hotel industry in terms of luxury, technological innovation, and size. The Midland Grand Hotel at St Pancras, for example, opened on 5 May 1873 with 'two hundred and fifty private sitting and bed rooms', over twice the number as the Great Western Hotel that had opened less than twenty years earlier.[6] The railways were thus integral to the burgeoning hotel industry, and indeed, the two grew hand-in-hand throughout the nineteenth century. As Derek Taylor and David Bush suggest, 'the railways produced hotels in two different ways: by creating the traffic for others to risk putting up new buildings or by building hotels themselves' (1974, p. 18). British hotels were thus borne out of the new mobilities enabled by nineteenth-century innovations in transport technology.

The impetus of the rapid spread of the railway network upon the hotel in Britain was therefore considerable. By the late nineteenth century, the emergence of trade journals such as *Hotel World*—first published on 4 January 1882—confirmed the health of the hotel industry. 'Never', proclaimed the editorial of that initial issue, 'have the prospects of the trade been brighter, nor the future more hopeful, than on the opening of this New Year' (1882, p. 4). That *Hotel World*'s first issue was published exactly twenty years after the Companies Act of 1862 is no great coincidence, and the editorial noted the dramatic changes undergone by the British hotel industry 'within the last twenty years', adding that, during this period, 'no city in the world has made more rapid strides in the construction of big hotels than London' (1882, p. 4). Thanks to a heady combination of the changes in corporate legislation that occurred in the mid-nineteenth century, and the growth of the railways that happened around the same time, 'hotel building', the editor concluded, had never been 'so much in vogue'

---

[5] For further and more detailed discussion of this legislation and its repercussions on the hotel industry, see Chap. 6.

[6] Advertisement for the Midland Grand Hotel, *The Pall Mall Gazette*, 2550, 18 April (1873), p. 15. The materials used to build Midland Grand Hotel at St Pancras were, as far as possible, sourced 'from places accessible by the Midland Railway. The facing bricks are from Nottingham, the stone is Ancaster, red Mansfield, and Park Spring, the slates are from the Swithland and Groby quarries, Leicestershire'. See: 'The Midland Railway Hotel', *The London Journal and Weekly Record of Literature, Science, and Art* (57: 1476), 24 May (1873), pp. 324–325 (p. 325).

as at this precise moment (1882, p. 4). The speed with which hotels proliferated in the second half of the nineteenth century does indeed suggest a craze for the building and establishment of hotels, the extent of which can be measured by the expansion of the hotel directory published by *Hotel World* itself. In its first issue, *Hotel World*'s 'Official Hotel Directory' was a small section that took up little more than half a page, listing seventy-six hotels in Britain and Ireland, a mere nine of which were in London. By December 1895, the directory had grown from a section to a supplement, listing 365 hotels in London alone. Just five years later, *The Official Hotel Directory of the British Isles* had become a standalone publication, with the July 1900 issue devoting fifteen pages to a list of London hotels, and over 100 pages to 'provincial hotels'. The growth of this one publication alone is evidence of the startling rate at which the British and Irish hotel industry grew in the last decades of the nineteenth century.

The history of the hotel in Britain is thus intertwined with that of the railways, and is implicated firmly in the emerging mobilities that this new mode of transport enabled. As Charlotte Mathieson points out, while it had been

> initially envisaged that railways would primarily assist in the industrial transportation of goods and materials, [...] it soon became clear that passenger transport was where the main potential was to be found, with the speed and cost of the railways appealing to a wider social demographic than could access road transportation. (2015, p. 6)

The railway network opened up the possibilities of travel in Britain like never before, affording a level of mobility to those whose lives had previously been relatively static. The new hotels that rose up both in and around railway stations catered to this newly mobile population. They offered accommodation for the commercial traveller or salesman, a profession permanently and irrevocably altered by the railways. Importantly, however, they also catered to the holidaymaker, to the individual, or family travelling for leisure. As Mathieson notes, 'the popularity of domestic leisure travel established earlier in the century [...] evolved, becoming available to new sections of the population through the working-class excursion trains to the seaside and other tourist destinations' (2015, p. 7). In the nineteenth and early twentieth centuries, the experience of the literary hotel guest was predominantly, as the readings in this book demonstrate, one of leisure, an experience that was, thanks to the new mobilities created by the rail network, no longer limited to the affluent classes.

The railways were of course not the only mode of transport to have an impact on the hotel industry in Britain. The advent of the transatlantic ocean liner in the mid-nineteenth century played a key role in the British awareness of the aforementioned 'American system'. British travellers to the United States reported back on the new luxuries and innovations they found in American hotels, while American travellers to Britain, having already grown accustomed to their own hotels, expected to find in British establishments what they now considered to be basic amenities, such as electric lights, lifts, and hot running water. The speed with which these same innovations were introduced in British hotels of the mid-to-late nineteenth century was a consequence of these transatlantic voyages. And, in the late nineteenth century, even the bicycle made its presence felt on hotels, with one of the earliest British hotel guides being that published by the Bicycle Touring Club for its members in 1879. This guide featured advice on hotels in which bicycles could be 'housed and cleaned', which offered rooms 'specially reserved for bicyclists', and even those which offered a 'bicyclists' tariff'.[7] Indeed, the impor..nce of the hotel for those early cyclists is immortalised in H.G. Wells's *The Wheels of Chance: A Bicycling Idyll* (1896), in which Mr Hoopdriver breaks up his cycling holiday with a number of brief sojourns in hotels.

In the early twentieth century, the hotel industry in Britain was directly affected again by the rise of the motorcar, which first began to capture the public imagination in the 1890s following the production of a three-wheeled 'motorwagen' designed by German engineer Karl Benz in 1885. While the initial availability of the motorcar was limited—only twenty-five of Benz's vehicles were sold between 1888 and 1893—numbers rose steadily. In France there were about 3000 motorcars owned by 1900, and this figure rose to 50,000 by 1909, and to 100,000 by 1913. In Britain, as production increased and prices became more affordable, the number of privately owned cars also continued to rise, and Sean O'Connell notes a sharp increase between the two world wars, 'from just over 100,000 in 1918 to slightly over two million in 1939' (1998, p. 19). With more and more people—couples, friends, and families—having access to a car, motoring holidays, daytrips, and weekends away became an increasingly realistic option for many. The surge in vehicle numbers inevitably had an impact on the roads and on the very geography of Britain, and Hugh

---

[7] *Bicycle Touring Club: Revised Prospectus Regarding Hotels*, 1 May (1879). See the archive of the Cyclists' Touring Club held at the University of Warwick (MSS.328/C) for further information.

Davies observes that 'it was clear even by the 1930s that traffic was growing so fast that the existing network, however well developed, would not be able to carry the traffic which seemed likely to want to use it' (2006, p. 69). The rise of the motorcar contributed significantly to the development of the already flourishing hotel industry, as more roadside and rural hotels were established by those quick to spot a business opportunity in servicing the needs of both weary motorists and eager holidaymakers. The Trust House hotel chain, for example, catered specifically to the motorist, with a guaranteed affordability and standardised comfort. Ever responsive to emerging transport technologies, the hotel industry in Britain grew and adapted throughout the nineteenth and twentieth centuries to meet the needs of an increasingly mobile population.

The Literary Hotel

The initial growth of the hotel industry in Britain was therefore concomitant with the rapid growth in new types of transport—specifically the rail network—in the first half of the nineteenth century, and it is following these developments that the hotel begins to figure frequently as a literary setting. While hotels can be found in British and Irish fiction from at least the early nineteenth century, it is only following the development of the national rail network and the opening of Britain's first railway hotels at Euston that hotels gradually begin to proliferate in literature, coming to be predominant in the first decades of the twentieth century. This indisputable relationship between the hotel and new transport technologies is not only the reason behind the increased frequency with which the hotel features in literature towards the end of the nineteenth century and in the first part of the twentieth century, but it also underpins a tendency for authors to explore ideas of transience and rootlessness through the space of the hotel, notions which are, for many critics, particularly characteristic of modernist literature. Noting the prevalence of travel in modernist literature, Alexandra Peat suggests that this 'attests to modernism's obsession with narratives of both geographical and cultural movement' (2011, p. 131). Charles Burdett and Derek Duncan also highlight the centrality of mobility to modernist narratives, maintaining that modernism

> can be seen as a metropolitan art of diaspora, the art produced in the wake of waves of migration and displacement that brought together millions of men and women of different nationalities, religions, and social classes in the

great cities of Western Europe and the United States. The formal alterity of
modernist art is therefore the consequence of travel and of the unpredictable fusions and fragmentations that occur when cultures are forced into
unusual proximity. (2002, p. 5)

While the suggestion that modernism's innovation and experimentation is
directly, or indeed solely, attributable to travel somewhat oversimplifies
the impact of new and emerging mobilities upon it, this impact should
nevertheless not be underplayed. There is, in modernist literature, an
overwhelming sense of fluidity across spaces, a proliferation of transitions
across thresholds and boundaries which leads Andrew Thacker to remark
that spaces in modernism 'cannot, it seems, be kept apart [...]: rooms
bleed into streets, anguished minds migrate to lands overseas' (2003,
p. 7). Modernism's preoccupation with mobility constructs it, not so
much as an 'urban art', as it has traditionally been conceived, but as one
which is instead a literature of the shifting, liminal spaces of the in-between.

This emphasis on mobility and movement in modernist literature in turn
produces protagonists who, constantly travelling in between places, are
rarely, if ever, at home, and who inhabit instead the unstable, transitory
space of the hotel. Hotels feature heavily in many of the canonical texts of
modernist fiction. The 'Sirens' episode of Joyce's *Ulysses* (1922), for example, opens in the bar and restaurant of the Ormond Hotel. References to
the Cannon Street Hotel in London and the Hotel Metropole in Brighton
add to the atmosphere of seediness crafted by T.S. Eliot in 'The Fire
Sermon' section of *The Waste Land* (1922). One of the principal settings of
Ford Madox Ford's *The Good Soldier* (1915) is the Hotel Excelsior in
Nauheim, and similarly, Woolf's *The Voyage Out* (1915) is set primarily in a
hotel in the fictional South American resort of Santa Marina. Hotels, as
Bettina Matthias observes, 'offer innumerable narrative opportunities that
require little causal preparation: they are spaces where people meet acciden-
tally and where stories emerge almost naturally from these chance meetings' (2006, p. 5). More specifically, the variety of different spaces within
the hotel—the lounge, the lobby, the corridors, the back areas, and the
bedrooms—constructs it as the perfect literary setting, providing as it does
a cross-section of society, all, as Elizabeth Bowen's Sidney Warren reflects,
'doing appropriate things in appropriate attitudes as though they had been
put there to represent something' (2003 [1927], p. 79). Despite being
such a prominent setting, however, hotels have been largely overlooked in
criticism of modernist literature, which tends to focus largely, as noted

above, on the notion of the modernist metropolis (Bradbury 1976; Williams 1996; Parsons 2000; Wilson 1992) or else, more recently, explores the private domestic space in modernist literature (Rosner 2005; Gan 2009). Yet existing in between the public and private spheres, the hotel encapsulates the instability and transience that permeates modernist literature.

The lacuna of critical work on the hotel extends, however, far beyond modernist literature. To date there is only one book-length study of the hotel in the literature of the nineteenth and early twentieth centuries, and one recent edited collection on the hotel in nineteenth-century writing (Matthias 2006; Elbert and Schmid 2018). While there has, in the last few years, been a welcome surge of research on the hotel in early-twentieth-century British fiction by scholars such as Randi Saloman (2012, 2015), Robbie Moore (2012), and Charlotte Bates (2003), the body of work on this space remains markedly insubstantial when compared to that on the city and the home in modernity.[8] The reasons behind this relative dearth of critical debate on the hotel are difficult to ascertain, particularly given the diverse ways in which it is employed by authors of this period to interrogate the experience of modern life. Existing in between the public space of the city street and the private space of the home, the hotel is thereby removed from both. In this sense the hotel exists in isolation—as Siegfried Kracauer suggests, 'if a sojourn in a hotel offers neither a perspective on nor an escape from the everyday, it does provide a groundless distance from it' (1995, p. 177). The hotel does indeed offer a space away from the everyday, where the everyday is understood as the quotidian existence of the public and private spheres, but Kracauer is mistaken in his claim that the hotel 'offers neither a perspective on nor escape from' these dominant spaces. Rather, the hotel is uniquely positioned to provide insight into both spheres, as well as opening up discussions of marginality, alienation, and liberation by providing a necessary alternative to these spaces, which are so often presented as an unshifting binary.

Despite the focus of the discussion thus far upon modernism, and despite—or rather because of—the title of this book that denotes its focus upon modern, as opposed to modernist literature, I want to pause here to

[8] Other work on the hotel includes: Siegfried Kracauer's, "The Hotel Lobby", in *The Mass Ornament: Weimar Essays*, ed. and trans. Thomas Y. Levin (Cambridge: Harvard University Press, 1995), pp. 173–185; D.J. van Lennep's, "The Hotel Room", in *Phenomenological Psychology: The Dutch School*, ed. Joseph J. Kockelmans (Dordrecht: Martinus Nijhoff, 1987), pp. 209–215; and Douglas Tallack's, "'Waiting, Waiting': The Hotel Lobby", *Irish Journal of American Studies*, 7 (1998): 1–20.

clarify how this book engages with and problematises modernism as a term and concept. In their introduction to *Bad Modernisms*, Douglas Mao and Rebecca Walkowitz explicitly term and identify 'New Modernist Studies' as a critical movement that has aggressively sought to move beyond the confines of high modernism to expand the range of writing which might be considered modernist. The resulting expansion and revision of the modernist canon, however, has triggered critical anxieties regarding the preservation of modernism as a distinct field. The so-called New Modernist Studies is primarily concerned with the expansion beyond the high canonical Modernism of writers such as Joyce, Woolf, and Eliot. While Mao and Walkowitz locate the New Modernist Studies as having been 'born on or about 1999 with the invention of the Modernist Studies Association' (2008, p. 737), and with the journal *Modernism/Modernity*, it in fact emerged a little earlier than this, with the publication of works such as Bonnie Kime Scott's *The Gender of Modernism* in 1990, and Sydney Janet Kaplan's *Katherine Mansfield and the Origins of Modernist Fiction* in 1991. Kime Scott and Kaplan were part of a movement which aggressively sought to move beyond the confines of high Modernism, and to expand the range of writing which might be considered Modernist. With the subsequent inclusion of authors such as Katherine Mansfield and Jean Rhys, the range of the modernist project expanded considerably. This idea of expanding the field, of bringing in and reconceiving previously neglected authors as modernist, is therefore central to the New Modernist Studies project. As Mao and Walkowitz observe, 'were one seeking a single word to sum up transformations in modernist literary scholarship over the past decade or two, one could do worse than light on *expansion*' (2008, p. 737; emphasis in original). However, there is, they note, more than one type of expansion. As with many other fields of literary scholarship, modernist studies has, they argue, expanded over the past few decades in 'temporal, spatial and vertical directions' (Mao and Walkowitz 2008, p. 737). The temporal and spatial directions are fairly self-explanatory, involving, respectively, broadening the period of focus of modernist studies and extending its geographical area of exploration. However, it is the notion of vertical expansion that is of particular relevance here, and it is this direction that has since proved to be the most controversial among a number of modernist scholars. For Mao and Walkowitz, vertical expansion involves the reconsideration of 'quite sharp boundaries between high art and popular forms of culture', the 'critique and reconfigur[ation]' of canons, the re-evaluation of 'works by members of marginalized social groups', and the extension of 'scholarly inquiry [...] to matters of production, dissemination, and reception' (2008, p. 738). Recent scholarship in modernist studies has indeed focused on these areas, such as the wealth of work on modernist magazines, as well as the impact of existing and new media on modernist literature, and the extensive work on authors previously neglected on account of their gender, nationality, and class background. However, it is in the reconsideration and interrogation of those 'boundaries between high art and popular forms of culture' that further work needs to be done, a claim further reinforced by the fact that it is here that Mao and Walkowitz have met with the most resistance from other modernist scholars.

In their attempts to define and draw together this emerging field, Mao and Walkowitz are widely regarded as being at the vanguard of New Modernist Studies, which Max Brzezinski identifies as 'a critical movement of which they are the leading spokespeople and practitioners' (2011, p. 109). However, Brzezinski's identification appears in the midst of a rather scathing attack on New Modernist Studies, in which he dismisses it as little more than 'a gossamer-like attempt to consolidate the current inchoate status quo of the work on modernism currently being produced by an institutionally powerful generation of scholars' (2011, pp. 120–1). Yet while Brzezinski's critique purportedly stems from a Marxist reading of the movement as symptomatic of 'global capitalism' (Puchner 2012, p. 93), a 'rebranding' of modernist studies into 'a marketable intellectual commodity' (Brzezinski 2011, p. 109), his anger can be traced back to an anxiety regarding the 'vertical expansion' advocated by New Modernist Studies. Such anxiety is exemplified in his claim that 'there is no reason to believe that expansion in content should be celebrated in and of itself', and in the subsequent, rather dramatic comparison he draws between the expansion of modernist studies and expansion in terms of 'military operations, imperial occupation, and capitalism's overproduction crises or creative destructions' (Brzezinski 2011, p. 121). This same anxiety regarding the vertical expansion at the heart of New Modernist Studies is expressed by Charles Altieri, who maintains that, 'as the content of modernism expands, its enduring force dwindles' (2012, p. 769). For Altieri, as for Brzezinski, the risk posed by this vertical expansion to reconsider those 'boundaries between high art and popular forms of culture' is a dilution and a 'dwindling' of the 'enduring force of modernism'.

Yet while these critiques of New Modernist Studies may reveal a deep-seated anxiety regarding the potential pollution of modernism by the inclusion or consideration of these 'popular cultural forms', they do nevertheless offer some pertinent points regarding the limitations of the New Modernist Studies as it is currently understood. Both Altieri and Brzezinski highlight the somewhat nebulous nature of Mao and Walkowitz's claims regarding the vertical expansion of modernist studies, and question what, precisely, a reconsideration of the 'boundaries between high art and popular forms of culture' would look like, and what this can add to an understanding of modernism. Altieri is primarily concerned with the lack of critical attention paid to the selection of materials to be read alongside each other, suggesting that, 'as the field of study expands and depends more on analogy, the likelihood grows that critics will not even try to find organizing concepts that they try to show are somehow within the phenomena' (2012, p. 768). Brzezinski is similarly alert to the importance of establishing a clear justification for bringing together a range of cross-cultural forms, arguing that 'methodological elaboration is more important than the choice of subject matter: to celebrate critical interest in new content is to say nothing about context, about how and why it is interesting' (2011, p. 121). For both, what is lacking from this notion of vertical expansion in the New Modernist Studies is a clear methodology, and a more careful and nuanced approach to the selection of texts to be read alongside each other. These are valid points, though they are nevertheless ones that a number of scholars collected under the umbrella of New Modernist Studies have already begun to address. To cite only one example, Laura Frost reads the work of D.H. Lawrence alongside E.M. Hull's popular desert romance, *The Sheik* (1919), in order to reveal the way both authors 'contributed to the modern exploration of sexuality and eroticism' (2006, p. 97). Through careful close reading, Frost charts a clear line of influence from Hull to Lawrence, arguing that 'many British genre novels' of the late nineteenth and early twentieth centuries 'exerted an important influence', and maintains that, '[t]he case of Lawrence and Hull suggests that "clichéd" popular fictions underpin modernism's supposedly "innovative" representations of sexuality and eroticism in spite of the modernist repudiation of this "badness"' (2006, p. 98). Frost's argument here is illuminating, and clearly demonstrates the benefits of reading modernist and popular literature alongside each other in order to reconsider not only the direction of lines of influence across literary forms of the early twentieth century, but also to reveal the shared concerns of modernist and popular literature in terms of their mutual exploration of female sexuality.

In her willingness to engage in an in-depth comparative reading of modernist and popular texts, Frost demonstrates how such an approach can afford a rich understanding of the ways in which texts existing in these apparently disparate categories were involved in a similar project of innovation in terms of the representation of female sexuality. Frost's work is an excellent starting point, though further work remains to be done in this area. Primarily, there is a clear need to move away from previous discussions of 'expansion' in the sense of expanding the modernist canon. The point here is not so much to further expand the range of texts that might be considered modernist, but to reconceive the hierarchical structure of modernist, middlebrow, and popular, where modernism is prized as the most important literary form of the early twentieth century, and where middlebrow and popular literature are effectively relegated as that which might merely afford some extra insight into modernism, or as a selection of texts which might, if they are fortunate, be brought in under the banner of modernism. Crucially, this approach involves a reconsideration of how value is attached to some texts and not others, and when reading these texts together, it is vital to resist positioning popular and middlebrow literature as modernism's 'other', as that against which modernism defines itself, but which is of less value, both critically and culturally. Rather, as critics we should afford the same critical attention to these texts, to understand them as carrying the same value as modernist literature, and as making their own significant contribution to the literatures of modernity. It is through this democratisation of terminology that texts in all three categories can come to be understood as participating in the same practices. This does not necessarily involve dismantling the boundaries of modernist literature—rather, this approach encourages an interrogation as opposed to a breaking down of these boundaries, and demands further consideration of how modernist literature differs from middlebrow and popular literature in its treatment of the same kinds of questions.

This book is engaged in just such a project, and throughout I consider how, as a space of dynamic movement, the hotel reconfigures the long-established critical boundaries of modernist, middlebrow, and popular literature by demonstrating that authors previously distanced by such divisions are engaged in remarkably similar explorations of form, style and subject. Through my readings of the work of authors who have previously been understood as diametrically opposed to one another, such as Arnold Bennett and Virginia Woolf, H.G. Wells and James Joyce, Henry James and Dorothy Richardson, the book charts how they employ the spaces of the hotel to think through the social and cultural conditions of modernity, particularly in terms of class, gender, and sexuality. Perhaps unsurprisingly, the unique insight afforded by the hotel into those latter concepts of gender and sexuality means that it is a space frequently employed by women writers. Authors such as Elizabeth Bowen, Jean Rhys, and May Sinclair all use the hotel to think through the societal and cultural upheavals of modernity, and to challenge gendered distinctions of the public and private. Their novels demonstrate the ways in which the hotel became a crucial space for women in modernity, within which they were freed from the judgemental gaze of the street and the domestic responsibilities or expectations of the home. As such, the hotel as setting offers a unique opportunity for women writers to fully interrogate the subjectivities of their female protagonists, and to comment on the lives of women in the early twentieth century. But, as I caution above, the hotel defies any attempts at straightforward categorisation, and while it may at times function in the narratives explored here as a space of sexual freedom for women, it also functions, often simultaneously, as a space in which women are entrapped and coerced by their male lovers. Similarly, it is a space in which female characters are both incarcerated and in which they seek refuge—a space in which they are freed from the responsibilities of the domestic role, but also a space to which those women who are *excluded* from the home are consigned. The hotel is, then, a vital imaginative space for women writers in the late nineteenth and early twentieth centuries, and a consideration of the hotel narrative in this period grants these authors—both canonical and non-canonical—the critical attention that they have too often been denied.[9] It is through the space of the hotel that we can come to redistribute cultural value that has previously been so unevenly assigned. As the readings of the hotel contained within this book conclusively demonstrate, this space is used by all of these writers, both male and female, to contemplate abstract concepts such as the nature of selfhood and subjectivity, as well as to explore new ways of structuring, framing, and driving their narratives.

* * *

In their structure and organisation, the five further chapters of this book enact the mobility that I explore within each by moving through the individual spaces of the hotel. Following Thacker's assertion that '[w]e should reconnect the representational spaces in literary texts not only to the material spaces they depict, but also reverse the movement, and understand

[9] I am grateful to my anonymous reviewer for their suggestions on this point.

how social spaces dialogically help fashion the literary *forms* of texts' (2005, p. 63; emphasis in original), Chap. 2 analyses the hotel as a 'textual space', and charts the development of a 'hotel narrative' from the late nineteenth to the early twentieth century. I explore how the hotel necessarily shapes narrative form and structure through the movement along its corridors from room to room, creating an episodic structure well suited to genre fiction such as the detective or mystery novel, as exemplified by Bennett's *The Grand Babylon Hotel* (1902). But I argue that this same 'hotel narrative' structure can be found in modernist works, such as Ford Madox Ford's *The Good Soldier* (1915) and Virginia Woolf's *The Voyage Out* (1915). I posit the hotel narrative as fragmented and often non-linear, beginning *in media res* and lacking resolution, and maintain that, while literary criticism has tended to identify these qualities as defining features of modernist literature, my analysis of the hotel narrative reveals experiments with narrative and form to be widespread across the literatures of modernity.

Chapter 3 considers the hotel lobby, which, as a space of movement across boundaries, can itself be understood as a boundary between the street and the inner spaces of the hotel. The chapter explores the various ways in which the lobby is figured as a space of transition, one through which characters are continually passing, and ceaselessly traversing this semi-public threshold between the public and the semi-private. As a space of transition, the lobby is also inevitably a space of anticipation for these characters—both the anticipation of the kind of space into which they are moving, and of the future movements for which this space holds the potential. The opening pages of Bowen's *The Hotel* (1927), for example, show Miss Pym scanning the letter racks in the lobby for clues regarding forthcoming arrivals, anticipating future romance and passion. In Winifred Holtby's *South Riding* (1936), Sarah Burton breathlessly enters the 'warm, half-empty lobby' of her Manchester hotel only to come face to face with Robert Carne, before whom she stands 'expectant and happy' in anticipation of their potential passion (2011 [1936], pp. 365–6). However, this sense of anticipation, and its powerful association with waiting, can also develop into stagnation, lack of purpose, and an absence of hope, in line with Siegfried Kracauer's positioning of the hotel lobby as a 'space of unrelatedness' characterised by 'an aimless lounging, to which no call is addressed' (1995 [1927], p. 179). The lobby in Henry Green's *Party Going* (1939), for example, is compared by one character both to a doctor's waiting room and purgatory, and I argue that the palpable sense of disillusionment conveyed by the lobby's links to illness and death here is indicative of the anxieties of late 1930s Britain as it edged closer to war. Published towards the end of the previous decade, the hotel lobby in Jean Rhys's *Quartet* (1928) is also a space of anxiety, though the anxiety in this case stems from Marya Zelli's awareness that her movements are constantly monitored from the desk of the *patronne*, signifying the scrutiny of marginalised subjects in interwar Europe. This chapter considers the way in which the hotel lobby is figured variously—and often simultaneously— across modern fiction as a space of anticipation, stagnation, and anxiety.

Chapter 4 considers the communal areas—rooms such as the lounge and dining room—which are less public than the lobby, but more so than the bedrooms and other spaces that extend beyond. These public areas are often presented in novels of the early twentieth century as spaces offering a vital sense of community to those isolated by the hotel lifestyle. However, I problematise the notion of these spaces as sanctuary through an interrogation of the ways in which inclusion into these spaces often rests upon the successful performance of specific gendered and classed identities. Moving into the more private space of the hotel bedroom, Chap. 5 demonstrates how the type and location of room is used across British fiction of the late nineteenth and early twentieth centuries to codify social standing and class identity. This chapter reads novels such as Bowen's *The Hotel* (1927) and Rhys's *Good Morning, Midnight* (1939) alongside contemporary hotel guides and tariffs to reveal the way in which authors use the type of hotel, and the floor on which the room is situated, to indicate the social class of their characters. This chapter also builds on recent criticism regarding the gendered experience of space in modernity in its exploration of the ways in which the hotel room functions for the female protagonists in novels such as Dorothy Richardson's *Oberland* (1927) as 'a room of one's own', a private space away from the demands of the domestic sphere. I maintain that the hotel can in this way be read as a space of empowerment, which restores a sense of agency to its female guests through enabling them to perform an active resistance to domestic routine and drudgery. Finally, this chapter explores the cultural connotations of the hotel bedroom concerning illicit sexual activity. I argue that these powerful associations position the hotel bedroom as a complex and contradictory space that offers characters—and particularly women—the freedom to explore their sexuality and their desires away from both the moral constraints of the home and the judgemental gaze of the public sphere, as in Bowen's *The House in Paris* (1934). However,

I discuss the way in which such connotations also contribute to the coercive potential of the hotel bedroom for men wishing to take advantage of women, as in Wells's *Ann Veronica* (1909). This chapter demonstrates how the hotel bedroom of modernity is figured variously and often frustratingly simultaneously in the literature of this period as a space of respite, refuge, coercion, and threat, marking it as a complex and multifarious space for those characters who inhabit it. Finally, Chap. 6 explores the hidden areas from which the hotel is managed by its staff, those areas referred to in Bennett's *Imperial Palace* (1930) as 'the bowels of the hotel', and considers the female staff who undertake the task of cleaning the hotel bedrooms, and who thereby permit the female guest to escape the drudgery of domesticity only by becoming entrapped in it themselves. Recalling the day of the housewife in its repetitive nature, the job of the chambermaid and her presence throughout these texts raises unavoidable problems when considered from a feminist perspective, as the burden of work is transferred onto other women, and onto those who are likely from a less privileged background. However, this chapter alternatively posits the chambermaids and other hotel staff as figures of considerable agency and power in fiction during this period, who follow and scrutinise. Issues of class here link back to notions of gender and surveillance, where the maid, who literally cleans up the dirt of these characters, knows in detail the personal behaviours and secrets of the guests who dismiss her.

REFERENCES

Adey, Peter. 2010. *Mobility*. London: Routledge.

Ahmed, Sara. 2006. *Queer Phenomenology: Orientations, Objects, Others*. Durham: Duke University Press.

Altieri, Charles. 2012. Afterword: How the 'New Modernist Studies' Fails the Old Modernism. *Textual Practice* 26 (4): 763–782.

Anon. 1853. American Hotels. *Reynolds's Miscellany of Romance, General Literature, Science, and Art*, 10.244, 102, March 12.

———. 1882. Editorial. *The Hotel World: A Weekly International Record of Hotel and Other News*, 1.1, 4, January 4.

Bates, Charlotte. 2003. Hotel Histories: Modern Tourists, Modern Nomads and the Culture of Hotel-Consciousness. *Literature & History* 12 (2): 62–75.

Bauman, Zygmunt. 1991. *Modernity and Ambivalence*. Ithaca, NY: Cornell University Press.

Berger, Molly W. 2011. *Hotel Dreams: Luxury, Technology, and Urban Ambition in America, 1829–1929*. Baltimore: The Johns Hopkins University Press.

Berman, Marshall. 2010 [1982]. *All That Is Solid Melts into Air: The Experience of Modernity*. London: Verso.

Biddle, Gordon. 1997. Hotels. In *The Oxford Companion to British Railway History*, ed. Jack Simmons and Gordon Biddle, 212–213. Oxford: Oxford University Press.

Bond, Emma. 2018. *Writing Migration Through the Body*. Cham: Palgrave.

Bowen, Elizabeth. 2003 [1927]. *The Hotel*. London: Vintage.

Bradbury, Malcolm. 1976. The Cities of Modernism. In *Modernism: A Guide to European Literature, 1890–1930*, ed. Malcolm Bradbury and James McFarlane, 96–104. London: Penguin.

Brzezinski, Max. 2011. The New Modernist Studies: What's Left of Political Formalism? *Minnesota Review* 76: 109–125.

Burdett, Charles, and Derek Duncan. 2002. Introduction. In *Cultural Encounters: European Travel Writing in the 1930s*, ed. Charles Burdett and Derek Duncan, 1–8. Oxford: Berghahn Books.

Carter, Oliver. 1990. *An Illustrated History of Railway Hotels, 1838–1983*. St Michael's: Silver Link Publishing.

Casey, Edward S. 1993. *Getting Back into Place: Toward a Renewed Understanding of the Place-World*. Bloomington: Indiana University Press.

———. 2000. *Remembering: A Phenomenological Study*. 2nd ed. Bloomington: Indiana University Press.

de Certeau, Michel. 1984. *The Practice of Everyday Life*. Trans. Steven Rendall. Berkeley: University of California Press.

Cresswell, Tim. 2006. *On the Move: Mobility in the Modern Western World*. London: Routledge.

Davidoff, Leonora. 1995. *Worlds Between: Historical Perspectives on Gender and Class*. Cambridge: Polity.

Davies, Hugh. 2006. *From Trackways to Motorways: 5000 Years of Highway History*. Stroud: Tempus.

Elbert, Monika, and Susanne Schmid, eds. 2018. *Anglo-American Travelers and the Hotel Experience in Nineteenth-Century Writing: Nation, Hospitality, Travel Writing*. New York: Routledge.

Evans, Meryle. 1952. Knickerbocker Hotels and Restaurants, 1800–1850. *New York Historical Quarterly* 36: 382–383.

Forster, E.M. 1990 [1908]. *A Room with a View*. London: Penguin.

Frost, Laura. 2006. The Romance of Cliché: E.M. Hull, D.H. Lawrence, and Interwar Erotic Fiction. In *Bad Modernisms*, ed. Douglas Mao and Rebecca L. Walkowitz, 94–118. Durham and London: Duke University Press.

Gan, Wendy. 2009. *Women, Privacy and Modernity in Early Twentieth-Century British Writing*. Basingstoke: Palgrave Macmillan.

Grosz, Elizabeth. 1994. *Volatile Bodies: Toward a Corporeal Feminism*. Bloomington: Indiana University Press.

———. 1995. Bodies—Cities. In *Space, Time, and Perversion: Essays on the Politics of Bodies*, 103–110. London: Routledge.

Harvey, David. 1990. *The Condition of Postmodernity*. Oxford: Blackwell.

Holtby, Winifred. 2011 [1936]. *South Riding*. London: BBC Books.

Kracauer, Siegfried. 1995. The Hotel Lobby. In *The Mass Ornament: Weimar Essays*, ed. and trans. Thomas Y. Levin, 173–185. Cambridge: Harvard University Press.

Levander, Caroline Field, and Matthew Pratt Guterl. 2015. *Hotel Life: The Story of a Place Where Anything Can Happen*. Chapel Hill: The University of North Carolina Press.

Mao, Douglas, and Rebecca Walkowitz. 2008. The Changing Profession: The New Modernist Studies. *PMLA* 123 (3): 737–748.

Mathieson, Charlotte. 2015. *Mobility in the Victorian Novel: Placing the Nation*. Basingstoke: Palgrave Macmillan.

Matthias, Bettina. 2006. *The Hotel as Setting in Early Twentieth-Century German and Austrian Literature: Checking in to Tell a Story*. Rochester, NY: Camden House.

Merleau-Ponty, Maurice. 2002 [1945]. *Phenomenology of Perception*. Trans. Colin Smith. Abingdon: Routledge.

Moore, Robbie. 2012. Henry James, Hotels, and the Invention of Disposable Space. *Modernist Cultures* 7 (2): 254–278.

Mulholland, Terri. 2017. *British Boarding Houses in Interwar Women's Literature: Alternative Domestic Spaces*. Abingdon: Routledge.

O'Connell, Sean. 1998. *The Car and British Society: Class, Gender and Motoring, 1896–1939*. Manchester: Manchester University Press.

Parsons, Deborah. 2000. *Streetwalking the Metropolis: Women, the City and Modernity*. Oxford: Oxford University Press.

Peat, Alexandra. 2011. *Travel and Modernist Literature: Sacred and Ethical Journeys*. Abingdon: Routledge.

Puchner, Martin. 2012. The New Modernist Studies: A Response. *Minnesota Review* 79: 91–96.

Rosner, Victoria. 2005. *Modernism and the Architecture of Private Life*. New York: Columbia University Press.

Sala, George Augustus. 1861. American Hotels and American Food. *Temple Bar: A London Magazine for Town and Country Readers* 2: 345–356.

Saloman, Randi. 2012. Arnold Bennett's Hotels. *Twentieth Century Literature* 58 (1): 1–25.

———. 2015. 'Do You Think You're at the Gresham?' Accepting Imperfection in 'The Dead'. *Modernist Cultures* 10 (2): 159–177.

Sandoval-Strausz, A.K. 2007. *Hotel: An American History*. New Haven: Yale University Press.

Smith, Albert. 1858 [1855]. *The English Hotel Nuisance*. 2nd ed. London: Bradbury & Evans.

Tallack, Douglas. 1998. 'Waiting, Waiting': The Hotel Lobby. *Irish Journal of American Studies* 7: 1–20.

Taylor, Derek, and David Bush. 1974. *The Golden Age of British Hotels*. London: Northwood.

Thacker, Andrew. 2003. *Moving Through Modernity: Space and Geography in Modernism*. Manchester: Manchester University Press.

———. 2005. The Idea of a Critical Literary Geography. *New Formations* 57: 56–73.

van Lennep, D.J. 1987. The Hotel Room. In *Phenomenological Psychology: The Dutch School*, ed. Joseph J. Kockelmans, 209–215. Dordrecht: Martinus Nijhoff.

Walsh, Joanna. 2015. *Hotel: Object Lessons*. London: Bloomsbury.

Williams, Raymond. 1996. *The Politics of Modernism: Against the New Conformists*. Edited by Tony Pinkney. London: Verso.

Wilson, Elizabeth. 1992. *The Sphinx in the City: Urban Life, the Control of Disorder, and Women*. Berkeley: University of California Press.

Young, Iris Marion. 2005. House and Home: Feminist Variations on a Theme. In *On Female Body Experience: 'Throwing Like a Girl' and Other Essays*, 123–154. Oxford: Oxford University Press.

CHAPTER 2

Along the Corridor: Charting the Hotel Narrative

Ostensibly, this book begins with a consideration of the hotel corridor, and yet this chapter differs slightly from those that follow, each of which focuses on a particular space within the hotel, and on the ways in which that space functions in fiction of the late nineteenth and early twentieth centuries. While the space and function of the hotel corridor itself is discussed at points throughout this chapter, the corridor here operates more as a spatial metaphor through which to consider the ways in which the hotel—and specifically movement through the hotel, as through the hotel corridor—impacts upon narrative. More specifically, this chapter teases out the relationship between the space of the hotel and narrative form. The relationship between space and narrative form is itself a complex one, and is one that has garnered increasing critical attention in recent years. Edward Soja (1989) and Fredric Jameson (1991) are widely credited with identifying the 'spatial turn' in cultural studies, an articulation that has become, as Karen Elizabeth Bishop notes, 'one of the most significant interdisciplinary preoccupations of the early twenty-first century' (2016, p. 20). The interdisciplinary nature of this preoccupation is wide-ranging, yet for the purposes of this book, the focus will be upon the nexus of critical literary studies and geography, which has recently developed into the distinct school of thought now known as literary geographies.[1] In order to fully

---

[1] The increasing critical significance of this field led to the establishment of the journal, *Literary Geographies,* in 2015.

© The Author(s) 2019
E. Short, *Mobility and the Hotel in Modern Literature,*
Studies in Mobilities, Literature, and Culture,
https://doi.org/10.1007/978-3-030-22129-4_2

consider the relationship between the hotel space and narrative form, it is first necessary to sketch out the various ways in which the link between spatiality and narrative has been hitherto understood in literary criticism and theory.

THE HOTEL OF FICTION: SPATIALITY AND NARRATIVE FORM

When considering the precise nature of the relationship between space and narrative, perhaps the first and most obvious facet of this relationship is the function of space *within* narrative, or in other words, the way in which it functions as a setting for events which take place over the course of the narrative. Indeed, narrative itself has largely been regarded in criticism as that which is primarily shaped by time, rather than space. As Marie-Laure Ryan, Kenneth Foote, and Maoz Azaryahu point out, '[s]pace has traditionally been viewed as a backdrop to plot, if only because narrative, by definition, is a temporal art involving the sequencing of events' (2016, p. 1). While the bulk of the discussion in this chapter will challenge this notion that space has no role in the shaping and structuring of narrative, it is worth pausing here to consider the question of space as setting in more detail. Setting is defined by Ruth Ronen as 'the *actual immediate* surrounding of an object, a character, or an event' (1986, p. 423; emphasis in original). Ronen makes a further distinction between setting and frame, arguing that while frames 'are fictional places and locations which provide a *topological determination* to events and states in the story', settings, on the other hand, are 'formed by a set of fictional places which are the *topological focus* of the story. A setting is the zero point where the *actual* story-events and story states are localised' (1986, p. 423; emphasis in original). A frame, then, is the wider, more generalised space in which the story takes place and the setting is the more specific, and smaller space, which exists within the frame, and in which the events and action of the narrative occur. For example, the eponymous Grand Babylon Hotel in Arnold Bennett's 1902 novel is the primary setting of the events of the narrative, but it is located within the wider frame of the city of London.

The frame of a narrative is undoubtedly important, for example, in terms of the significance of the country or region in which a particular hotel is located. The eponymous hotel in Elizabeth Bowen's 1927 novel is, for instance, situated on the Italian Riviera, a fact which is particularly pertinent to determining the class status of the guests at the hotel. Yet the hotel as setting in itself warrants further analysis here, specifically with regard to what kind of setting this is, and what it allows authors to do. Perhaps first and foremost is the fact that, as acknowledged in the Introduction to this book, hotels enable authors to bring otherwise disparate and unconnected individuals and groups of people together under one roof. The ability to offer this cross-section of society is important, as it further allows for, and indeed typically encourages, the interrogation of societal boundaries and expectations. Not only do hotel guests and staff exist in close proximity, giving intimate insight into the tensions in which this can result, but the peculiar anonymity afforded by the hotel means that guests can occasionally, as Bettina Matthias notes, 'choose to play with their identity' (2006, p. 4). Such is the case in H.G. Wells's 1905 novel, *Kipps*, in which the eponymous protagonist, a lower middle-class orphan, receives a sizeable and unexpected windfall from his grandfather. One of the many things that this windfall enables Kipps to do is to stay at the luxurious Royal Grand Hotel in London. However, as is demonstrated in the discussion of the dining room in Chap. 4, Wells ultimately reveals the apparent impossibility of true social mobility in a particularly excruciating scene in the hotel dining room, in which Kipps feels himself thoroughly exposed and unmasked.

It is already becoming clear, then, that the hotel is much more than the average setting. It is more than a background, and to regard it solely as such would be to effectively overlook its significance. Indeed, in his discussion of the role of space in narrative, Wesley Kort notes the tendency of readers to refer to 'setting' when taking 'note of space in a narrative' (2004, p. 15). Yet the very term 'setting', Kort argues, 'condemns the language of place to inherently passive and secondary roles. "Setting" suggests background, necessary, perhaps, but never, like the other languages of narrative, foregrounded' (2004, p. 15). According to Kort, 'the term sounds empty as well as passive' (2004, p. 15). The three other 'languages of narrative' that Kort refers to here include that 'of character', 'of actions and events', and 'of the teller's interests or attitudes' (2004, p. 14). Each of these four languages should be understood as playing an equally important role in the development of narrative, though crucially, the shifting dynamics of these languages means that any one of them may be temporarily subordinate to the others at points throughout the narrative. However, Kort asserts that too often place and space are relegated to a lesser role by the term 'setting', maintaining that this 'is an inadequate term for covering the possibilities of language and space in narrative discourse because place and space need not stand only as background and need not lack force and significance' (2004, p. 15). Instead, he argues that 'spatial language in a narrative can be active, meaningful, and primary' (Kort 2004, p. 15). To regard space in narrative as active means to regard it not as mere setting or background, but as that which decisively shapes the form, structure, and possibilities of narrative. The hotel is uniquely placed to demonstrate this 'active, meaningful, and primary' quality of space in narrative.

Indeed, it is the inherent mobility of the hotel that prevents it from being relegated to mere background, and the movement and transience by which this space is characterised marks it as a space which is always already 'active, meaningful, and primary'. As noted in the Introduction, the hotel functions as a space of mobility on a number of levels. Firstly, it is a space that is brought into being and reified by the movement of people from one place to another, and is typically (though not always) a point on a journey or a destination in itself. By its very nature, the hotel—and particularly the hotel corridor—is a space that is imbued with an air of impermanence, existing as it does for guests who are always coming and going. Even for those guests whose stay in the hotel is indefinite, and which thereby appears on the surface to be more secure, the constant stream of arrivals and departures that sustains this space characterises the existence of anyone staying within the hotel as one which is both transient and ephemeral. Mobility is also, however, inherent in the architectural design of the hotel, which in itself is governed by the movements of hotel guests and staff. It is therefore a space that is both produced and continually constituted by mobility, and which is consequently never passive, but always active.

Yet the question remains as to what it means for a space to be active in terms of narrative. Kort maintains that space is active in the sense that the 'various locations in a narrative can be read as constituting a kind of "geographical synthesis" in the narrative analogous to the kind of synthesis of actions and events we refer to as the narrative's plot' (2004, p. 15).[2] He argues further that the 'geography' of a narrative, the locations by which it is constituted, 'can set limits and boundaries to the narrative world, determining, for example, what occurs, what is possible, and what can and cannot be expected' (Kort 2004, p. 15). In evidence here are the first indications of a link between space and plot, and more importantly, of the connection between space and narrative form. On this understanding, the

---

[2] Here, Kort cites: J. Nicholas Entrikin, *The Betweenness of Place: Towards a Geography of Modernity* (Baltimore: Johns Hopkins University Press, 1991), p. 128.

space of the narrative, and the various locations that make up its geography, is more than just a passive background—instead, it decisively shapes the narrative, dictating what actions and events can take place, and effectively ruling out those that cannot. In terms of narrative possibilities, however, the hotel is perhaps a more flexible location than most. The very nature of this space—its transience and impermanence, and its (apparent) openness to all—means that almost anyone might arrive, and almost anything might happen. But that word 'almost' is important here, as there are nevertheless still parameters for the action and events that are likely to take place within the hotel, parameters which will become clear throughout this book. The focus here, however, is upon the relationship between space and narrative form and structure, and specifically, on how to conceive of the hotel as a space which effectively drives the narrative forward in literature of the late nineteenth and early twentieth centuries.

As a route into thinking about the ways in which the space of the hotel shapes and/or dictates narrative form, Andrew Thacker's conception of 'textual space' is particularly useful. Thacker maintains that, when considering the relationship between literature and geography and space, it is crucial to 'reconnect the representational spaces in literary texts not only to the material spaces they depict, but also reverse the movement, and understand how social spaces dialogically help fashion the literary *forms* of texts' (2005, p. 63; emphasis in original). Here, Thacker further articulates and extends Kort's arguments, making explicit the importance of recognising how space can directly influence narrative form. Thacker goes on to envisage a 'critical literary geography' that

> would trace how social space intrudes upon the internal construction of spatial forms. *Literary texts represent social spaces, but social space shapes literary forms.* The term *textual space* could then refer to this interaction between spatial forms and social space in the written text. Emphasis should be devoted to spatial features of literature such as typography and layout on the page; the space of metaphor and the shifting between different senses of space within a text; or the very shape of narrative forms, found in open-ended fictions or novels that utilise circular patterns for stories. (2005, p. 63; emphasis in original)

This 'critical literary geography' proposed by Thacker has since been taken up by numerous others, and indeed, writing ten years after Thacker, Sheila Hones acknowledges the arguments outlined above as an 'important predecessor of current literary geography' (2015, p. 1). Following Thacker's insistence that 'to investigate a novel as a spatial text must amount to more than simply considering how that text represents an interesting location', I am concerned here less with the way in which hotels are represented in the novels considered in this book (though this will be touched upon), but more with the various ways in which authors employ the space of the hotel, and particularly, in this chapter, in how they use this space to inform and construct their narratives.

There is nevertheless one final and significant critical perspective to acknowledge before embarking on a fuller consideration of the precise way in which the space of the hotel affects and shapes narrative form—that of Joseph Frank's 1945 concept of spatial form, which Thacker and others credit as being a key instigator of discussions of space and modernist narratives. Frank himself returns to the arguments of Gotthold Ephraim Lessing, the eighteenth-century German Enlightenment thinker, on form in art versus form in literature. Frank cites Lessing's arguments:

> Form in the plastic arts [...] is necessarily spatial because the visible aspects of objects can best be presented juxtaposed in an instant of time. Literature, on the other hand, makes use of language, composed of a succession of words proceeding through time; and it follows that literary form, to harmonize with the essential quality of its medium, must be based primarily on some form of narrative sequence. (Frank 1963 [1945], p. 6)[3]

Lessing's arguments, then, are in essence a fairly traditional understanding of visual art as spatial, and literary and/or narrative art as temporal. Yet Frank claims that modernist literature makes a decisive break from this more traditional understanding, in that it moves towards spatial, rather than temporal, form. He argues that modernist writers—among whom he includes T.S. Eliot, Ezra Pound, James Joyce, and Djuna Barnes—'ideally intend their reader to apprehend their work spatially, in a moment of time, rather than as a sequence' (Frank 1963 [1945], pp. 8–9). Time, then, is still a key factor here, but importantly, in spatial form, the temporal aspect of the narrative must be non-sequential, and ideally, events must be presented simultaneously.

Frank cites the significance of Imagism in this regard, an image being, according to Pound, 'that which presents an intellectual and emotional complex in an instant of time' (Pound 1913, p. 200). In order to fully

---

[3] See also: Gotthold Ephraim Lessing, *Laocoon: Or, the Limits of Poetry and Painting*. Translated by William A. Steel (London: J.M. Dent & Sons, 1930).

illustrate his point regarding spatial form and how it might be recognised, however, Frank turns first to a scene from Gustave Flaubert's 1856 novel, *Madame Bovary*, rather than to a more recognisably modernist novel.[4] Referring to the country fair scene, Frank notes three levels of action—the crowd, the speech-making officials, and the whispering lovers in a room overlooking the scene below—and argues that these are presented as if taking place simultaneously 'by cutting back and forth between the various levels of action in a slowly rising crescendo' (1963 [1945], p. 15). Labelling the scene as 'cinematographic' as well as an example of spatial form—and indeed, for Frank at least, the two may well go hand in hand— he maintains that the scene

> illustrates, on a small scale, what we mean by the spatialization of form in a novel. For the duration of the scene, at least, the time-flow of the narrative is halted; attention is focused on the interplay of relationships within the immobilized time-area. (1963 [1945], p. 15)

While it is important to point out here that this is one of several ways in which to read the relationship between space and narrative form, it is nevertheless a significant one in terms of the prioritisation of space over time, and how this can aid recognition of spatial form.

Virginia Woolf's first novel, *The Voyage Out* (1915), contains evidence of a very similar kind of spatialisation of form to that which Frank recognises in Flaubert's *Madame Bovary*. Woolf's novel centres, as the title indicates, on a journey from England to South America, focusing on the experiences of twenty-four-year-old Rachel Vinrace, who travels out with her aunt and uncle, the Ambroses. In terms of the key locations of the novel, much of the action takes place either in London, at sea, in the villa in which Rachel resides with her aunt and uncle when they arrive in Santa Marina, and on the boat on which a group takes an expedition upriver to a nearby village. However, there is one other significant location in the novel, which is that of the hotel in Santa Marina. In a brief history of Santa Marina given in Chapter Seven of the novel, the narrator observes that the hotel was converted 'quickly' from an old monastery to answer the increasing

---

[4] Frank does go on, however, to discuss spatial form in reference to Joyce's *Ulysses* (1922) and Barnes's *Nightwood* (1936). In addition to this, critics such as William A. Johnsen recognise and articulate the links between Flaubert's 1856 novel and modernism. See: William A. Johnsen, '*Madame Bovary*: Romanticism, Modernism, and Bourgeois Style', *MLN* 94 (4) (1979): 843–850.

tourist demand, as 'the fashion spread', and 'a famous line of steamships altered its route' to serve the town (Woolf 2009 [1915], p. 98). These brief remarks locate the hotel very much as the domain of tourists, as opposed to travellers, the latter being the group with which the Ambroses and Rachel might well associate themselves, however inaccurately, due to the fact that the villa in which they stay was built by Helen Ambrose's brother some years earlier, 'in the very spot which had now become so popular' (Woolf 2009 [1915], p. 98). This effective relegation of the hotel as a space for tourists is echoed later on in the novel when even its own guests seek refuge from the hotel in the Ambroses' villa:

> It was now the height of the season, and every ship that came from England left a few people on the shores of Santa Marina who drove up to the hotel. The fact that the Ambroses had a house where one could escape momentarily from the slightly inhuman atmosphere of an hotel was a source of genuine pleasure. (Woolf 2009 [1915], p. 255)

Here, the idea of the hotel as a place from which to escape is made explicit, and the reason for the flight of these guests, who clearly regard themselves as more discerning, is attributed to the 'slightly inhuman atmosphere of the hotel', hinting at a distaste for what they regard as the inherent artificiality and constructed nature of the hotel as touristic space.

Yet the space of the hotel in Santa Marina reveals the underlying characteristics, drives, and desires (not always positive) of many of its British guests in a number of different ways, which extend far beyond their own desire to escape the space. As noted above, there are distinct similarities to be drawn between scenes at the hotel in *The Voyage Out* and the scene of the agricultural fair in Flaubert's novel. While largely absent from the narrative structure is the cutting back and forth that Frank observes between the levels in the scene in question from *Madam Bovary* (instead, there is more linearity to Woolf's narrative), the scene in Woolf's novel nevertheless moves and is structured according to the architecture of the hotel. This movement begins towards the end of Chapter Eight, when Helen Ambrose is led by her excitable niece, Rachel, on a nocturnal mission to investigate the local hotel. As they walk in the darkness up the road to the hotel, they are suddenly 'confronted by a large square building', as the hotel comes into view (Woolf 2009 [1915], p. 109). That these two women are 'confronted' by the hotel gives a sense not only of its considerable size (thus suggesting that this is or can at least be likened to a grand hotel), but also hints at the potentially patriarchal nature of the space, an idea that is reinforced by its former existence as a monastery. More significant, however, is the architectural structure and layout of the hotel, which is revealed by the 'row of long windows' which run along the front of the hotel (Woolf 2009 [1915], p. 109). These windows, as Woolf's narrator makes explicitly clear, not only allow Helen and Rachel to see into each of the downstairs rooms, but further, '[e]ach window revealed a different section of the life of the hotel' (Woolf 2009 [1915], p. 109). It is in this way, with the steady procession of windows giving rise to a series of different vignettes one after another, that the hotel plays a key role in the spatialisation of form.

The architecture of the hotel thus breaks down the narrative into separate moments, each detailing the activity taking place within a distinct space of the hotel. This results in a narrative that is effectively compartmentalised, and structured according to the movement through each of these rooms. In terms of the rest of the novel, however, this structure is comparatively brief, lasting only for the final part of Chapter Eight, and the first part of Chapter Nine, and just as Frank observes of the agricultural fair scene in Flaubert's novel, the scenes which take place within the hotel might well be considered as being 'of minor importance to [the] novel as a whole' (Frank 1963 [1945], p. 16). Regardless of their importance to the overall plot (though they are of some importance, given the opportunity they provide for introducing those characters residing at the hotel), this thirteen-page section of the novel is nevertheless highly significant in terms of its experimentation with spatial form. This experiment is, however, one which reveals itself gradually, as initially, in Chapter Eight, the descriptions of activities taking place within the individual rooms are framed by the perspectives of Helen and Rachel, as they creep along the outside of the hotel, peering into the rooms one by one. After strategically placing themselves 'into one of the broad columns of shadow which separated the windows', they 'gazed in', and first 'found themselves just outside the dining-room. It was being swept; a waiter was eating a bunch of grapes with his leg across the corner of a table' (Woolf 2009 [1915], p. 109). The overtly casual position of the waiter, together with the darkness outside, indicates that dinner has already been served, and that the guests have now left the dining room. This is supported by the next window, that of the kitchen, which reveals the staff 'washing up' (Woolf 2009 [1915], p. 109). At this point, the narrative still follows the movements and point of view of Helen and Rachel:

Moving on, they became lost in a plantation of bushes, and then suddenly found themselves outside the drawing-room, where the ladies and gentlemen, having dined well, lay back in deep armchairs, occasionally speaking or turning over the pages of magazines. (Woolf 2009 [1915], p. 109)

That the scenes revealed through the window are coloured by the perspective of the two watching women is reinforced by their occasional asides to one another, such as Rachel's comment to Helen, regarding the guests in the drawing room, that 'They're all old in this room' (Woolf 2009 [1915], p. 109) and Helen's caution, 'Take care or we shall be seen' (Woolf 2009 [1915], p. 110). While the space of the hotel undoubtedly plays a role here, the narrative is primarily focused on, and structured by, the movements and intentions of two characters. At the end of Chapter Eight, however, Helen and Rachel flee the grounds of the hotel, having been spotted by someone (who is later revealed to have been Mr Hirst), and this framing perspective is removed. It is from this point on that the narrative takes on an increasingly spatial form.

The first half of Chapter Nine of Woolf's *The Voyage Out* is structured not according to the perspective of characters, but by the spaces of the hotel itself. Specifically, the narrative in these nine pages is shaped by a movement through the hotel bedrooms. The chapter opens with a temporal marker, the narrator noting that an hour had passed since Helen and Rachel's swift departure, 'and the downstairs rooms at the hotel grew dim and were almost deserted, while the little box-like squares above them were brilliantly irradiated. Some forty or fifty people were going to bed' (Woolf 2009 [1915], p. 113). Here, the narrative falls briefly back on temporality as the primary structuring mode, but this is merely to indicate the parameters of what Frank refers to as an 'immobilized time area' (1963 [1945], p. 15). While time does move forward over the ensuing pages, its passage quickly becomes less dominant in the narrative, with the emphasis instead switching to a spatialisation of form.

This focus on space begins with a description of the thinness of the walls between the hotel bedrooms:

The thump of jugs set down on the floor above could be heard and the chink of china, for there was not so thick a partition between the rooms as one might wish, so Miss Allan [...] determined, giving the wall a smart rap with her knuckles. It was only matchboard, she decided, run up to make many little rooms of one large one. (Woolf 2009 [1915], p. 113)

The sounds from the floor above, and, later, from the neighbouring room, give a sense not only of the lack of privacy in this hotel bedroom, but also of the insubstantiality of the hotel itself, and the economy that has gone into its creation. Together with the aforementioned remarks on the hotel as a space for tourists, the 'matchboard' walls identified by the disapproving Miss Allan serve to reinforce an idea of artificiality, cheapness, and above all a capitalist desire to fit as many guests as possible into the hotel. The intrusive nature of the sounds from neighbouring rooms is emphasised by the way in which they preclude concentration. Miss Allan, who is 'writing a short *Primer of English Literature*—Beöwulf to Swinburne', is 'deep in the fifth book' of Wordsworth's 'Prelude'

> when a pair of boots dropped, one after another, on the floor above her. She looked up and speculated. Whose boots were they, she wondered. She then became aware of a swishing sound next door—a woman, clearly, putting away her dress. It was succeeded by a gentle tapping sound, such as that which accompanies hair-dressing. It was very difficult to keep her attention fixed upon the 'Prelude'. Was it Susan Warrington tapping? She forced herself, however, to read to the end of the book. (Woolf 2009 [1915], p. 113)

This passage is significant for what it reveals about the phenomenological effect of thin hotel walls upon occupants.[5] Miss Allan's thoughts and actions are repeatedly interrupted by the noises she hears through these walls, explicitly hindering her ability to focus on the task at hand. Her attention inevitably wanders to identifying the various sounds coming from the next room, and to attempting to decide upon their originator, to the extent that she has to consciously 'force herself' to finish her book. However, the thinness of the bedroom walls plays another important role here in terms of narrative form, in that the sounds heard by Miss Allan prefigure, and to an extent engender, the movement of the narrative into the next room.

The adjoining room is indeed occupied, as Miss Allan predicts, by Susan Warrington, and the narrative moves 'through the wall' to the next vignette: 'Very different was the room through the wall, though as like in shape as one egg-box is like another. As Miss Allan read her book, Susan Warrington was brushing her hair' (Woolf 2009 [1915], pp. 113–4). There is, here, a slight cut backwards in time, given that the narrative leaves Miss Allan to move into Susan Warrington's room only once Miss

[5] See Chap. 5 for further discussion of this.

Allan has 'turned out the light' (Woolf 2009 [1915], p. 113). So the narrative is at this moment not strictly linear in terms of its movement through time (though it does proceed as such from this point on), further emphasising the prioritisation of space in terms of form. Unlike Miss Allan, Susan Warrington is undisturbed in her actions—which include 'meditating' on her feelings for fellow hotel guest Arthur Venning, writing in her diary, and praying—by any noises from adjoining rooms, which is likely because William Pepper, who occupies the room next door to her, is asleep. With this next guest unconscious, the narrator takes a step forward:

> A glance into the next room revealed little more than a nose, prominent above the sheets. Growing accustomed to the darkness [...] one could distinguish a lean form, terribly like the body of a dead person, the body indeed of William Pepper, asleep too. (Woolf 2009 [1915], p. 115)

Where previously the narrator has limited themselves to largely anonymous and impersonal descriptions, here, with no character actions to relate other than sleep, they become more visible, more overtly agential. Just shy of slipping into the first person, they 'glance' into the room, 'growing accustomed to the darkness', and attempt to 'distinguish' the form of the sleeping guest. This raises the possibility that the narrative is at this point, as in Chapter Eight, framed by the perspective of a character, in this case the narrator. This problematises the notion of spatial form, as it suggests that the impact of space upon narrative structure is diminished, and that the movement through the rooms merely follows the movement of the narrator as character, rather than the narrative itself.

In the same paragraph in which the form of a sleeping William Pepper is identified, the narrator also moves rapidly through the adjoining few rooms, giving, for the first time, their room numbers:

> Thirty-six, thirty-seven, thirty-eight—here were three Portuguese men of business, asleep presumably, since a snore came with the regularity of a great ticking clock. Thirty-nine was a corner room, at the end of the passage, but late though it was—'one' struck gently downstairs—a line of light under the door showed that someone was still awake. (Woolf 2009 [1915], p. 115)

The speed with which these descriptions are given creates the impression of someone moving quickly down a corridor, and the notion of the corridor is reinforced by the absence of description of the interiors of the rooms. The narrator makes assumptions about the unconscious state of the guests within based only on the snores that can be heard outside the rooms. A description is then given of the precise location of room number thirty-nine, and the narrator adds another temporal marker ('"one" struck gently downstairs'), before making one final observation, again from the corridor, as to the 'line of light under the door'. All of these details and observations contribute to the suggestion that, in this particular paragraph, the narrative is determined by the perspective of a character—the narrator—moving through space, rather than by the space itself. However, once the narrative moves into the next room—room number thirty-nine, with the 'line of light under the door', which is occupied by Mr and Mrs Hughling Elliot, both of whom are awake—the narrator once again fades into the background. In this account of night falling across the hotel, the narrator comes more to the fore, or comes increasingly into focus as a character, when describing rooms in which guests are absent or unconscious, retreating again into impersonality when the rooms are occupied by guests who are awake and active in that space. In the latter instances, where the narrator retains a level of impersonality, the narrative form seems driven entirely by the space of the hotel itself, whereas in the former, the narrative appears to be framed and shaped by the perspective of the narrator as an inquisitive character moving through the hotel corridor. This raises key questions, then, as to whether the narrative and narration across these few pages is shaped and driven primarily by character (whether that be the narrator as character, or the named characters in the plot), or solely by space itself.

One way to answer these questions might be to point to issues with the development of the narrator in *The Voyage Out*. Joanne Frye, for example, is overtly critical of the narrative voice in Woolf's first novel, arguing that it 'is very uneven: here it points clumsily to a significant "moment"; here it insists that we notice a landscape; here it comments on a character's emotions' (1980, p. 411). For Frye, Woolf is still, in this her earliest work, grappling with establishing a sophisticated and effective impersonal narrative voice. However, Frye does acknowledge that this early attempt at a narrative voice has moments of power, particularly 'when it withdraws into the patterns of imagery', and she maintains further that this pattern is often 'sustained through a use of perspective and landscape peculiar to this novel' (1980, p. 411). The passage under consideration, which gives an account of night passing in the hotel, is used by Frye as an example of one of several 'impersonal descriptions which help to provide the novel's understructure and which move away from the apparently personal level of the novel into a mood neither of social breadth nor of individual emotional depth' (1980, p. 413). Yet as the discussion thus far has shown, this passage detailing the hotel at night does not sustain this level of impersonality throughout, and this may well be attributable to what Frye terms Woolf's 'overall, though still clumsy, control of an impersonal narrative voice' (1980, p. 403). The problems that the rather inconsistent narrative voice poses for a reading of the spatialisation of form in this passage might, however, also be resolved by a further consideration of the significance of the relationship between subjects and space.

The complication presented by a narrative voice which fluctuates between impersonality and personality, between background and foreground, is that it makes it unclear whether or not the progression and structure of the narrative is governed by the actions of characters (either those of the narrator as character or the other characters in the novel) or by the space of the hotel. Yet it might well be understood, however, as being driven and shaped by both. The narrator is more present, more noticeable, when describing those hotel rooms in which no activity (other than sleeping) is taking place, and is more impersonal, or less noticeable, when giving an account of the hotel rooms in which guests are awake and active. In this sense, it is perhaps not space alone that is dictating the movement of the narrative, but rather, the relationship between the individual spaces of the hotel rooms and the characters who occupy them, a relationship which is brought into being when the characters are engaged in activities that are themselves shaped and/or supported by the room itself. Susan Warrington, for example, sits at her dressing table brushing her hair and, looking 'with extreme solicitude at her own face in the glass', meditates upon life and love, before moving across to the writing table in the room to update her diary (Woolf 2009 [1915], pp. 114–5). Miss Allan's relationship with her hotel room is no less evident, though somewhat more fraught, as her attempts to read in bed are continuously interrupted by the noises that surround her from the above and neighbouring rooms. Later on in the chapter, the narrative moves into the room of St John Hirst, which adjoins that of his friend, Terence Hewet. Hirst—who, it is noted, occupies the room in which, previously, 'the boots had dropped so heavily upon Miss Allan's head'—sits 'deep in an armchair', 'reading the third volume of Gibbon's *History of the Decline and Fall of Rome* by candle-light' (Woolf

2009 [1915], p. 116),[6] only to be interrupted by the entrance of Hewet. In describing their conversation and their movements around the room—as Hirst, for example, bends 'over the basin' to wash, before 'hopping briskly across the room'—the narrator once more retreats into impersonality, as the focus shifts to the relationship between these characters and the space of the hotel room (Woolf 2009 [1915], p. 117). Even in those moments where the narrator comes to the fore, however, and the narrative is framed by the perspective of the narrative voice, the direction of the narrative is still nevertheless driven by the space of the hotel. In this sense, space here remains dominant, particularly so when it is paired with the actions of the characters who occupy that space, and a spatialisation of form is clearly in evidence.

This brief section of Woolf's *The Voyage Out*, which charts nightfall across the hotel in Santa Marina, conforms clearly to what Frank refers to as 'the spatialization of form in a novel' (1963 [1945], p. 15). For these few pages, the structure and movement of the narrative is dictated by the space of the hotel, rather than by the passage of time. While Frank cites a passage from Flaubert's 1856 novel, *Madame Bovary*, to exemplify this, he nevertheless argues that the spatialisation of form is something that can be firmly linked to modernism, and to writers like Eliot, Joyce, and Barnes who 'ideally intend their reader to apprehend their work spatially, in a moment of time, rather than as a sequence' (1963 [1945], pp. 8–9). This connection made by Frank between modernism and spatial form not only falls in with a critical tradition of identifying modernist literature as that which is formally and technically innovative and experimental, but it also prefigures more recent debates, taken up by those such as Thacker, regarding the centrality of space to modernist literature. As a canonical and high-modernist writer, Woolf here, then, provides an ideal example of this affinity between modernism and spatial form. Yet I want now to turn to the work of non-modernist authors such as Arnold Bennett to investigate the extent to which they too might be regarded as being involved in similar experiments with the spatialisation of form, in the creation of their own hotel narratives, before turning back to the modernist fiction of Ford Madox Ford to consider an alternative type of hotel narrative, one based on experience rather than architecture.

[6]That Hirst is reading his book 'by candle-light' is worth noting here, as in all the rooms described so far, lights have been 'turned off', indicating the presence of electric lights. The lack of electric lights, and the fact that his room is on an upper floor, reveals this to be a cheaper room than those occupied by Miss Allan, Susan Warrington, and the Elliots. See Chap. 5 for further discussion of the social code of hotel bedrooms.

THE HOTEL NARRATIVE

The preceding discussion of Woolf's *The Voyage Out* demonstrated the way in which narrative form is shaped and structured by space, and specifically by the space of the hotel. Yet, this spatialisation of form in Woolf's novel takes place only across a few pages, with the narrative reverting back to a more temporally dominated form once the account of the night in the hotel has passed. While analysis of this passage does reveal the way in which writers—and particularly, in this case, modernist writers—employed the space of the hotel as more than mere setting or background, it is necessary to look beyond such brief passages in order to find more concrete evidence of the effect of the hotel space on narrative form. In this section, I read two early-twentieth-century novels an attempt to delineate a previously unrecognised narrative form, which I term the hotel narrative. I explore how the hotel necessarily shapes narrative form and structure through the movement along its corridors from room to room, creating an episodic structure well suited to genre fiction such as the detective or mystery novel, as exemplified by Bennett's *The Grand Babylon Hotel* (1902). But I argue that the space of the hotel also has a definite, if less immediately apparent, effect on the narrative structure of modernist works such as Ford Madox Ford's *The Good Soldier* (1915) through the role and significance of the narrator, John Dowell. I argue that the hotel's inherent impermanence constructs it as a space in which moments of transition regularly occur, either propelling the narrative forward, or, alternatively, engendering moments of crisis for those characters who reside within. I posit the hotel narrative as fragmented and often non-linear, and maintain that, while criticism has tended to identify these qualities as defining features of modernist literature, the analysis of the hotel narrative in the second half of this chapter reveal experiments with narrative and form to be widespread across literature of the early twentieth century.

Published in novel form in 1902, after having been first serialised in *The Golden Penny* in 1901, *The Grand Babylon Hotel* was Arnold Bennett's second novel in an extremely prolific writing career that spanned just over thirty-five years,[7] in which Bennett published no fewer than thirty-four novels, along with several collections of short stories, plays, and numerous works of criticism, journalism, and non-fiction. In terms of his literary

---

[7] From 1895, when he began work on his first novel, *A Man from the North* (1898), until his death from typhoid fever in 1931.

output, Bennett is perhaps most well remembered today for his novels and short stories set primarily in the Staffordshire Potteries,[8] particularly *The Old Wives Tale* (1908) and *Clayhanger* (1910), though several of his other novels, *The Grand Babylon Hotel* included, engage with a far broader, more urban, and more international range of locations. Yet, Bennett has unfortunately, until relatively recently,[9] been neglected in literary criticism. As Randi Saloman notes in her introduction to the recent Broadview edition of *The Grand Babylon Hotel*:

> Time has not been kind to Arnold Bennett. Arguably the most recognized, most popular writer in England in the early years of the twentieth century, with a distinctive appearance and a staggering output of novels, short stories, plays, and articles, today Bennett is neglected disproportionately by academics and general readers alike. (2016, p. 11)

The reasons behind Bennett's relative obscurity are manifold. It can be attributed, at least in part, to Bennett's reputation 'as a commercially driven popular writer rather than a serious literary figure' (Saloman 2016, p. 11).[10] In this sense, it is the very popularity of his novels during his own lifetime that has since afforded him such a lack of critical acclaim. This is, of course, inextricably bound up with a much more widespread critical disregard for the popular, which has, until recently, seen late-nineteenth- and early-twentieth-century writers such as Marie Corelli, Elinor Glyn, A.E.W. Mason, and Bennett himself—all bestselling authors in their day—overlooked and ignored by literary scholarship on the period. This lacunae of work on

[8] Six small towns—Tunstall, Burslem, Hanley, Stoke, Fenton, and Longton—which today make up the city of Stoke-on-Trent in the West Midlands of England. Bennett himself was born in Hanley in 1867, moving later to Burslem with his family, and the area was depicted as 'the Five Towns' in his writings, omitting Fenton.

[9] Recent scholarship on Bennett includes a collection of essays, entitled *An Arnold Bennett Companion*. Edited by John Shapcott (Leek: Churnet Valley Books, 2015); John Squillace's monograph, *Modernism, Modernity, and Arnold Bennett* (Lewisburg, PA: Bucknell University Press, 1997); and a Broadview edition of *The Grand Babylon Hotel*. Edited by Randi Saloman (Peterborough, ON: Broadview Press, 2016).

[10] Virginia Woolf was also fairly damning about Bennett's immense rate of production, remarking in her 1924 essay, 'Character in Fiction' (which had evolved out of her previous essay, 'Mr Bennett and Mrs Brown'), that: 'I am not going to deny that Mr Bennett has some reason when he complains that our Georgian writers are unable to make us believe that our characters are real. I am forced to agree that they do not pour out three immortal masterpieces with Victorian regularity every autumn'. See: Virginia Woolf, 'Character in Fiction', in *Selected Essays*, ed. David Bradshaw, 37–54 (Oxford: Oxford University Press, 2008), p. 51.

popular fiction of the late nineteenth and early twentieth centuries can also, however, be attributed to the positioning of modernism as the preeminent object of literary study. Yet this tendency has, as discussed in the Introduction, recently been disrupted by the surge of literary scholarship that has sought, if not to destabilise or undermine modernism's elevated position, then to at least reconsider the boundaries of modernism itself. My tracing here of the hotel narrative falls under the auspices of this approach, as it reveals experiments with narrative and form to be widespread not just in modernist literature, but across the literatures of modernity.

Bennett's own relationship with modernism has long been regarded as particularly fraught, and indeed this tension is another reason behind the lack of critical attention afforded to his work in the years since his death. More specifically, however, his relative obscurity might well be attributed to Virginia Woolf, and her 1924 essays 'Mr Bennett and Mrs Brown' and 'Character in Fiction' (the latter an essay that emerged out of the former, and which was published in *The Criterion* in July 1924). These essays were in part a reaction to a review Bennett had written of her own novel, *Jacob's Room* (1922), which Woolf had judged to be unfavourable. In fact, as John Squillace notes, Bennett's supposed 'attack', in an essay titled 'Is the Novel Decaying?' (1923), 'was balanced by praise' (Squillace 1997, p. 16), Bennett writing that 'I have seldom read a cleverer book than Virginia Woolf's *Jacob's Room*. [...] It is packed and bursting with originality, and it is exquisitely written' (Bennett 1968 [1923], p. 88). However, Bennett did nevertheless level some criticism at Woolf and her contemporaries, and his comments had largely to do with their lack of attention to the creation of character. In a novel, Bennett argues, 'Style counts; plot counts; invention counts; originality of outlook counts; wide information counts; wide sympathy counts. But none of these counts anything like so much as the convincingness of the characters' (1968 [1923], p. 87). Bennett's evident regard for Woolf's skill as a writer is tempered somewhat by his claim that, in *Jacob's Room*, 'the characters do not vitally survive in the mind because the author has been obsessed by details of originality and cleverness' (1968 [1923], p. 88). It is this particular criticism with which, perhaps unsurprisingly, Woolf takes issue in her own essay, and her argument rests both on the clear and explicit distinctions that she makes between the 'Georgian' writers—among whom she counted herself, E.M. Forster, James Joyce, D.H. Lawrence, and T.S. Eliot—and the 'Edwardians', who included John Galsworthy, H.G. Wells, and Bennett himself, as well as on her claim that, 'on or about

December, 1910, human character changed' (p. 38). Woolf pits what she regards as the older generation against the younger, with her central contention being that the 'tools' of the Edwardian writers are simply no longer adequate to depict human character in all its complexity. Of the 'Edwardians', she writes:

> it seems to me that to go to these men and ask them to teach you how to write a novel—how to create characters that are real—is precisely like going to a bootmaker and asking him to teach you how to make a watch. (Woolf, p. 44)

Woolf's fairly scathing critique here marks the work of Bennett, Wells, and Galsworthy as crude and workmanlike, in stark opposition to the complexity and dexterity of the writers of the younger generation, among whom she regards herself. For her, these three writers, and Bennett in particular, are too much concerned with the material, and with detailed descriptions of the spatial surroundings of characters, than upon character itself, arguing that with these details, Bennett 'is trying to make us imagine for him; he is trying to hypnotise us into the belief that, because he has made a house, there must be a person living there' (Woolf, p. 47). It is true that in Bennett's novels, and specifically in *The Grand Babylon Hotel*, space is foregrounded, playing a central role not only in characterisation, but in narrative form and structure. Yet it is in this significance of space that clear similarities between the work of Woolf and Bennett begin to emerge. Woolf, as demonstrated in the previous section of this chapter, utilises the space of the hotel in *The Voyage Out*, its architectural layout, to construct a spatial form, and this is precisely what Bennett does in *The Grand Babylon Hotel*. Indeed, Gloria Fromm observes this connection between the two writers, suggesting that Woolf herself likely recognised that 'they were too similar', and that this recognition may well have underpinned Woolf's determined efforts in 1924 to distinguish her own craft from Bennett's (1982, p. 29). It is in the space of the hotel, however, and how these two authors employ it in their creation of narrative form, that these similarities are undeniably present.

This is not to suggest, however, that Bennett and Woolf's spatialisation of form is identical, or that they utilise the space of the hotel in precisely the same way. For one thing, as noted above, the space of the hotel appears sporadically in Woolf's first novel, shaping its form only momentarily. In Bennett's *The Grand Babylon Hotel*, on the other hand, twenty-one of the novel's thirty chapters take place primarily within the eponymous hotel, and the architecture of the hotel is integral to the way in which the events of the plot unfold throughout. There is also the question of genre, which is more pertinent to Bennett's novel than to Woolf's. Like many of her works, Woolf's *The Voyage Out* seemingly evades any genre classification more precise than that of 'novel', and it has certainly not been discussed critically in terms of genre fiction. Bennett's *The Grand Babylon Hotel*, however, is categorised by the author himself as a 'fantasia', though precisely what this term denotes is unclear. Part mystery, part thriller, part detective fiction, the novel never sits particularly comfortably within any one genre, and yet it is nevertheless one which is driven, in part, by suspense, a factor which, Squillace notes, is typically 'eschewed by modernists' such as Woolf (1997, p. 183). While this in itself is yet another indication of the differences in the way in which modernist and popular fiction is approached and valued by critics (questions of genre are rarely raised in relation to any modernist writing), genre is here worth considering in terms of its relation to narrative form.

Bennett's novel, as noted, is resistant to easy categorisation, encompassing as it does key aspects of a number of genres. However, given that the story revolves around an initial crime—the murder of Reginald Dimmock, discovered in Chapter Five—followed by a series of other, connected crimes, it might productively be read as a form of detective fiction. Theodore Racksole, the American millionaire who buys the Grand Babylon Hotel in the second chapter of the novel, here functions as the detective, accompanied in no small part by his daughter Nella, who is, if anything, more adventurous and takes more risks in her search for the truth. Both characters attempt to solve the mysterious death of Dimmock, and the even more perplexing disappearance of his body, when the police fail to make progress with the case. Observing that 'the arrangement of narrative elements is fundamentally the same in the majority of classical detective novels' (Hühn 1987, p. 453), Peter Hühn charts the typical way in which the narrative of such novels unfolds:

> Most classical detective novels start out with a community in a state of stable order. Soon a crime (usually a murder) occurs, which the police are unable to clear up. The insoluble crime acts as a destabilising event, because the system of norms and rules regulating life in the community has proved powerless in one crucial instance and is therefore discredited. In other words, the narrative incapability on the part of society's official agents, their inability to

discover and tell the story of the crime, thus threatens the validity of the established order. At this point, the detective takes over the case, embarks on a course of thorough investigations, and finally identifies the criminal, explaining his solution at length. (1987, p. 452)

In Bennett's novel, the Grand Babylon Hotel, with its guests and staff, is itself the 'community in a state of stable order'. The police's inability to solve the crime does indeed destabilise this community, to the extent that Racksole, as owner of the hotel, takes it upon himself to act as detective and investigate the case himself. It is Racksole and Nella, rather than the police, who restore order to the hotel.

Yet the failure of the police is not the Racksoles' only or even most pressing motivation to solve the crime. In fact, it is made clear very early on that Theodore Racksole has always had little faith in the police, and that he held them 'in sorry esteem. He acquainted them with the facts, answered their queries with a patient weariness, and expected nothing whatever from that quarter' (Bennett 2016 [1902], p. 87). Instead, Racksole is largely driven by anger that such a crime could have been committed in 'his hotel' without his knowledge, and by the unwelcome realisation that he does not wield as much power in England as in America:

Over there he was a 'boss'; men trembled before his name; when he wished a thing to happen—well, it happened; if he desired to know a thing, he just knew it. But here in London, Theodore Racksole was not quite the same Theodore Racksole. He dominated New York; but London, for the most part, seemed not to take much interest in him; and there were certainly various persons in London who were capable of snapping his fingers at him—at Theodore Racksole. Neither he nor his daughter could get used to that fact. (Bennett 2016 [1902], pp. 87–8)

Racksole is not compelled into action by the threat that this crime, and the failure of the police to solve it, poses to 'the validity of the established order'. The established order here is that of London, and Racksole is motivated not by any desire to restore order to the imperial centre, but rather by his own insecurities triggering his apparent loss of status on arrival in England, a loss which he had seemingly not anticipated. In an earlier discussion with the hotel's previous owner, Félix Babylon, Racksole details his English heritage, noting that while he considers himself to be 'a true American', his English father 'began by being a bedmaker at an

Oxford college' (Bennett 2016 [1902], p. 71). In coming to England, Racksole's intentions were originally to 'build a house in Park Lane', to 'buy some immemorial country seat with a history as long as the A.T. and S. railroad', and to 'calmly and gradually settle down' (Bennett 2016 [1902], p. 71). As Saloman notes, 'Racksole romanticises England as the place where truth and history reside, and imagines his entry into English life will solidify his identity, rather than confront him with the need for self-definition' (2016, p. 25). However, rather than strengthening his sense of identity, England, and London in particular, undermines it, leaving Racksole unnerved and unsettled.

The initial source of Racksole's unease is the head waiter of the Grand Babylon Hotel, Jules (whose real name, it is later revealed, is Tom Jackson), who in the opening pages of the novel at first refuses Racksole's request for an 'Angel's Kiss' cocktail, on the basis that it is an American drink, and that, as he tells Racksole, 'This isn't an American hotel' (Bennett 2016 [1902], pp. 43–4). Soon after this incident, Jules thwarts Racksole's attempt to order 'Filleted steak for two, and a bottle of Bass' for himself and his daughter in the hotel dining room, telling him that Rocco, the head chef, would be unable to serve this dish. Racksole's indignation, his disbelief that he, 'the ineffable Racksole, who owned a thousand miles of railway, several towns, and sixty votes in Congress, should be defied by a waiter, or even by a whole hotel', is what spurs him on to seek out the hotel's owner, Félix Babylon, and purchase the establishment from him (Bennett 2016 [1902], p. 51). Having acquired the hotel, his first act is to summon Rocco, raise his wages, and order the previously denied steak and Bass, 'to be served by Jules—I particularly desire Jules' (Bennett 2016 [1902], p. 55). Thus, the novel establishes a palpable animosity between Racksole and Jules from the outset, a fraught and hostile relationship that sustains Racksole's later determination to uncover Jules as a master criminal. But it also sets up additional tensions over nationality and class that play out over the course of the text. Racksole's own identity, and the social order to which he has become accustomed—a hierarchy in which he occupies the uppermost position—are thus threatened first by London, and then by Jules, and finally by Racksole's lack of control over the crimes which take place within the hotel. These things combined compel him to take on the role of detective.

Lying at the heart of the crimes, and indeed of the very process of detection, is the space of the Grand Babylon Hotel itself. The aforementioned threat to identity felt by Racksole is only reinforced by the hotel that he has recently acquired. In keeping with his character as a 'dominating' New York businessman, he is determined to exert his own influence over the hotel, despite having been warned by Félix Babylon that, 'You think because you control a railroad, or an ironworks, or a line of steamers, therefore you can control anything. But no. Not the Grand Babylon' (Bennett 2016 [1902], p. 56). Key to the Grand Babylon's uncontrollable nature is its architectural layout. Beyond the relatively open spaces of the lobby, lounge, and dining room lie a maze of corridors, staircases, and hidden rooms and passageways. Racksole's efforts to exert order and his own influence over the hotel take the form of moving through and around the hotel in an attempt to familiarise himself with, and orient himself within, this space. Yet despite Racksole's attempts to master the space of the hotel, its complex layout at first thwarts and undermines him. His initial exploration of the hotel takes place in Chapter Three in the middle of the night, mere hours after he has purchased the establishment from Félix Babylon. Once he has entered the corridors of the hotel, however, Racksole almost immediately becomes *dis*oriented, and is 'not so sure that he could discover his own room', having 'forgotten whether it was on the first or second floor' (Bennett 2016 [1902], p. 63). He locates his room only by discovering, rather by accident, a 'very dark and narrow' staircase (most likely a service staircase), and, through a process of elimination, determining that his room must be on the second floor. As he walks the corridors, the hotel seems, to Racksole, 'vast, uncanny, deserted', though crucially he is not intimidated by this space, but instead wanders 'at ease to and fro, rather amused, rather struck by the peculiar sense of night and mystery which had suddenly come over him' (Bennett 2016 [1902], p. 64). Racksole's apparent confidence and assurance here is attributable in part to the luxury of the hotel, with its 'electric lights' and 'thick carpets', and in part to Racksole's own confidence, as a wealthy businessman and as the new owner of the space through which he moves (Bennett 2016 [1902], p. 64). It is during this initial exploration of the hotel that he observes Jules—the head waiter with whom, as previously discussed, Racksole is already at odds—tying a white ribbon around the handle of Room 111, the room assigned to his daughter, Nella (Bennett 2016 [1902], p. 64). Racksole's suspicions regarding Jules are thus heightened, and fail to diminish when it is revealed, a short while later, that the room is no longer occupied by Nella, but by Reginald Dimmock. And yet despite Racksole's suspicions, and despite his determination to orient himself within the space of the hotel, the hotel, at least initially, resists his attempts at orientation.

It is, in fact, the very labyrinthine structure of the hotel—a maze which Racksole is at first unable to successfully navigate—that enables the crimes committed within its walls to take place without Racksole's knowledge.

As a complex and often bewildering space, the Grand Babylon Hotel at first precludes the attempts of Racksole to attain mastery over it in order to reveal its secrets. But by the same token, this same space of the hotel—its architecture and its layout—holds the key to solving the crimes committed within it. Racksole's determination, and his repeated and sustained movements through the hotel, soon begin to pay off, as he discovers secret rooms and passageways that have been central to the execution of the crimes, and which now enable him to uncover those same activities. Yet this movement through the hotel also shapes and structures the narrative, in a similar kind of spatialisation of form to that seen on a much smaller scale in Woolf's *The Voyage Out*. The chapters of Bennett's novel—with titles including 'In the Gold Room', 'Rocco and Room No. 111', and 'In the State Bedroom'—are primarily structured according to the hotel space in which events occur, such as the dining room, lobby, state bedroom, and wine cellar. This movement through the individual rooms and spaces of the hotel creates, as it does in Woolf's novel, a series of vignettes or episodes, giving rise to a somewhat fragmented and episodic narrative structure. The fact that the novel was initially serialised should, of course, not be overlooked here, as this particular publication history certainly contributed to the episodic structure of the narrative. However, it is nevertheless the space of the hotel—and specifically the movement through the corridors and individual rooms—that shapes and indeed engenders the episodic structure of *The Grand Babylon Hotel*, a structure that is so well suited to genre fiction such as the detective novel.

Yet the episodic structure is, by its very nature, aligned with temporality as opposed to spatiality, and with a linear chronology. As Paul Ricoeur notes:

Thanks to its episodic dimension, narrative time tends towards the linear representation of time in several ways: first, the 'then' and 'and then' structure that provides an answer to the question 'What next?' suggests a relation of exteriority between the phases of the action; second, the episodes constitute an open-ended series of events that allows one to add to the 'then' an 'and then' and an 'and so on'; and finally, the episodes follow one another in accordance with the irreversible order of time common to human and physical events. (2002, p. 44)

By the 'relation of exteriority', Ricoeur might well be understood as referring here to the passage of time outside of and apart from the events that
take place, in that the passage of time is what links these moments, or
episodes, together in a linear chronology. Given the prominence of the
space of the hotel in Bennett's novel, however, it is worth exploring the
extent to which, departing from Ricoeur, this 'relation of exteriority'
might instead be conceived of spatially, so that the moments or episodes
in a narrative are linked less by the passage of time, and more by the movement through space. Determining whether or not Bennett's narrative follows a strictly linear chronology throughout can help to illuminate this.

The first six chapters of Bennett's *The Grand Babylon Hotel* do indeed
follow a linear chronology, adhering to this even when the narrative
changes track, in Chapter Eight, to follow Nella (rather than Racksole) in
her pursuit of Miss Spencer to Ostend, and her subsequent kidnapping on
a yacht by Jules. Leaving Nella on the yacht at the end of Chapter Ten,
having just been rescued from a sexual assault at the hands of Jules by
Prince Aribert, this linearity continues as the narrative returns to the
Grand Babylon Hotel and Racksole in Chapter Eleven, and continues
until the end of Chapter Fourteen, which ends with Racksole receiving a
telegram from his daughter, asking him to come immediately to Ostend.
Chapter Fifteen, however, sees an interruption, whereby the narrative
tracks back to re-join Nella and Prince Aribert on the yacht moments after
Jules has been knocked unconscious. It is only at the end of Chapter
Fifteen that the narrative time streams once again correspond, with Nella
arriving at the Hôtel Wellington in Ostend and sending the telegram to
her father. In the final chapters of the novel, however, the temporal linearity is repeatedly disrupted, as the narrative moves more according to the
spaces occupied and passed through by characters than to the passage of
time. This is particularly in evidence in Chapters Twenty-Seven and
Twenty-Eight, in which events take place simultaneously, but in different
spaces of the hotel. In Chapter Twenty-Seven, Racksole interrogates the
now captured Jules in the attic bedroom of the Grand Babylon (thereby
revealing the solution to the crime), while in Chapter Twenty-Eight, Nella
and Prince Aribert attend, in the hotel's Royal apartments, to Prince
Eugen, who has, as a result of Jules's plot against him, taken an overdose
of laudanum. While these are relatively minor interruptions to the linear
chronology, they are nevertheless significant moments at which the narrative becomes far more spatially dominated, rather than temporally. This,
together with the centrality of the space of the hotel to both the criminals'

ability to carry out their crimes, and to the erstwhile detectives' capacity to solve those crimes, marks Bennett's *The Grand Babylon Hotel* as a novel which engages with and experiments in questions of spatial form.

Linearity, or rather its absence, is a far more pertinent question when considering the narrative of Ford Madox Ford's 1915 novel, *The Good Soldier*. Written in the nine months preceding the outbreak of the First World War, the novel concerns the thwarted and tragic relationships and affairs of a central group of four people, one of whom, John Dowell, relates the events that have taken place as the novel's somewhat unreliable narrator. On its initial publication, the novel received largely (though by no means completely) favourable reviews, with many critics remarking specifically on the novel's complex narrative structure, which shifts backwards and forwards between incidents that are often only partially recalled by Dowell, and which is at the mercy of the narrator's predilection towards digression. Writing in the *New Republic*, novelist Theodore Dreiser was overtly critical of the novel, suggesting that Ford, 'in spite of the care he has bestowed upon [the story], has not made it splendid in the telling' (1915, p. 155). Of the narrative structure, he continues: 'A story may begin in many ways. [...] once begun, it should go forward in a more or less direct line, or at least [...] should retain one's uninterrupted interest. This is not the case in this book' (Dreiser 1915, p. 155). The reviewer of the *Saturday Review* was similarly unimpressed, writing that 'we are asked to become listeners whilst Dowell gives his reminiscences in broken and spasmodic gusts', acknowledging that, while '[i]t is all very cleverly done [...] we draw from it neither pleasure nor profit' (Anon 1915a, p. iv). Yet there were also a number of contemporary critics in favour of Ford's intricate narrative technique. Among these was the reviewer from the *New York Times*, who, while acknowledging that the 'story is related in an odd, rambling sort of way, going forward then back again almost to the starting point', nevertheless recognised this as an attempt to convey the 'psychology' of the characters, ultimately praising the novel's 'artistry, force, and truthfulness' (Anon 1915b, p. 86). Fellow writer Rebecca West, herself a friend of Ford's, claimed that the novel was 'a much, much better book than any of us deserve', and praised Ford's technique which, she argued, 'has the supreme triumph of art, that effect of effortlessness and inevitableness' (1915, p. 6). It is in this reference to art, however, that the motivation behind Ford's convoluted narrative structure might be discerned, and more specifically in Ford's self-professed alliance with the movement known as literary impressionism.

Literary impressionism was a term first used by the French critic Ferdinand Brunetière in his 1879 essay on the novelist Alphonse Daudet, 'Impressionism in the Novel'. In this essay, Brunetière drew clear parallels between the impressionist movement in visual art and that which he identified as emerging in literature. Max Saunders notes that Ford 'proclaimed himself as an impressionist figure from an early stage, and became literary impressionism's most prolific exponent' (2010, p. 267). However, Ford's actual association of himself with the movement was initially less a proclamation, and more an (apparently) humble acquiescence. In an essay entitled, 'On Impressionism', published in two parts in *Poetry and Drama* in 1914, Ford wrote: 'A few years ago, if anybody had called me an Impressionist I should have languidly denied that I was anything of the sort [...]. But one person and another in the last ten years has called me Impressionist with such persistence that I have given up resistance' (1914, p. 167). In his following account of impressionism, Ford emphasised the multiplicity inherent in the method, arguing that it is 'perfectly possible that a piece of Impressionism should give a sense of two, of three, of as many as you will, places, persons, emotions, all going on simultaneously' (1914, p. 173). Here, along with the notion of plurality, the idea of linear chronology begins to be dismantled, as several 'places, persons, emotions' are conveyed, in the impressionist work, 'simultaneously', as opposed to one after another. Impressionism is, in this sense, concerned more with conveying accurately the perception of a moment, rather than giving an account of a series of events.

Sensory perception and experience are thus integral to literary impressionism. As Julia van Gunsteren observes,

> Literary Impressionists started from perception. For them the surrounding world is not well ordered but constitutes an indistinct and obscure picture made up of an irreversible flood of confused and ever changing sense impressions. Through sensory experience they discover a new relationship with the everyday world. (1990, p. 51)

This emphasis on the connection between the subject and the surrounding world is closely attuned to the phenomenological approach of thinkers such as Maurice Merleau-Ponty (2002 [1945]), and more recently Sara Ahmed (2006) and Iris Marion Young (2005), all of whom explore how this relationship between the body and space is mediated, and indeed made possible, through the senses. However, as Jesse Matz points out, such approaches are based on a rigorous process of philosophical reasoning, and he therefore cautions against aligning literary impressionism too closely with phenomenology, maintaining that to equate the two 'is to attribute too much philosophical systematicity to the outlook of the Impressionist writer, who could never aspire to transcend error in the manner of his or her philosophical counterpart' (2004, p. 27). Instead, he argues for an approach that recognises literary impressionism's inherent ambivalence, an 'ambivalence that characterizes the Impressionist's use for the perceptual theories systematically achieved in phenomenological philosophy. We need not therefore', he suggests, 'rule out phenomenology, but rather place it at a distance, and think of it as the horizon toward which Impressionism reaches as it looks beyond its empirical ground' (Matz 2004, p. 27). It is no doubt important to recognise that literary impressionism is more flexible in its approach to thinking through and representing sensory perception, but considering this literary method in terms of phenomenology nevertheless proves useful, particularly when it comes to considerations of the importance of space in impressionist narratives.

Emphasising the importance of the spatial in literary impressionism, Maria Kronegger notes that, in these texts, 'space is qualified by light, the signature of time. The reader is intended to seize the works of Flaubert, Proust, James, Pound, Joyce, and Mansfield spatially in a moment of time, rather than as a time sequence' (1973, p. 48). Once again, the emphasis here is on a lack of chronological linearity, which is, in impressionist literature, eschewed in favour of conveying a moment 'spatially'. Kronegger's argument here recalls Frank's assertion, in his aforementioned 1945 article on spatial form, that modern literature moves closer to the plastic or visual arts in its capacity to represent objects, characters, landscapes, and emotions, 'juxtaposed in an instant of time' (Frank 1963 [1945], p. 6). Both Kronegger and Frank also cite Flaubert, Kronegger placing the author firmly in the category of impressionist writers, with Frank upholding his novel, *Madame Bovary*, as an early exemplar of spatial form. This shared admiration for Flaubert is by no means coincidental, and neither is the fact that Ford himself, in his essay 'On Impressionism', refers to Flaubert as a fellow impressionist. Dismissing the attempts of Futurist painters to convey the lived experience of reality, Ford argues that 'those Futurists are only trying to render on canvas what Impressionists *tel due moi* have been trying to render for many years. (You may remember Emma's love scene at the cattle show in *Madame Bovary*)' (1914, p. 175).

Citing the very same scene in *Madame Bovary* that is used by Frank to illustrate the concept of spatial form, Ford himself here draws a clear and decisive connection between impressionism and spatial form in literature.

There is also, however, another crucial link to be made between literary impressionism and psychology. More specifically, literary impressionism attempts to give an effective and realistic account of the mind and its thought processes, and of the effect of perception upon the mind of the character. Rather than giving an accurate and precise account of the events in the story and how they unfolded chronologically, Ford's *The Good Soldier* is instead primarily concerned with conveying the way in which its narrator, John Dowell, recalls and perceives those events. It is this focus on representing the consciousness of Dowell, rather than on establishing narrative coherence, that both marks this novel as impressionist and contributes substantially to the disordered and fragmented narrative structure. Indeed, Rebecca Bowler suggests that this narrative incoherence is most revealing about Dowell's own character and personality, arguing that Dowell ultimately fails 'in the act of looking back and trying to reorder and aestheticize [his] past into some kind of coherent whole', as he is 'too short-sighted and too wilfully self-protective' to be able to succeed in this project (Bowler 2016, p. 14). Yet while this is an undeniably accurate description of Dowell's flawed character, there is another way to read his often overwhelming inability to recount the events of the plot in an ordered and chronological fashion, and that is to understand it as an effect of space, and specifically, of the hotel existence, upon his subjectivity.

Hotels certainly feature heavily throughout Ford's *The Good Soldier*, and indeed, it is in the dining room of the Hotel Excelsior in Nauheim, Germany, that Dowell first encounters Edward and Leonora Ashburnam, the couple with whom his life will, from that point on, become intricately entangled thanks to the affair between Edward and Dowell's own wife, Florence. In the second sentence of the novel, Dowell establishes that he and his wife 'had known the Ashburnams for nine seasons of the town of Nauheim' (Ford 2002 [1915], p. 13). A spa resort town, Nauheim is described in the 1910 *Baedeker* guide to Northern Germany as 'a town with 5,000 inhabitants, in a healthy situation on the N.E. slopes of the Taunus Mts.', and as possessing 'warm saline springs, impregnated with carbonic acid gas, which attract 30,000 patients annually. [...] The water is used both for drinking and for baths; its curative properties, more especially in cardiac diseases, are of considerable repute' (Baedeker 1910, p. 337). Both Dowell's wife, Florence, and Edward Ashburnam have been diagnosed with suffering from cardiac disease (though Florence's condition, as Dowell later reveals, is largely fictitious), hence their repeated visits to the town. The extensive list of hotels given in the Baedeker indicates the popularity of the resort, and the considerable number of hotels with anglicised names suggests a largely English-speaking tourist population.[11] However, despite the significance of the space of the hotel in Ford's novel, and despite a number of key incidents taking place within this space, by no means do all of the events in *The Good Soldier* take place within the hotel. As such, the hotel space does not structure the narrative in the same way as it does in Bennett's *The Grand Babylon Hotel*, or indeed in the brief moments in Woolf's *The Voyage Out*. Rather, the influence of this space upon the narrative form of the novel is mediated through Dowell as narrator.

The narrative of *The Good Soldier* does not follow a straightforward linear chronology. Rather, it is disordered and fragmented, moving from present to past events in no particular order, and with frequent digressions and asides from Dowell as narrator. Critical discussions of the novel's narrative structure have tended to focus on its temporality. Richard Hood, for example, provides a comprehensive account of the time frame of Dowell's 'narrative recounting', and points out that this is 'an experienced action' for both Dowell and the reader (1988, p. 451). Hood's emphasis on the narrative structure as 'experienced action' again draws parallels with literary impressionism, and indeed, the way in which the disjointed chronology contributes to this effect is undoubtedly central to unlocking the novel's meaning. But to focus solely on the temporal here is to overlook the spatial characteristics of the narrative, and the way in which the structure is influenced and shaped by particular kinds of spaces. While the narrative does move backwards and forwards in time, or, as Ford himself terms it, 'backwards and forwards over [Dowell's] past' (1924, pp. 129–30), it is scenes and locations, rather than moments in time, that dominate and structure the narrative, including Branshaw, India, and the numerous hotels in which Dowell stays. Dowell's recollections are thus characterised spatially, rather than temporally. This spatial aspect of the narrative is made explicit at the beginning of Part Four, the concluding section of the novel, in which Dowell himself acknowledges that 'I have, I am aware, told this story in a very rambling way so that it may be difficult

[11] These include the Bristol Hotel, the Prince of Wales Hotel, the Augusta Victoria Hotel, Park Hotel, and the Railway Hotel.

for anyone to find their path through what may be a sort of maze' (Ford 2002 [1915], p. 147). This spatial, maze-like quality is also highlighted by David Bradshaw who, remarking on the complexity of the narrative structure, argues that 'the layout of [Dowell's] story is […] obstructive. In fact, it is […] like a labyrinth: with every page we turn, another dark passage lies before us' (2002 [1915], p. xiii). This rambling, tortuous, and at times seemingly impenetrable structure seems at odds, however, with the relatively ordered space of the hotel. While the extensive corridors and back areas of an establishment like Bennett's Grand Babylon Hotel might prove initially confusing for those, like Racksole, who try to familiarise themselves with the space, there is nevertheless some level of regularity in the rooms which are, typically, arranged one after another along a corridor. In order to understand the impact of the hotel space upon Ford's novel, it is perhaps necessary to reconceive the manner in which space can influence a narrative, and to move from a consideration of the architectural to that of the experiential, in keeping with the text's impressionist nature.

Dowell's own past is key to understanding the way in which the space of the hotel functions in this narrative. Little detail is given by Dowell about his childhood and upbringing, and the earliest point in his memory to which he refers are the weeks when he was courting Florence, a time in his life during which he 'had no occupation—I had no business affairs. I simply camped down there in Stamford, in a vile hotel' (Ford 2002 [1915], p. 67). Dowell is thus a character who, from the very first, has frequented hotels more than any other kind of space. Indeed, in Part One Chapter Three, Dowell explicitly acknowledges his transient, fractured existence spent moving between hotels, recounting how he 'had no attachments, no accumulations' (Ford 2002 [1915], p. 25). Reflecting on the contrasting nature of home, he remarks:

> In one's own home it is as if little, innate sympathies draw one to particular chairs that seem to enfold one in an embrace, or take one along particular streets that seem friendly, when others may be hostile. And, believe me, that feeling is a very important part of life. I know it well, that have been for so long a wanderer upon the face of public resorts. (Ford 2002 [1915], p. 25)

For his adult life at least, Dowell has, by his own admission, had no real home. Despite referring to Paris as 'our home' in the opening pages of the novel, the flat he and Florence share there is little more than a pied-à-terre in which they reside only fleetingly, as the couple spend their winters 'somewhere between Nice and Boudighera', and their summers (from July to September) in Nauheim (Ford 2002 [1915], p. 13). Yet Dowell often refers to, and appears to yearn for, the stability that might be provided by a home, remarking on the way in which such a space can give its occupant 'some sort of anchorage', hinting at a sense of being tethered, rooted, and with steady, firm foundations (Ford 2002 [1915], p. 25). In terms of narrative structure, this foundation or 'anchorage' provides not just a stable basis for a character, but further functions as a steady point of origin for any story they might tell. Those 'little, innate sympathies' in the home that 'draw one to particular chairs' have an effect on the character which can translate into similar 'innate sympathies' that guide a story along a familiar path, one which follows a linear structure of beginning, middle, and end. In this sense, the type of narrative structure engendered by the space of the home is one of familiarity, comfort, and order.

As has already been established, however, this is not the type of narrative constructed by Dowell in *The Good Soldier*. In this narrative, there is no such familiarity, no such regularity, and any order that exists is of a very different, almost indiscernible kind. This is a hotel narrative, but it is one unlike that which is found in, for example, Bennett's *The Grand Babylon Hotel*, or in Woolf's *The Voyage Out*. In those novels, the form of the narrative can be aligned with the movement around a hotel, or along a hotel corridor, whereby the architectural space of the hotel itself structures the narrative. There is thus a particular kind of order to those narratives, albeit a fragmented one, but there is no such regularity to the narrative structure of *The Good Soldier*. This might well, as Hood argues, be attributed to the fact that Dowell is himself working through, and working out, the narrative as he tells it, with the various observations and realisations that come to light during this process taking the form of digressions and interruptions to the narrative. To read the spatial back into this disjointed narrative, however, means to understand it as that which has been necessarily shaped by Dowell's own transitory existence moving through and between hotels. The significant amount of time spent in these transitory, impermanent spaces can be read in this way as shaping his very ability to piece together a coherent story. The constant digressions and interruptions within the narrative replicate those which the hotel existence has for so long forced upon him, in the form of interruptions from other guests, from hotel staff, and of the movement from one hotel to another. *The Good Soldier*, then, offers a hotel narrative of a very different, though no less valid, kind to that which is found elsewhere in the novels of Bennett and Woolf, and the novel signals a distinguishing shift between the architectural hotel narrative, and the experiential hotel narrative.

* * *

Far more than a mere setting or background, the hotel functions in the novels explored here—and indeed throughout this book—as an active and engaging space, one which has the capacity to influence and shape the very structure of a narrative. The importance of space in literature, and specifically the spatialisation of narrative form, is identified by Frank as being characteristic of the experimental nature of modernist writing. And indeed, as this chapter has shown, this very spatialisation of form is clearly in evidence in Woolf's *The Voyage Out*, in which a key passage of the novel is structured according to the architectural space of the hotel. And yet charting the hotel narrative reveals these experiments with narrative and form to be present not just in modernist literature, but in earlier and more popular texts such as Bennett's *The Grand Babylon Hotel*. The narrative of Bennett's 1902 novel is almost entirely dominated by the space of the hotel—it is central to the criminals' ability to carry out their crimes, as well as to the erstwhile detectives' capacity to solve those crimes, and it also shapes and engenders the novel's episodic narrative structure. There are also, in Bennett's novel, moments at which the linear chronology slips, and the spatiality of the hotel overtakes the temporality that structures more traditional narratives. However, far more extreme in its disruption of linearity is Ford's *The Good Soldier*, which shifts backwards and forwards through the memories of narrator John Dowell, and the stories he has been told by others, according to no apparent logic or order. This lack of chronological linearity might well be attributed to Ford's own commitment to literary impressionism, as opposed to any kind of spatialisation of form. After all, tracking the hotel narrative in this novel is complicated by the fact that the majority of the events take place outside the space of the hotel. Yet there is a way in which to conceive of the two techniques—literary impressionism and spatial form—not as mutually exclusive, but rather as mutually intertwined, and indeed interdependent, and that is through a focus on Dowell himself. It is Dowell's own past experiences constantly moving through and between the transitory, impermanent spaces of hotels, that leads to the development of a different kind of hotel narrative, one that is experiential as opposed to architectural, and one that, in line with literary impressionism, effectively conveys the embodied consciousness of Dowell as that which has been irreversibly affected by his hotel existence.

REFERENCES

Ahmed, Sara. 2006. *Queer Phenomenology: Orientations, Objects, Others*. Durham: Duke University Press.

Anon. 1915a. Review of Ford Madox Ford's *The Good Soldier*. *Saturday Review*, 119, iv, June 19.

———. 1915b. Review of Ford Madox Ford's *The Good Soldier*. *The New York Times Book Review*, 86, March 7.

Baedeker, Karl. 1910. *Northern Germany as Far as the Bavarian and Austrian Frontiers*. Leipzig: Karl Baedeker.

Bennett, Arnold. 1968 [1924]. Is the Novel Decaying? In *The Author's Craft and Other Critical Essays*, ed. Samuel Hynes, 87–88. Lincoln: University of Nebraska Press.

———. 2016 [1902]. *The Grand Babylon Hotel*. Ed. Randi Saloman. Peterborough, ON: Broadview Press.

Bishop, Karen Elizabeth. 2016. Introduction. In *Cartographies of Exile: A New Spatial Literacy*, ed. Karen Elizabeth Bishop, 1–22. London: Routledge.

Bowler, Rebecca. 2016. *Literary Impressionism: Vision and Memory in Dorothy Richardson, Ford Madox Ford, H.D. and May Sinclair*. London: Bloomsbury.

Bradshaw, David. 2002 [1915]. Introduction. In *The Good Soldier*, vii–xxxvi. London: Penguin.

Brunetière, Ferdinand. 1879. Impressionnisme dans le roman. *La Revue des Deux Mondes*, 446–459, November 15.

Dreiser, Theodore. 1915. The Saddest Story. *New Republic*, 3, 155–156, June 12.

Ford, Ford Madox (Hueffer). 1914. On Impressionism: First Article. *Poetry and Drama* 2 (6): 167–175.

Ford, Ford Madox. 1924. *Joseph Conrad: A Personal Remembrance*. London: Duckworth.

———. 2002 [1915]. *The Good Soldier*. London: Penguin.

Frank, Joseph. 1963 [1945]. Spatial Form in Modern Literature. In *The Widening Gyre: Crisis and Mastery in Modern Literature*, 3–62. New Brunswick, NJ: Rutgers University Press.

Fromm, Gloria. 1982. Re-Mythologizing Arnold Bennett. *Novel* 16 (1): 19–34.

Frye, Joanne S. 1980. *The Voyage Out*: Thematic Tensions and Narrative Techniques. *Twentieth Century Literature* 26 (4): 402–423.

van Gunsteren, Julia. 1990. *Katherine Mansfield and Literary Impressionism*. Amsterdam: Rodopi.

Hones, Sheila. 2015. Literary Geographies, Past and Future. *Literary Geographies* 1 (2): 1–5.

Hood, Richard A. 1988. 'Constant Reduction': Modernism and the Narrative Structure of *The Good Soldier*. *Journal of Modern Literature* 14 (4): 445–464.

Hühn, Peter. 1987. The Detective as Reader: Narrativity and Reading Concepts in Detective Fiction. *Modern Fiction Studies* 33 (3): 451–466.

Jameson, Fredric. 1991. *Postmodernism, or, The Cultural Logic of Late Capitalism*. London: Verso.

Kort, Wesley A. 2004. *Place and Space in Modern Fiction*. Gainesville: University Press of Florida.

Kronegger, Maria Elisabeth. 1973. *Literary Impressionism*. New Haven: College & University Press.

Matthias, Bettina. 2006. *The Hotel as Setting in Early Twentieth-Century German and Austrian Literature: Checking in to Tell a Story*. Rochester, NY: Camden House.

Matz, Jesse. 2004. *Literary Impressionism and Modernist Aesthetics*. Cambridge: Cambridge University Press.

Merleau-Ponty, Maurice. 2002 [1945]. *Phenomenology of Perception*. Trans. Colin Smith. Abingdon: Routledge.

Pound, Ezra. 1913. A Few Don'ts by an Imagiste. *Poetry: A Magazine of Verse* 1 (6): 200–206.

Ricouer, Paul. 2002. Narrative Time. In *Narrative Dynamics: Essays on Time, Plot, Closure, and Frames*, ed. Brian Richardson, 35–46. Columbus: The Ohio State University Press.

Ronen, Ruth. 1986. Space in Fiction. *Poetics Today* 7 (3): 421–439.

Ryan, Marie-Laure, Kenneth Foote, and Maoz Azaryahu. 2016. *Narrating Space/ Spatializing Narrative: Where Narrative Theory and Geography Meet*. Columbus: The Ohio State University Press.

Saloman, Randi. 2016. Introduction. In *The Grand Babylon Hotel*, ed. Randi Saloman, 11–30. Peterborough, ON: Broadview Press.

Saunders, Max. 2010. *Self-Impression: Life-Writing, Autobiografiction, and the Forms of Modern Literature*. Oxford: Oxford University Press.

Soja, Edward. 1989. *Postmodern Geographies: The Reassertion of Space in Critical Social Theory*. London: Verso.

Squillace, John. 1997. *Modernism, Modernity, and Arnold Bennett*. Lewisburg, PA: Bucknell University Press.

Thacker, Andrew. 2005. The Idea of a Critical Literary Geography. *New Formations* 57: 56–73.

West, Rebecca. 1915. Mr. Hueffer's New Novel. *Daily News and Leader*, 6, April 2.

Woolf, Virginia. 2008 [1924]. Character in Fiction. In *Selected Essays*, ed. David Bradshaw, 37–54. Oxford: Oxford University Press.

———. 2009 [1915]. *The Voyage Out*. Oxford: Oxford University Press.

Young, Iris Marion. 2005. House and Home: Feminist Variations on a Theme. In *On Female Body Experience: 'Throwing Like a Girl' and Other Essays*, 123–154. Oxford: Oxford University Press.

CHAPTER 3

Anticipation and Stagnation in the Lobby

Existing in between the street and the inner spaces of the hotel, the hotel lobby is always a space of movement across boundaries. More specifically, it is in and through the lobby, typically the site of a constant stream of arrivals and departures, that the mobility of the hotel is primarily enacted, at least in terms of its guests. For certain members of hotel staff, on the other hand, most notably the concierge, the hotel lobby is a space in which they remain fixed, always on hand to register guests and to assist them in their queries. The hotel lobby is thus characterised by this tension between mobility and stasis, a tension that unfolds in a variety of different ways throughout the novels explored in this chapter. This chapter charts the development in literature of this space, tracking its rising level of significance in fiction, from the pre-First World War entrance hall, a space of meetings between characters and of low-level surveillance, to the interwar lobby, an altogether more symbolic space of thwarted anticipation, boredom, paralysis, and anxiety which speaks far more directly and explicitly to the ideologies of the period between the wars, and in which that tension between mobility and stasis is increasingly pronounced.

Like the hotel itself, the lobby has been largely overlooked in criticism, with the exception of a handful of pieces that consider its cultural significance from a range of perspectives. The earliest of these is Siegfried Kracauer's essay, 'The Hotel Lobby', which formed part of his larger study of the detective novel (1922–1925), and which is, as such, ostensibly focused on the way in which the lobby functions in genre fiction, though

© The Author(s) 2019
E. Short, *Mobility and the Hotel in Modern Literature*,
Studies in Mobilities, Literature, and Culture,
https://doi.org/10.1007/978-3-030-22129-4_3

it does extend to a more philosophical rumination on the broader nature of this space. Marc Katz picks up on and updates Kracauer's arguments in his article, 'The Hotel Kracauer' (1999), as does Douglas Tallack (1998) in his reflection on the hotel lobby in literature and film. Tallack defines the hotel lobby, not as a 'specifically memorable' space, but as one that is 'associated with events and even stories' (1998, p. 3). For Tallack, the lobby is only noticeable in fiction and film when something occurs within it, making it 'a space which *takes place* in narratives' (1998, p. 3; emphasis in original). However, to understand the lobby in this way is to regard it solely as setting, as a space which is only brought into being through the events that take place within it. But, as my discussion at the beginning of the previous chapter made clear, to define space as mere setting is to effectively disregard it as passive, and to 'condemn' it, as Kort argues, 'to an inherently secondary' role (2004, p. 15). What is needed instead is a reading of the hotel lobby that takes into account its own power and agency. Such a reading as the one I put forward in this chapter will foreground the way in which the space of the lobby, rather than functioning as a mere backdrop for events, instead determines what can take place within it, and in doing so actively shapes and drives the narrative.

THE PRE-WAR ENTRANCE-HALL

In literature written and published prior to the end of the First World War, the hotel lobby possesses a different kind and level of significance to that of lobbies found in fiction of the interwar years. Indeed, the very term typically used to refer to it in literature of this earlier period—entrance hall—denotes more a space to be passed through than a space in which people wait or linger, as is implied by the more interwar usage of the term lobby (a term more commonly associated, as noted by the OED, with 'waiting-places'). In late-nineteenth- and early-twentieth-century literature, the hotel lobby, or entrance hall, is rarely a space in which guests spend any significant amount of time. The reasons behind this shift in symbolic weight are in part bound up in the rising popularity of the hotel between the wars, which was in itself largely due to the rapid developments in technologies of travel that took place in the years following the First World War.[1] Such developments further contributed to an idea of the

[1] For further discussion of these developments in transport technologies, see the Introduction to this book.

hotel as a destination in and of itself, as opposed to a merely incidental place of rest.[2] As such, the hotel lobby of interwar literature is a space in which characters spend considerably more time than they do in the hotel entrance hall of pre-war literature. In the latter, characters tend to move through this space, pausing only at the hotel reception or bureau, and as a result, it functions in such literature both as a convenient meeting place for characters, and as a space in which characters are watched and monitored by the hotel staff behind the reception desk.

Just as less time is spent by guests in the fictional hotel entrance halls of late-nineteenth- and early-twentieth-century literature, so too are descriptions of this space limited to fairly cursory details. In the mid- to late-nineteenth-century novels of Anthony Trollope and Wilkie Collins, both authors in whose work hotels feature heavily, the hotel entrance hall barely features at all. If it is mentioned, it is as a space in which characters spend little to no time, only moving through it to another, more well-defined, space within the hotel, such as a coffee room or bar. In Trollope's *Can You Forgive Her?* (1865), for example, the first novel in the *Palliser* series, Alice Vavasor, her cousin George, and his sister Kate return to their hotel in Basel following a stroll along the Rhine, only to move swiftly from 'the front steps of the hotel, through the hall and on to the stairs' (Trollope 2004 [1865], p. 93). The entrance hall of the hotel in Port St. Mary Wilkie Collins's *Armadale* (1866) is described merely as the passage, into which protagonist Allan Armadale 'lounged [...] on the chance of discovering somebody to talk to' (Collins 1995 [1866], p. 117). However, despite the very brief amount of time spent in this passage, it is nevertheless the site of the second meeting between Allan Armadale and the local doctor Mr Hawbury, a meeting which leads to Allan and Ozias Midwinter borrowing Hawbury's pleasure boat, and which consequently leads to Allan and Midwinter becoming stranded on the wreck of *La Grace de Dieu*, onboard which Allan's father was murdered by Midwinter's father several years previously. As such, while the amount of time spent in the passage of the hotel may initially appear negligible, the nature of this space, which occasions the chance meeting between Allan and Hawbury, has a direct and significant impact upon the course of the narrative.

---

[2] Though as I discuss in Chap. 4, the notion of the hotel as destination, and further as status symbol, was already coming to prominence in the first decade of the twentieth century.

A similar and still more palpable narrative impact is felt in Henry James's *The Ambassadors* (1903), in which Lambert Strether first makes the acquaintance of Maria Gostrey in the entrance hall of a Chester hotel. The appearance and layout of the hall itself is given markedly scant attention, save for the mention of the 'young woman in the glass cage', a receptionist who initially appears, in her 'glass cage', to be more ornament than conscious agent, her only action here being to deliver a telegraph to Strether from his friend Waymarsh, and to inform him of his imminent arrival (James 2008 [1903], p. 2). Turning away from the receptionist, however, Strether finds himself, 'in the hall, facing a lady who met his eyes as with an intention suddenly determined, and whose features—not freshly young, not markedly fine, but on happy terms with each other—came back to him as from a recent vision' (James 2008 [1903], pp. 2–3). The 'intention' with which Maria Gostrey meets Strether's gaze at once marks her not only as far more agential and engaging than the hotel receptionist, but signals the importance of her character to the narrative as a whole. Strether quickly realises that he has seen Gostrey before, having 'noticed her at his previous inn, where—again in the hall—she had been briefly engaged with some people of his own ship's company' (James 2008 [1903], p. 3). As in Collins's *Armadale*, this is not the first time that the two characters have encountered one another, but unlike in Collins, their initial glimpse of each other did not amount to an introduction between them, though it did, importantly, take place in yet another hotel entrance hall. Significant also is the fact that, in this second instance, dialogue between the two hotel guests is only occasioned when Gostrey overhears the receptionist pronounce the name of Strether's friend, Waymarsh, and 'was moved to ask, by his leave, if it were possibly a question of Mr. Waymarsh of Milrose Connecticut' (James 2008 [1903], p. 3). The particular nature of this space, and specifically the incorporation within it of a bureau or reception desk at which names of other guests will be spoken aloud—either in enquiry or information—enables Maria Gostrey to glean information regarding Strether's friendships, and consequently his own identity. The hotel entrance hall is here firmly established as a space in which the likelihood of a chance acquaintance between people, and of a relationship then developing between them, is significantly increased, and it thus functions as a useful location in which authors can bring otherwise disparate characters together.

In Arnold Bennett's *The Grand Babylon Hotel* (1902), focus is once more placed upon the hotel reception desk—or the bureau, as it is called in this case—with this being the only feature of the entrance hall described in any detail. Occupied by Miss Spencer, the bureau is 'a fairly large chamber, with two sliding glass partitions which overlooked the entrance-hall and the smoking-room' (Bennett 2016 [1902], p. 44). Immediately, the bureau is defined as a space of observation, the glass partitions allowing its occupant to not only keep track of arrivals and departures to the hotel, but also to survey the meetings and conversations between guests taking place in the smoking room. That the bureau overlooks the particularly masculine space of the smoking room, and not the more feminine space of the drawing room, is of further significance. The gendering of this room is made explicit within the novel itself on the preceding page, the narrator remarking that, 'The Grand Babylon Hotel was a hotel in whose smoking-room one behaved as though one was at one's club' (Bennett 2016 [1902], p. 43). Populated solely by men—and importantly, by men of a certain class, background, and occupation—the smoking room of the Grand Babylon Hotel is a space in which discussions concerning lucrative business deals and political manoeuvrings are likely to take place.[3] For corrupt hotel staff with ulterior motives, such as Miss Spencer and Jules, the head waiter, the ability to observe this area is therefore a very attractive prospect.

Yet in Bennett's novel, the space of the bureau itself is also gendered, this time as feminine, and the unique nature of this is emphasised by the narrator, who notes that the bureau 'served chiefly as the lair of Miss Spencer, who was as well known and as important as Jules himself. Most modern hotels have a male clerk to superintend the bureau. But the Grand Babylon went its own way' (Bennett 2016 [1902], p. 44). At this early point in the novel, the anonymous and apparently neutral narrator reveals themselves to be not entirely impartial, with a marked bias towards the hotel itself (rather than towards any particular character). The narrator proclaims (and indeed, rather overestimates, given the presence of a female receptionist/clerk in James's *The Ambassadors*) its superiority over other 'modern hotels', none of which, with their 'vagaries', are as modern as the Grand Babylon, which strives for gender equality in its staffing decisions (Bennett 2016 [1902], p. 44). However, this apparent equality between Miss Spencer and Jules is quickly betrayed by the narrator as illusory, in the description of the 'gracious and alluring contours of her figure', which 'were irreproachable' (Bennett 2016 [1902], p. 44). Added to this is the observation that 'in the evenings she was a useful ornament of which any

[3] See Chap. 4 for further discussion on the gendering of public spaces within the hotel.

hotel might be innocently proud' (Bennett 2016 [1902], p. 44). Like James's hotel receptionist trapped in her glass cage, Miss Spencer's physical appearance, and her role as an item of decoration, is revealed here to be just as important as her abilities as a member of staff.

Further contributing to Miss Spencer's decorative function is her lack of mobility. The hotel entrance hall is, as has already been discussed, a space of inherent mobility, encompassing and engendering as it does the all the various comings and goings of the hotel guests. However, despite Miss Spencer's 'unrivalled' and extensive 'knowledge of Bradshaw, of steamship services, and the programmes of theatres and music-halls', she herself

> never travelled, she never went to a theatre or music-hall. She seemed to spend the whole of her life in that official lair of hers, imparting information to guests, telephoning to the various departments, or engaged in intimate conversations with her friends on the staff. (Bennett 2016 [1902], pp. 44–5)

A purely static figure (at least while employed by the hotel), Miss Spencer is confined to the space of the bureau, existing to be observed by guests as much as she is there to observe them. Yet there are numerous indications that Miss Spencer's motionless, ornamental quality is intentionally crafted to enable her to gather information on unsuspecting hotel guests. 'Always admirably dressed [...] she looked now just as she had looked an indefinite number of years ago. Her age—none knew it, save herself and perhaps one other', and this impenetrability permits her to scrutinise the guests without their full awareness (Bennett 2016 [1902], p. 45). The bureau is thus in Bennett's novel a site of surveillance, the location from which Miss Spencer is able to monitor the movements of the hotel guests, her own agency and purpose masked by the unthreatening and inscrutable nature of her appearance.[4]

These early examples of hotel entrance halls in literature in some respects function very differently to those found in the later fiction of the interwar period. Where hotel guests tend to linger in the lobbies of hotels between the wars, in the late nineteenth and early twentieth centuries the entrance hall is primarily a space to be moved through. The speed with which characters pass through this space does slow down from the novels of the mid-to-late nineteenth century, such as those of Trollope and Collins, to those

---

[4] Of course, the extent to which this is Miss Spencer's agency operating here, rather than that of Jules, is debatable.

of the early twentieth century, such as those of James and Bennett, and this deceleration can at least in part be attributed to the increasing presence and significance of the hotel itself in society. And despite the clear differences between literary depictions of these early entrance halls and of the lobbies of the interwar years, there are nevertheless similarities to be found, not least in the way in which authors across the period—from Collins in 1866 to Henry Green in 1939—are able, by virtue of the nature of the space, to use the hotel lobby to bring otherwise disparate characters together. More striking, however, is the motif of surveillance in the entrance hall that finds its beginnings in Bennett, and that comes to fruition in the anxiety and paralysis of later interwar novels, such as those by Rhys and Green.

MOBILITY AND STASIS IN THE INTERWAR LOBBY

It is in literature of the interwar period that the hotel entrance hall comes to be figured more decisively as the lobby. No longer a mere incidental passageway between the outside world and the interior of the hotel, as the entrance hall might well be understood, the lobby is instead a specific and bounded space which serves a particular function in hotels, and an increasingly symbolic function in interwar hotel fiction. As the point of arrival and departure to and from the hotel, the lobby is by its very nature always already a space of movement and transition from one place to another, but it is also a space of stasis, and of a lack of mobility. This section explores the various ways in which the lobby is figured as a space of both mobility and stasis in four interwar novels—Elizabeth Bowen's *The Hotel* (1927), Jean Rhys' *Quartet* (1928), Winifred Holtby's *South Riding* (1936), and Henry Green's *Party Going* (1939). In *South Riding*, the lobby of a hotel off Manchester's Piccadilly plays a brief yet significant role as the unexpected meeting place of protagonist Sarah Burton, a headmistress of a rural school in Yorkshire, and Robert Carne, the father of one of her pupils and a local, struggling landowner. While the episode in the hotel spans the course of only one chapter, the space nevertheless offers up the rare possibility of the consummation of their mutual attraction. Unlike Holtby's novel, hotels dominate the remaining three texts, and indeed, this focus is explicitly announced by the title of Bowen's first novel, *The Hotel*, which follows, for a few weeks of one summer, the lives of a group of British guests at a luxurious, unnamed hotel on the Italian Riviera. The nature and type of this hotel thus dictates that the characters featured are, in terms of their class backgrounds, somewhat limited in scope, with the

lowest class arguably represented by James Milton, a middle-class reverend who is keen to escape his professional identity during his brief sojourn
in the hotel. Similarly limited in the scope of its representation is Henry
Green's 1939 novel, *Party Going*, which centres on a wealthy group of
'bright young things' who become delayed, and then trapped, in a station
hotel when fog prevents them from embarking on their continental holiday. The novel does enact a critique of their privilege not simply through
their own self-involved and often ridiculous behaviour, but through scenes
depicting their servants waiting with their luggage on the platform, denied
access to the hotel itself. However, despite these brief interludes, the focus
is first and foremost on the upper-class characters within the hotel. Quite
the opposite is the case in the fourth and final novel explored here, Jean
Rhys's *Quartet*. Originally published as *Postures* in 1928, Rhys's first novel
was republished under its new title in 1929, and follows protagonist
Marya Zelli, who is characterised by her distinct lack of privilege and
background. Whereas in Bowen and Green's novels, the action takes place
in one hotel, in Rhys's novel Marya is continually displaced from one
hotel to the next, occupying a total of six hotels over the course of the
narrative, each of which speak to her lack of privilege, albeit in various
different ways. Each of these authors employs the space of the hotel, and
more specifically the hotel lobby, to think through the social and cultural
conditions of modernity, particularly in terms of class, gender, and, in the
case of Rhys, national identity.

Before embarking on a more thorough reading of the significance and
function of the hotel lobby in these four novels, it is worth pausing to
consider, or more specifically, to map the type and layout of the hotel
lobby in each text. In Rhys's novel, descriptions of the hotel spaces that lie
outside the bedroom are sparse at best, and only one hotel lobby is
described in any detail—that of the Hôtel de l'Univers. Situated in the
Rue Cauchois in Montmartre, it is in this hotel that Marya is residing with
her husband Stephan when the novel begins. Indications of the nature of
this hotel, and of its particular frugality, are given in the novel's opening
chapter. Marya's living arrangements are referred to as '[a] bedroom, balcony and *cabinet de toilette* in a cheap Montmartre hotel', to get to which
Marya has to climb 'five flights of steep, uncarpeted stairs' (Rhys 2000
[1929], p. 10). The absence of a lift here confirms that the hotel is at the
cheap end of the scale, and correlates with the lower tariffed hotels featured in popular hotel guides such as *The Official Hotel Directory*.[5] Only

---

[5] See discussion in Chap. 5 on the impact of lifts on hotel room tariffs.

the vaguest sketch is given of the lobby itself, the novel merely delineating the stairs that lead to the rest of the hotel, and the 'hotel bureau' behind which is 'a small sitting-room' where the hotel's *patronne*, 'Madame Hautchamp and her husband spent more than half their lives, quite happily as far as one could see' (Rhys 2000 [1929], p. 21). That no indication of the décor and furnishings of the lobby itself are given—save for the uncarpeted stairs—suggests that they are not worthy of note, with the implication being that this space functions solely as an entrance, exit, and, as I discuss later, a space of surveillance.

Described as 'second-rate', the Manchester hotel in which Sarah spends the night after Christmas shopping in the city en route to her sister's in Bradford-on-Avon is, while not particularly upmarket, at least decidedly more comfortable than the Hôtel de l'Univers, and this is indicated almost immediately upon her entrance into the hotel by the space of the lobby (Holtby 2011 [1936], p. 365). Pushing 'her way round the revolving doors of that establishment [...], burdened with frivolous purchases, [Sarah] struggled into the warm, half-empty lobby' (Holtby 2011 [1936], pp. 365–6). Despite being 'half empty', the warmth of this lobby positions it in stark contrast to the 'uncarpeted stairs' of Marya's Paris hotel, and conveys a sense of welcome, rather than of sparse utility. The source of the physical warmth emanates from the lobby's fireplace, in front of which stands Robert Carne, who provides Sarah with a different source of emotional warmth in his smile of 'radiant welcome' (Holtby 2011 [1936], p. 366). The 'small glass-covered table' to which he leads her (Holtby 2011 [1936], p. 366), together with the 'leaping' fire and 'the palms doing their best to appear exotic', depicts a lobby which is, if not exactly opulent, at least cosy and pleasant, and a space in which one might comfortably spend time, as Sarah and Robert then do (Holtby 2011 [1936], p. 367).

The hotel lobby in Bowen's novel is a different kind of space again, and is one that is described in rich detail throughout the novel. While this is still a space of arrivals and departures, it is, unlike Rhys's hotel lobby, a space which is furnished to such a degree that lobby and lounge are here one and the same. The hotel's front swing doors open into this lounge/lobby, from which the stairs and lift ascend, and also located here are the concierge's desk, an announcements board, and a letter rack. The 'looking-glassed walls' (Bowen 2003 [1927], p. 157), and 'the crude and vivid glitter' of the lounge, decorated with 'glazed stuffs' and 'noisy colours' (Bowen 2003 [1927], p. 154), create a sense of an attempt, at least, at art deco elegance, and the grouped furniture—armchairs and sofas—seems designed to encourage guests and visitors to pause and spend time in this space, as opposed to just passing straight through it.

Like Bowen's eponymous hotel, the hotel in Green's novel is unnamed, as is the railway station in which it is situated. However, given that the group are waiting for the boat train to take them to the South of France, it can be safely assumed that the action takes place in Victoria Station, from the Eastern side of which, from 1929 onwards, departed the *Golden Arrow* train to the continent. This would mean that the hotel in which the party gathers is the Grosvenor Hotel, which to this day has an entrance on the station platform. As in Bowen's eponymous hotel, the hotel lobby in Green's novel is merged and synonymous with the lounge—some time after the group have arrived in the hotel, the narrator observes that 'Julia's fears had left her earlier when Max had arrived in the lounge downstairs' (Green 1978 [1939], p. 447). Where the lobby in Green's novel differs from Bowen's is in its lack of comfort and order—rather, Green's hotel lobby is a space of muted chaos and discomfort, and while there is a sense of opulence in the décor, most notably, the 'vast chandelier with thousands of glass drops' that hangs from the ceiling, the additional detail that it is 'rather dirty' connotes that any glamour this space may once have had is faded to say the least (Green 1978 [1939], p. 414). These four rather contrasting hotel lobbies each speak to different facets of modernity, and specifically to the various ideologies, experiences, and atmospheres of the interwar period.

The movement inherent to the hotel lobby—the way in which it is necessarily characterised by the constant comings and goings of guests and visitors—marks it first and foremost as a space of anticipation. This anticipation in the hotel lobby takes a number of forms, one of which is, for example, the anticipation of the guest who, upon arrival, does not yet know the spaces beyond the lobby into which they are yet to move. The question of mobility is, of course, central here, as the anticipation of discovering what lies beyond the lobby is denied those who do not have the ability—financial or otherwise—to book a room. Yet another kind of anticipation engendered by the hotel lobby is that concerning the potential for events or activities that might take place within the hotel, and it is this that is most prominent in Holtby's *South Riding*. Sarah's unexpected encounter with Robert in the lobby of her Piccadilly hotel stirs in her a previously dormant but undeniably palpable sexual desire for the man standing before her. Standing 'before him, passive, expectant, happy',

Sarah feels that '[a]ll possible journeys had led toward this end', conveying a sense of inevitability regarding, not only their meeting, but the consummation of their unspoken desire for one another (Holtby 2011 [1936], p. 366). Sarah's expectation of this is occasioned not by their meeting, nor by its unexpected nature, but rather by the space in which they meet.

As I discuss at length in Chap. 5 of this book, hotels, existing as they do away from the moral codes of the home and the scrutiny of the public place, provide a truly unique space in which women in the early twentieth century were able to explore and act on their sexual desires. Yet the potential sexual freedom offered by the hotel space is concomitant with a strong cultural association of the hotel with illicit sexual behaviour and promiscuity, an association which often resulted (as seen in texts such as H.G. Wells's 1909 novel *Ann Veronica*) in men attempting to use the space of the hotel to sexually manipulate and coerce women.[6] The 'passivity' attributed to Sarah here is in this respect troubling, suggesting as it does a willingness to submit to Robert's advances, whenever he should choose to make them. Yet her 'passive, expectant, happy' demeanour can be read, alternatively, as a willingness to give herself up more to the inevitability of their affair taking place within the hotel, in which they would both be active and willing participants, rather than to surrender herself entirely to Robert. This agency is made clear by the repeated evidence of her desire for him in their initial meeting in the lobby, the first indication of which is the 'involuntary gasp' that she emits when she sees him (Holtby 2011 [1936], p. 366). Almost orgasmic in nature, and accompanying a loss of physical control as she drops one of her packages, this gasp is immediately followed by a second, as she exclaims 'Oh!', causing Robert to turn and see her (Holtby 2011 [1936], p. 366). This orgasmic tone is continued in her 'singing joy which had no reason and no justification', together with her 'witless pleasure', both of which bears traces of (or rather prefigures) the notion of feminine *jouissance* (Holtby 2011 [1936], pp. 366, 367). This connection is further drawn out in the fact that, face to face with Robert, '[s]he had no words', and thus occupies the pre-linguistic space of the Lacanian Imaginary that goes hand in hand with *jouissance* (Lacan 2006 [1966]). The power of Sarah's desire for Robert is therefore made strikingly apparent over the course of their brief meeting in the hotel lobby, and is indeed engendered by the space itself.

[6] See Chap. 5 for a more detailed discussion of sexual coercion in the hotel.

A third kind of anticipation created by the hotel lobby is the anticipation of future arrivals to the hotel. This particular anticipation is woven through Bowen's novel, beginning, in the opening pages, with Miss Pym scanning the letter racks in the lobby for clues regarding forthcoming arrivals:

> She read the announcements pinned to the notice-board, looked along the letter-rack and read the names on the envelopes stuck prominently on the concierge's desk to await new arrivals. These long-forecast shadows for ever darkening the threshold of the Hotel excited Miss Pym; for some new arrival that never arrived she was storing up tenderness. (Bowen 2003 [1927], p. 8)

The sense of excitement here, together with this 'tenderness', hints that Miss Pym's anticipation is again bound up with sexual desire. In this way, both Bowen and Holtby's exploration of the hotel lobby, and the anticipation it engenders, corresponds with and prefigures Kracauer's notion of the 'erotic desire' that permeates the space of the hotel lobby. However, while Sarah's desire in Holtby's novel is directed very firmly towards Robert, Bowen's novel comes closer to Kracauer's conception of the peculiar nature of desire in the hotel lobby as that which 'roams about without an object' (Kracauer 1995, p. 178). Miss Pym's desire has no object— rather, she 'stores up tenderness' for '*some* new arrival', as opposed to a named, specific person. Building on Kracauer, Marc Katz highlights further the sexuality inherent in the lobby, arguing:

> The hotel […] is a site of exchanges of all sorts—information, money, services, goods. And among these we might include identity as well, since as sites of displacement, hotels tend to magnify that sense of the performative that is concomitant with urban anonymity. This is what gives the lobby its particular promiscuous energy. (1999, p. 139)

While the otherwise reserved Miss Pym might seem an unlikely conduit for this 'promiscuous energy', it is worth acknowledging here that her perusal of the letter racks comes immediately after a 'quarrel' between herself and her close friend, Miss Emily Fitzgerald. This quarrel has triggered the 'violent […] exit' of Miss Fitzgerald from the Hotel, and the novel opens to her standing in the road outside. In fact, the entire reason that Miss Pym is waiting in the lobby is to give her friend 'a little longer to get away' after 'this crisis of ungovernable agitation' (Bowen 2003 [1927],

p. 7). The language of 'crisis', and of 'ungovernable agitation' denotes that this is more than a spat between mere friends. Indeed, as Petra Rau maintains, this novel 'begins with a sapphic disruption' (2006, p. 225). As Rau explains, the separation in the opening pages between Miss Pym and Miss Fitzgerald, along with their reunion at the end of the novel, provides 'the novel's sapphic frame [which] does not just envelope and curb but actually forecloses heterosexual development as narrative teleology' (2006, p. 225). In this sense, Miss Pym's anticipation for the potential arrivals can be understood as encapsulating that 'erotic desire' and 'promiscuous energy', transferred or, as Katz suggests, 'exchanged' at the moment of frustrated crisis from Miss Fitzgerald to this nameless 'new arrival'. However, while Rau's queering of the novel here is undoubtedly percep- tive, it fails to take into account the importance of the hotel space itself in the foreclosure and frustration of heterosexual development.

Despite its seemingly rich potential for the fulfilment of erotic desire, the hotel lobby all too often delivers only frustration and thwarted pas- sion in the literature of the interwar period. In Holtby's *South Riding*, the union between Sarah and Robert that she had so eagerly anticipated in the hotel lobby just hours before is prevented by Robert suffering a severe attack of angina upon reaching her bedroom. Having left him in the lobby after their initial meeting, Sarah returns to her room, which she had only moments before described to Robert as 'a terrible room up on the fifth floor that looks like a scene set for a Russian tragedy' (Holtby 2011 [1936], p. 367). However, the intensity of the anticipation engen- dered within her by the lobby is such that it carries over into this space, and she finds that the 'ugly room' 'could not depress her' (Holtby 2011 [1936], p. 368). Instead, her sexual desire is once more palpable as she shivers 'more with excitement than with the chill damp room', and, pre- paring herself for dinner with Robert, and for their subsequent expected union, she 'redresses herself without remorse in the satin under-garments she had bought for her sister' (Holtby 2011 [1936], p. 368). Again, Sarah's sexual agency here is clearly in evidence, as she consciously and meticulously readies herself for the much-awaited event that, she imag- ines, will satiate her desire. When she returns to her 'ugly room' after their dinner to await Robert's arrival, the room seems to her instead, 'a lovely room', 'my bridal chamber', such is the influence of the hotel lobby and the excitement it engenders (Holtby 2011 [1936], p. 378). Yet due to Robert's sudden illness, their illicit liaison never takes place, and, '[w]renched suddenly from the crest of expectation [...], she felt herself violated, outraged' (Holtby 2011 [1936], p. 381). The anticipation created and sustained by the hotel lobby is here thwarted, only to be replaced with disappointment, anger, and frustration.

The frustration with which Bowen imbues the opening scene of her novel extends far beyond the sexual and sapphic frustration that festers between Miss Pym and Miss Fitzgerald, as the anticipation of characters throughout the novel is consistently forestalled. Miss Pym stores up tenderness 'for some new arrival *that never arrived*', meaning that her anticipation is articulated just as it is simultaneously doomed to disappointment. While the anticipation of other characters for impending arrivals may not be doomed, in the sense that those expected do actually arrive, their anticipation of the moment of arrival is nevertheless thwarted. The arrival of Ronald Kerr, for example, is eagerly awaited by the majority of the guests in the hotel, and most notably by his mother, Mrs Kerr, who, upon learning of her son's visit, 'gazed delightedly at the future' and talks excitedly about her son 'in a glow of speculation' (Bowen 2003 [1927], p. 71). Less eager is Sydney Warren, the young protagonist of the novel who has formed a deep attachment to Mrs Kerr, and whose anticipation of Ronald's arrival, though arguably equal to Mrs Kerr's, is coloured more with apprehension than excitement. When Mrs Kerr, in her bedroom, tells her the news that Ronald will soon be joining them at the Hotel, she feels 'powerless', 'bewildered', and 'angry', and the room, to Sydney, 'appeared to be much constricted' (Bowen 2003 [1927], p. 70). Like Sarah's shifting perception of her own bedroom in Holtby's *South Riding*, Mrs Kerr's bedroom—a space in which Sydney had only moments beforehand felt such a degree of comfort that she exclaimed, 'leaning her side and elbow against the side of the sofa [...] "I could stay like this for the rest of the afternoon"'—now becomes claustrophobic with her own wary anticipation of Ronald's arrival (Bowen 2003 [1927], p. 68). Her palpable unease stems from the threat she feels is posed by Ronald to the relationship that she has built with Mrs Kerr, a relationship that, while close, is filled with insecurity on Sydney's part. Earlier in the novel, Sydney's anxiety regarding Mrs Kerr's opinion of her is made starkly apparent, as she wonders not just 'What did Mrs Kerr think of her?—but rather—Did Mrs Kerr ever think of her? The possibility of not being kept in mind seemed to Sydney [...] a kind of extinction' (Bowen 2003 [1927], p. 17). Sydney's existential dread stems not simply from the overwhelming need for one's sense of self to be confirmed by the recognition of the other, but, more pertinently, from her sapphic desire for Mrs Kerr, from the fact that, as Rau points out, having 'fallen in love with' Mrs Kerr, reality is therefore, for Sydney, 'circumscribed by her lesbian desire; indeed living this desire seems the only reality imaginable' (2006, p. 225). Sydney's conscious decision that the future of herself and Mrs Kerr 'must not be devastated by the descent upon them of Ronald', indicates the extent to which his imminent arrival represents, for her, a clear threat to the continuation of this desire (Bowen 2003 [1927], p. 71).

Yet despite these varying levels and strains of anticipation, Ronald's eventual appearance at the Hotel is eventually overshadowed by a dance taking place in the dining room that same evening, an event which means that all other communal spaces in the Hotel, including the lobby, 'had been drained of their usual occupants' (Bowen 2003 [1927], p. 81). Ronald himself, it becomes clear, has also been anticipating this moment of arrival in the lobby:

> He had been sustained till now by the brilliant certainty of being expected and awaited, but he was tired after his journey and the lounge, from which the palms had all been taken away to decorate the dining-room, now seemed repellent, mean and artificial. (Bowen 2003 [1927], p. 81)

The hotel lobby/lounge, the location for all three characters—Sydney, Mrs Kerr, and Ronald himself—of Ronald's imagined and expected arrival, here ultimately disappoints. Already unimpressed and 'irritat[ed]' by the apparent chaos and irregularity, and by the concierge's manner, which he 'felt [...] lacked *empressement*', Ronald instructs the concierge to inform his mother of his arrival (Bowen 2003 [1927], p. 81). 'The concierge went away, but nobody came, though he waited', leaving Ronald to make his own way through to the dining room, where, confronted by the 'twirling forms' of the ball (Bowen 2003 [1927], p. 81), he is only very gradually 'apprehended' by Sydney (Bowen 2003 [1927], p. 83). Despite Sydney's attempts to speak to him, which are coldly rebuffed by Ronald, the much-awaited moment of reunion with his mother, Mrs Kerr, is denied to both Sydney and reader as Ronald is led out of the room by another guest to find his mother elsewhere, beyond the lobby. In Bowen's novel, the intense anticipation created by the space of the lobby is an anticipation that is always inevitably thwarted, and which is thereby revealed to be illusory. Instead of the excitement of arrival, the hotel lobby here becomes, as Ronald discovers, a space of interminable waiting.

Anticipation is therefore rarely if ever fulfilled in Bowen's hotel lobby. Ronald is left waiting there by the concierge, and throughout the novel, the lobby is regularly populated with characters waiting: waiting, like Miss Pym, for unspecified arrivals or departures; waiting for an expedition, like the party led by Mr Lee-Mittison, who stand in a group in the lobby 'eyeing each other blankly' (Bowen 2003 [1927], p. 32); or simply waiting, like Colonel Duperrier, who on a rainy afternoon wanders 'sadly' through the 'groves of chairs' in the lounge/lobby (Bowen 2003 [1927], p. 53). That Duperrier finally settles next to Joan Lawrence, a young guest writing a letter, and that it gives him 'a restful, anchored feeling to sit beside somebody who was doing something', emphasises his own lack of purpose (Bowen 2003 [1927], p. 55). This inertia is encapsulated by Kracauer's argument that 'the hotel lobby accommodates all who go there to meet no one. It is [...] a space that encompasses them and has no function other than to encompass them' (1995, p. 175). For Kracauer, the hotel lobby is purposeless save for its existence as a space in which people gather. In this understanding, there is no direction or motivation behind the occupation of the hotel lobby, except to wait, to linger before moving on elsewhere. Yet this lack of momentum inevitably raises the question of movement and mobility, and specifically of how we understand the hotel lobby in these terms.

This section began by locating the lobby first and foremost as a space of mobility, as a space of transition between one place and another. And yet, as my reading of Bowen's novel has shown, the hotel lobby is just as often characterised not by activity, but rather by a static waiting. This contradictory nature of the lobby is highlighted by Tallack, who observes that a 'combination of movement and stasis' is inherent to this space, a blend which, he argues, 'suggests a reading of the hotel lobby as emblematic of certain aspects of modernity' (1998, p. 4). Indeed, it is this tension between mobility and paralysis that so closely aligns the hotel lobby with the interwar years in Britain and Europe, a period of anticipation and excitement, but also of uncertainty and anxiety. Kracauer, too, hints that the hotel lobby may not be the space of dynamic mobility that it first appears, and that it may rather be a space of stagnation, in which, '[l]acking any and all relation, [the guests] drip down into the vacuum with the same necessity that compels those striving in and for reality to lift themselves out of the nowhere towards their destination' (1995, p. 176). Key to Kracauer's argument here is this notion of the lack of 'any and all *relation*'—for him, the stasis of the lobby is underpinned by the absence of any real connections between people in this space. As Tim Cresswell maintains, 'mobility [is] socially produced motion', and is therefore bound up with agency and with relationships between people (2006, p. 3), yet for Kracauer, these relationships are precluded by the space of the hotel lobby. According to him, there is no sense of coherent community in the hotel lobby, in that those gathered there share nothing in common save for the fact that they are contained within, or 'encompassed' by, this space. In Bowen's novel, the only real sense of community within the hotel is found in the more distinctly feminine space of the drawing room, where the female guests of the hotel sit 'in a semi-circle with a firelight on their knees' (Bowen 2003 [1927], p. 52).[7] Excluded from this atmosphere of warmth on account of his gender, Duperrier is left to wander the lobby/lounge, which 'with its grouped furniture was of an isolating vastness', and in which 'a man, from here unrecognisable, sat leaning his back against one radiator', while another guest, a Mr Miller, 'had drawn up as close as possible to another' across the room, the distance between them further emphasising the distinct absence of any kind of connection (Bowen 2003 [1927], p. 53). Without this sense of a community bound by a common purpose, the space of the hotel lobby imbues the movements of those within it—if indeed there are any movements at all—with an aimless quality, the 'drip [...] into the vacuum' posited by Kracauer denoting a lack of any and all agency or motivation.

While a sense of stasis is undeniably present in Bowen's hotel lobby, it is far more pronounced in Green's 1939 novel, *Party Going*. In the novel, written between 1931 and 1938 in the years leading up to the outbreak of the Second World War, the sense of frustrated mobility hinted at in Bowen becomes explicit. Having been ushered into the hotel by the station manager, the party suddenly find themselves trapped in the hotel as the doors are closed and locked to prevent the lobby from being overwhelmed by the rapidly amassing crowds on the station platform. The anticipation of future arrivals, or indeed departures, is thereby paused indefinitely. Yet even before the doors are locked, the hotel lobby engenders powerful feelings of claustrophobia in the characters, most notably Julia Wray. It is Julia who observes the aforementioned 'dirtiness' of the 'vast' hotel chandelier, conveying her distaste for the faded glamour of the establishment (Green 1978 [1939], p. 414). Yet as this description of the space continues, any

---

[7] See Chap. 4 for further discussion of this space in Bowen, and of gendered spaces of community within the hotel more generally.

sense of glamour or luxury, however faded, quickly dissipates. As she looks around the lobby, Julia observes that '[i]t was full of people and those who had found seats, which were all of them too low, lay with blank faces as if exhausted' (Green 1978 [1939], p. 414). The inertia of Colonel Duperrier seated next to Joan Lawrence in Bowen's novel pales in comparison to that in evidence here, where the occupants of the lobby are forced, by the 'too low' seats, to lie more horizontal than vertical. In addition to the lack of any kind of energy or movement, their 'blank faces' suggest not merely a lack of emotion or feeling, but a lack of identity. This loss of individualised identity is emphasised in the description a few lines later of the activities in which the lobby's occupants are engaged: 'Almost every woman was having tea as if she owned the whole tray of it. Almost every man had a dispatch case filled with daily newspapers' (Green 1978 [1939], p. 414). Nameless and faceless, the occupants are reduced to their respective gendered stereotypes of middle-class identity, and the homogeneity of their behaviours renders them anonymous. However, this is an anonymity in which there is no sense of freedom. Rather, as Kracauer suggests, the anonymity engendered by the hotel lobby 'does not foster the solidarity of those liberated from the constraints of the name; instead, it deprives those encountering one another of the possibility of association that the name could have offered them' (1995, p. 183). Once more, what is reinforced here is the lack of connections between people, and the way in which the hotel lobby denies the possibility of community to those who occupy it, a denial which reinforces the inevitability of stasis.

So it is that the more emphatic anonymity of Green's hotel lobby (at least, in Bowen's lobby, all of the characters have names) is concomitant with, or indeed is the primary cause of, the lack of mobility in this space, which here escalates to a kind of paralysis. Julia's observation that 'it was like an enormous doctor's waiting room and that it would be like that when they were all dead and waiting at the gates' betrays her rising panic (Green 1978 [1939], p. 414). That the lobby is likened here to a 'doctor's waiting room' links the space explicitly with illness, thus locating it within what Richard Overy refers to as 'the medicalization of the language of crisis' in the interwar period, a wider discourse 'of disease, physical decline or mental instability [that] could be applied metaphorically to the wider world of politics and social development' (2010, p. 4). In this way, the hotel lobby comes to function as a space in which the period's broader anxieties regarding the collapse of civilisation and impending war are articulated. However, while Overy maintains that this medicalised language

'suggested the possibility of a cure' (2010, p. 4), the fact that this depiction of the hotel lobby moves immediately from 'doctor's waiting room',
with its implications of illness, to death, with no points in between, appears
to deny the possibility of such a cure. Instead, it denotes a distinct absence
of hope, an absence which is made yet more explicit in this hotel lobby in
which the occupants lie, 'if there was anything to hope for, as though they
had lost hope' (Green 1978 [1939], p. 414). This hopelessness is reified
in the subsequent impenetrability of the hotel entrance once the steel door
'crashes' shut (Green 1978 [1939], p. 416).

As the novel progresses, and the sense of entrapment grows, the pervasive sense of anxiety within the lobby becomes tied more concretely to the
fear of impending war:

> Although all those windows had been shut there was a continual dull roar
> came through them from outside, and this noise sat upon those within like
> clouds upon a mountain so they were obscured and levelled and, as though
> they had been airmen, in danger of running fatally into earth. Clouds also,
> if they are banked up, will so occupy the sky as to dwarf what is beneath and
> this low roar, which was only conversation in that multitude without, lay
> over them in such a pall, like night coming on and there is no light when one
> must see, that these people here were obscured by it and were dimmed into
> anxious Roman numerals. (Green 1978 [1939], pp. 481–2)

A 'continual dull roar' comes through the closed windows from the
crowds gathered on the platform outside the hotel, and the noise 'sits
upon' and oppresses those within the lobby 'like clouds upon a mountain
so they were obscured and levelled and, as though they had been airmen,
in danger of running fatally into earth'. This noise, this 'low roar', is then
further described as lying over those within the lobby like 'a pall'. This
funereal imagery, together with that of the 'airmen in danger of running
fatally into earth', irrevocably blends war and death within the space of the
lobby. It echoes the fear and pessimism that was so widespread during the
1930s, and which was articulated by figures such as the Conservative
prime minister Stanley Baldwin, and anthropologist and pacifist Bronislaw
Malinowski who, in a lecture given at Harvard University in 1936, claimed
that while the First World War had seriously damaged Western civilisation,
another one 'may well destroy it' and would at the very least trigger 'a
slow death of humanity' (cited in Overy 2010, p. 177). This sense of
immobility and powerlessness is intensified by the structure of the sen-
tences, which, with their multiple dependent clauses that are as 'banked

up' as the clouds they describe, themselves enact a very palpable delay. As a space of paralysis and hopelessness, the hotel lobby in Green's *Party Going* thereby encapsulates the anxieties of interwar society regarding impending war and the consequent crisis of civilisation.

In Rhys's *Quartet*, an anxiety of a rather different kind is in evidence, though one that is no less powerful and pervasive. As discussed earlier, while the hotel lobbies in Bowen and Green convey at least some trace of luxury and glamour (even if, as in Green's novel, this is distinctly faded), the hotel lobbies in Rhys's first novel are largely marked, through their sparse decoration and furnishings, by a distinct lack of privilege. Marya Zelli, who lacks 'the necessary fixed background', and her husband Stephan, 'this stranger and alien', are confined to certain types of hotels not simply on account of their relative poverty, but also due to the way in which this poverty is inextricably linked to their precarious existence on the peripheries of society (Rhys 2000 [1929], pp. 10, 16). As Carol Dell'Amico notes, Rhys constructs Marya and Stephan 'as national/ethnic hybrids, characters most notable for their lack of identity', and she argues further that 'they are racialized, feminized, and (under) classed as a unit' (2005, p. 98). As such, the hotel in Rhys is bound up with the fate of the marginalised subject in interwar society. Marya and Stephan's indeterminate backgrounds mark them as foreign, as other, and thereby determine not only the kind of hotels in which they temporarily reside, but also the extent to which they are monitored by the hotel's management for the duration of their stay, a process which takes place within the space of the hotel lobby.

In the Hôtel de l'Univers, the hotel in which Marya and Stephan have a room when the novel opens, the *patronne*, Madame Hautchamp, maintains a constant presence, along with her husband, in the aforementioned 'small sitting-room behind the hotel bureau' in the lobby (Rhys 2000 [1929], p. 21). From this vantage point, Madame Hautchamp observes all the comings and goings in the hotel, and is thus able to give Marya, when she returns to the hotel one afternoon, a detailed account of her husband's earlier arrest. Marya, anxious under this apparent scrutiny, is 'aroused' by the inflection in Madame Hautchamp's voice 'to some useful instinct of self-defence, and she was able to say that [Stephan's arrest] was evidently a mistake' (Rhys 2000 [1929], p. 22). Marya's anxiety seems at first to be not entirely misplaced—the *patronne* of the hotel is described in the following chapter as 'the watching Madame Hautchamp', who carefully monitors '[a]ll the strange young couples who filled her hotel', observing that they were all 'internationalists who invariably got into trouble sooner or later' (Rhys 2000 [1929], p. 27). Delia Caparoso Konzett argues that Madame Hautchamp here enacts 'a racism that operates not so much systematically but in a more latent and insidious manner' (2002, p. 150). This prejudice is enacted through the surveillance that takes place in and through the hotel lobby, yet this is a rather different type of surveillance to that found in earlier, pre-war novels such as Bennett's *The Grand Babylon Hotel*. In fiction such as this, while guests are monitored by staff within the space of the lobby, the indication is rarely given that this is enacted for the purposes of potential exclusion. In Bennett's novel, for example, Miss Spencer, to an extent herself controlled by criminal mastermind Jules, keeps track of the movements of certain guests, and particularly of the occupation of particular rooms, for the sole purpose of allowing Jules, Rocco, and herself to carry out their planned crimes. However, the surveillance which takes place within the interwar hotel lobby is more often targeted specifically at marginalised subjects. As Katz suggests, the space can be understood in this sense as 'a quasi city gate', which serves 'as a kind of policing unit' in which hotel management, like Madame Hautchamp, act 'under a self-imposed moral and aesthetic imperative to bar access to indigents and undesirables' (1999, p. 140). In the semi-public space of the lobby, Marya feels exposed and threatened by Madame Hautchamp's ostensible monitoring of her movements, and fears her potential exclusion from the hotel.

Rhys's novel is indeed one that, as Dell'Amico notes, 'sets out to demonstrate the perniciousness of exclusion' (2005, p. 99), and yet despite Madame Hautchamp's surveillance, Marya's fears of exclusion from the Hôtel de l'Univers are ultimately unfounded. Her eventual departure from the hotel is triggered not by the *patronne*'s insistence upon her leaving, but rather by the insistence of Hugh Heidler, her eventual lover, that she come and stay with him and his wife in their apartment. In fact, rather than a figure who polices, Madame Hautchamp can be read conversely as a character who offers a level of support to Marya, and she is characterised by Dell'Amico not as enacting that aforementioned 'insidious racism', but, quite the opposite, as an 'internationalist-sympathizer' (2005, p. 106), who in fact takes pity on 'all the strange couples that filled her hotel—internationalists who got into trouble sooner or later' (Rhys 2000 [1929], p. 27). While Madame Hautchamp does not 'for one moment [allow] her sympathy to overflow a certain limit of business-like correctness', she is sympathetic nonetheless, helping Marya, for example, to sell her dresses in order to survive (Rhys 2000 [1929], p. 31). In this sense, her observation of Marya from the vantage point of the hotel bureau might alternatively be read not as surveillance or scrutiny, but rather as enacting a crucial level of care and protection.

The protection that Madame Hautchamp provides is reinforced by its conspicuous absence in the novel's final chapter, in which Marya visits her husband Stephan who, having been released from prison, is staying in the apartment of a fellow ex-inmate, Monsieur Bernadet. The rooms, located in the Rue Bleue in Montmartre, are 'on the third floor of a dark and dilapidated house', and Stephan informs Marya as they ascend the stairs that 'The concierge hates Bernadet, I shall have to be careful of her' (Rhys 2000 [1929], p. 134). Stephan's subsequent revelation that the reason the female concierge dislikes Bernadet is because he abused his wife effectively transforms his own comment that he 'shall have to be careful of her' into a sinister foreshadowing of Marya's violent assault at the hands of Stephan himself a few pages later, after she reveals to him the details of her affair with Heidler: 'He caught her by the shoulders and swung her sideways with all his force. As she fell, she struck her forehead against the edge of the table, crumpled up and lay still' (Rhys 2000 [1929], p. 143). As he leaves the building after having either killed or seriously injured his wife (the novel leaves her fate uncertain), Stephan repeats almost exactly that same phrase: 'As he went down the stairs he was thinking: "The concierge; I must be careful of the concierge." But the concierge's *loge*, when he passed it, was in darkness' (Rhys 2000 [1929], p. 143). Unlike Madame Hautchamp, whose presence in her hotel lobby is reliably constant, the concierge in Bernadet's apartment building is absent, thus allowing Stephan to leave the building and evade any repercussions of his violence. In this sense, the space of the hotel lobby becomes a space of reassurance, a space in which the ever-present and watchful *patronne* ensures the safety of her female guests, thereby standing in stark contrast to the other, more threatening spaces of the interwar city.

The Hôtel de l'Univers is, as was established at the beginning of this section, a particular type of hotel, one that is run-down, cheap, and possessing no trace of luxury. And yet passing through the lobby of this hotel nevertheless ensures a level of safety for Marya that is unavailable to her elsewhere. As a woman with no money and no 'fixed background', Madame Hautchamp's awareness of her movements marks a rare constant in her life, even if her presence is limited to the length of Marya's sojourn in the hotel. The hotel lobby in interwar literature is consistently characterised by this tension between mobility and stasis, between fixity and flux. In Bowen, the anticipation of movement—and specifically of the moment of arrival—is continually frustrated, leading to a perpetual and relentless state of waiting. In Green's novel, the lobby shifts from a space of stasis to one of paralysis, and the palpable sense of disillusionment conveyed by the lobby's links to illness, death, and *lack* of mobility is here indicative of the anxieties of late 1930s Britain and Europe as they edged ever closer to war. Marya's awareness that her movements are constantly monitored from the desk of the *patronne* might well be read as signifying the scrutiny of marginalised subjects in interwar Europe. However, as I have demonstrated, this same fixed presence can also mark the hotel lobby as a space of security and reassurance for those same subjects, offering a rare possibility of hope in an uncertain and anxious period.

*   *   *

The lobby and its inherent significance shift, perhaps more dramatically than any other space within the hotel, from late-nineteenth and early-twentieth-century depictions in literature through to fictional representations in the interwar period. As spaces that are primarily passed through rather than lingered in, the early entrance halls found in the work of Trollope and Collins, and to an extent James and Bennett, carry fairly little symbolic weight compared to the interwar lobbies of authors such as Holtby, Bowen, Green, and Rhys. In the novels of the latter authors, characters spend increasing amounts of time in the lobby, and this time is marked by anticipation and frustration, by boredom and paralysis, emotions which frequently bleed into one another and manifest simultaneously. And yet the tension between mobility and stasis that so clearly surrounds the interwar lobby, and which creates and sustains these powerful feelings within the characters, is also detectable in earlier novels in the figure of the hotel receptionist or concierge, who must remain fixed in the lobby in order to carry out their work of recording the movements of the hotel guests. In the work of James and Bennett, the gendering of this figure as a woman is particularly pertinent, opening up as it does questions of feminine mobility—or rather the lack of it—at the turn of the century (questions I explore in greater detail in the discussion of hotel staff in Chap. 6), and which extend into and are complicated by the particular nature of the interwar lobby.

Also present across both pre- and interwar novels is the issue of surveillance—in both Bennett and Rhys, the comings and goings of hotel guests are watched closely by the static hotel staff in the entrance hall or lobby. However, here again, there are differences to be traced in the precise nature and purpose of this surveillance. In literature depicting the pre-war entrance hall, surveillance tends to be carried out both for the purpose of security and, in the case of Bennett's novel, to aid in the nefarious activities of certain members of the hotel staff. In the interwar novels of authors like Rhys, however, this surveillance might be read in one of two ways. On the one hand, it might well be understood as a way in which hotel staff monitor marginalised subjects with a view to potentially expelling or excluding them from the hotel space and of policing or even limiting their mobility. This is what characters such as Marya fear, and in this way the surveillance of hotel staff only serves to fuel her anxiety concerning her precarious position in society. However, this surveillance might alternatively be read as a vital form of security—as the one constant in the lives of transient characters like Marya, and which, when absent, can prove fatal. In this instance, the stasis of the staff marks a point of security or consistency within an otherwise fluid—and precarious—life. Once more, then, it is this peculiar combination of mobility and stasis that so strongly characterises the hotel lobby, and which constructs it as a space that, though undeniably ambiguous, nevertheless powerfully articulates the shifting tensions of modernity.

References

Bennett, Arnold. 2016 [1902]. *The Grand Babylon Hotel*. Ed. Randi Saloman. Peterborough, ON: Broadview Press.

Bowen, Elizabeth. 2003 [1927]. *The Hotel*. London: Vintage.

Collins, Wilkie. 1995 [1866]. *Armadale*. London: Penguin.

Cresswell, Tim. 2006. *On the Move: Mobility in the Modern Western World*. London: Routledge.

Dell'Amico, Carol. 2005. *Colonialism and the Modernist Moment in the Early Novels of Jean Rhys*. New York: Routledge.

Green, Henry. 1978 [1939]. *Party Going*. In *Living, Loving, Party Going*, 384–528. London: Picador.

Holtby, Winifred. 2011 [1936]. *South Riding*. London: BBC Books.

James, Henry. 2008 [1903]. *The Ambassadors*. Oxford: Oxford University Press.

Katz, Marc. 1999. The Hotel Kracauer. *Differences* 11 (2): 134–152.

Konzett, Delia Caparoso. 2002. *Ethnic Modernism: Anzia Yezierska, Zora Neale Hurston, Jean Rhys, and the Aesthetics of Dislocation*. New York: Palgrave Macmillan.

Kort, Wesley A. 2004. *Place and Space in Modern Fiction*. Gainesville: University Press of Florida.

Kracauer, Siegfried. 1995. The Hotel Lobby. In *The Mass Ornament: Weimar Essays*, ed. and trans. Thomas Y. Levin, 173–185. Cambridge: Harvard University Press.

Lacan, Jacques. 2006 [1966]. *Écrits*. Trans. Bruce Fink. New York: W.W. Norton & Company.

Overy, Richard. 2010. *The Morbid Age: Britain and the Crisis of Civilization, 1919–1939*. London: Penguin.

Rau, Petra. 2006. Telling It Straight: The Rhetorics of Conversion in Elizabeth Bowen's *The Hotel* and Freud's *Psychogenesis*. In *Sapphic Modernities: Sexuality, Women and National Culture*, ed. Laura Doan and Jane Garrity, 217–231. Basingstoke: Palgrave.

Rhys, Jean. 2000 [1929]. *Quartet*. London: Penguin.

Tallack, Douglas. 1998. 'Waiting, Waiting': The Hotel Lobby. *Irish Journal of American Studies* 7: 1–20.

Trollope, Anthony. 2004 [1865]. *Can You Forgive Her?* London: Penguin.

CHAPTER 4

'The Intolerable Impudence of the Public Gaze': The Public Rooms of the Hotel

Given that the rise in the popularity and number of hotels in the Western world was concomitant with the increasingly rapid developments in technologies of travel in the mid-to-late nineteenth and early twentieth centuries, it would be reasonable to assume that the primary purpose of the hotel was, for the traveller at least, to provide a bedroom in which to sleep, a resting place in between destinations. Yet, the majority of hotels—both in the late nineteenth and early twentieth centuries and today—also offered their guests access to a range of other, more public rooms. The type and number of these rooms varied depending on the character—and importantly price—of the hotel, but most would include at the very least a dining room, a lounge, and a bar, with the possible additions of a smoking room, drawing room, reading room, and even ballroom. This chapter considers in detail these communal areas—rooms such as the lounge and dining room—which are less public than the lobby, but more so than the bedrooms and other spaces, such as the corridor, that extend beyond.

In fiction of the early twentieth century, these communal areas often function as spaces of community that are sought after by those characters who embody the hotel lifestyle—those who effectively live in hotels, or constantly move between them, a trend which becomes especially prominent in literature of the interwar period. Yet the reading of these spaces as sanctuary is, I argue, complicated by a number of factors. Firstly, spaces such as the drawing room and smoking room are often explicitly gendered,

© The Author(s) 2019
E. Short, *Mobility and the Hotel in Modern Literature*,
Studies in Mobilities, Literature, and Culture,
https://doi.org/10.1007/978-3-030-22129-4_4

to the extent that they demand the performance of traditional femininities and masculinities from those who occupy these respective areas. I examine the ways in which such spaces are consequently figured as exclusionary for those who do not, or will not, conform to such rigid gender identities. I demonstrate how novels such as May Sinclair's *Kitty Tailleur* (1908), in which the eponymous protagonist is, upon her entrance into the dining room of the Cliff Hotel, subjected to 'the intolerable impudence of the public gaze', reveal the ways in which gendered identity is constructed both by the spaces we occupy, and by the censorious gaze of the others within those spaces. The gaze of the other, and the lack of privacy so inherent to such communal spaces within the hotel, marks them further in novels such as H.G. Well's *Kipps* (1905), in which Arthur Kipps becomes increasingly anxious and paranoid in the dining room of the Royal Grand Hotel, as spaces in which class identity is constantly scrutinised and evaluated. This chapter demonstrates the preoccupation of the literature of the late nineteenth and early twentieth centuries with the impact of space upon the subject.

DESIGNING AND DIVIDING THE HOTEL: REPLICATING THE DOMESTIC

The origins of public rooms in hotels can be traced back at least as far as the basic social spaces—the dining room, bar, and coffee room—of coaching inns and taverns, the earliest of which were first introduced in England by the Romans (Boer 1972). To chart the development of the public room in the hotel specifically, however, it is necessary to look back at least to the early hotels of late-eighteenth-century America. The very first American hotel is identified by A.K. Sandoval-Strausz as the Union Public Hotel in Washington DC. Conceived of by merchant and financier Samuel Blodget, Jr., the 'internal arrangement' of the Union Public Hotel 'went far beyond that of any public house in the nation', with the ground floor 'consist[ing] of several public meeting rooms' (Sandoval-Strausz 2007, p. 22). The hotel was, however, fraught with severe financial difficulties from the outset. The cornerstone was laid in 1793, but it was some years before work was completed, and it was never used as a hotel. Instead, the building was established by the Federal Government as the first headquarters of the Postal Service and Patent Office. However, significantly, it was the Union Public Hotel's extensive public rooms that later led to its most auspicious role in accommodating Congress for fourteen months from

1814 to 1815, following the damage caused to the Capitol by the fires of the War of 1812 (Sandoval Strausz 2007, pp. 20–3). Public rooms were also an important feature of the next major American hotel, the City Hotel, which Sandoval-Strausz pinpoints as 'the nation's first functioning hotel' (2007, p. 25). Located on lower Broadway in Manhattan, construction began on the hotel in 1794, and its interior was, Sandoval-Strausz observes, 'designed to incorporate many different functions. Its exceptionally tall main and second stories were to house a ballroom, public parlors, bar, stores, offices, and a circulating library', and these public rooms quickly became 'sought-after venues for private cotillions, concerts, and at least one finishing school' (2007, p. 24). Following the construction of the City Hotel, a number of large American hotels were designed and never built, but were, Sandoval-Strausz argues, nevertheless significant due to the architectural coherence of their plans, a coherence which rested largely on the layout and function of the public rooms. One of the most notable and influential of these early hotels was that designed in 1797 for the city of Richmond by architect Benjamin Henry Latrobe. For Sandoval-Strausz,

> the most revealing aspect of the drawings was how they detailed the hotel's interior. Latrobe intended not only that the internal spaces of the hotel be numerous but that each was to have a specialized function for which it would be designed. The plan of the ground floor included a 'supper room,' 'liquor bar,' 'coffee bar,' and 'private dining room.' (2007, p. 27)

It was this 'complex subdivision and purpose-specific assignment of space', that, as Sandoval-Strausz points out, 'characterized hotel interiors', and set the hotel apart from the more generalised and 'undifferentiated interiors' of earlier inns and taverns (2007, pp. 27–8).

The same kinds of interior layouts were echoed in the earliest hotels established in Britain at the beginning of the nineteenth century, Woods' Hotel in London being a good example of this design. Located in the Furnival's Inns of Court in Holborn, London, the hotel was built in the first decades of the nineteenth century, and was demolished in 1898, along with the rest of the Inn, to make way for further development of the Prudential building.[1] In an article from a June 1882 edition of trade

---

[1] The earliest traceable reference to Woods' Hotel appears in a list of insolvent debtors published in the *London Gazette* on 2 February 1830, which gives the hotel as one of the

journal, *Hotel World*, Woods' Hotel is described as 'one of the few first-class hotels in the British metropolis where the comfort, and quiet of home-life, the regularity of a large establishment, and close proximity to "everywhere," are happily combined' (Anon 1882, p. 3). The article then goes on to give a detailed account of the hotel's public rooms, noting:

> While there is every convenience for gentlemen, the wants of families and ladies have been sedulously anticipated. There are two coffee-rooms, a 'general' one, and one for ladies; a service department and bar; a smoking room; a telephone, used equally by gentlemen in transacting business and by ladies in ordering a box at a theatre, a bonnet at a milliner's, or a doll for the baby; a large cigar-room where the choicest brands are kept in stock for patrons exclusively; and a capacious reading-room for ladies or gentlemen, where a large assortment of newspapers, periodicals, magazines, maps, guides, directories, &c., is ready to hand. (Anon 1882, p. 3)

The article's emphasis on the 'comfort, and quiet of home life' is worth noting here in relation to its public rooms, as it gives an indication of the way in which such rooms were designed, at least in part, to mimic the layout and familiarity of the domestic space. The description of the public rooms themselves further reveals the establishment of gendered divisions from room to room, with a separate coffee room for ladies. This provision of rooms specifically designated for women is an early example of the slow proliferation of public spaces geared towards women, of which the department store is perhaps one of the most well known. Scholarship on the department store at the turn of the century has tended to depict it as an emancipatory space for women, and has highlighted its unique role as an urban space outside of the home in which women were able to gather freely. Elizabeth Wilson, for example, observes the way in which 'department stores in their seduction of women created zones such as restaurants, rest rooms and even reading rooms where they could, towards the end of the century, go unchaperoned or certainly free of men's protection' (1992, p. 60). The public rooms of hotels such as Woods' hotel functioned in a similar way to provide spaces which women could occupy unaccompanied by male companions, thus contributing to the transformation of societal attitudes towards women in the public, urban space.

many residences of a William Adair Carter. For details on the demolition of Woods' Hotel and Furnival's Inn, see: Laurie Dennett, *A Sense of Security: 150 Years of Prudential* (Cambridge: Granta, 1998), pp. 148–150.

The public rooms hold further significance in terms of what they reveal about the hotels to which they belong. Beyond the initial spectacle of the lobby, the public rooms are most likely the next spaces into which guests and visitors to the hotel will move, and their interior design is therefore typically geared to reflect something of the hotel's character. In novels of the late nineteenth and early twentieth centuries, descriptions of hotel lounges, dining rooms, bars, and drawing rooms are replete with details of their décor and furnishings. In Ford Madox Ford's *The Good Soldier*, for example, 'the aspect of the dining-room of the Hotel Excelsior' in Nauheim, the space in which he first meets the Ashburnams, is burned on John Dowell's memory:

> [T]hat white room, festooned with papier-mâché fruits and flowers; the tall windows; the many tables; the black screen round the door with three golden cranes flying upward on each panel; the palm tree in the centre of the room; the swish of the waiter's feet; the cold expensive elegance. (Ford 2002 [1915], p. 27)

What resonates here is a sense of grandeur, albeit one that is somewhat restrained, 'the cold expensive elegance' conveying an atmosphere of refinement that lacks any kind of warmth or friendliness. This absence of warmth is heightened by the room's bare white walls, which stand in stark contrast to the 'black screen round the door'. The 'three golden cranes' which adorn this screen, together with 'the palm tree in the centre of the room', denote an attempt at a kind of opulent and Orientalist exoticism. Overwhelming in this extract, however, is the absence of any kind of truth in this space, signalled initially by the falsity of the 'papier-mâché fruits and flowers', and further reinforced by the mishmash of cultural appropriation represented by the screen and palm tree. In this brief description of its dining room, then, a great deal is revealed about the character of the Hotel Excelsior, though not all of it positive. While on the surface this space is depicted as one of elegance and glamour, underpinning this is a powerful sense of unreality and, crucially, of inauthenticity.

The lack of authenticity in the hotel space may well be more pro-nounced in some hotels than in others, but due to the attempt to echo the layout of the home in the architectural design of the hotel's public rooms, this falsity is always present to some extent. These public rooms—the din-ing room, the lounge, the drawing room, and even the writing and/or reading room—effectively map on to the blueprint of the typical domestic space to a greater or lesser degree depending on their number, size, and grandeur. In the nineteenth-century home, rooms were organised according to a careful demarcation of functions—as Stefan Muthesius points out, '[t]he overriding principle in the planning of a nineteenth-century house whether country mansion or cottage was the same: the differentiation of functions, the allocation of a separate room for each and every purpose' (1982, p. 45). These purposes varied depending on whether the room in question was to be used primarily by the family or by the servants, meaning that class played a significant role in the allocation of space. Those rooms occupied by servants were designed for more functional and utilitarian tasks and purposes—the kitchen for cooking, for example—whereas the rooms for the family—the sitting room, the drawing room, the study— tended, as Victoria Rosner notes, to be 'larger and given over to leisurely pursuits' (2005, p. 63). Alongside class, gender played an important role in the division of rooms, and this was indicated not simply by the room's name and intended purpose, but also by the level of privacy afforded to those occupying said rooms. Rosner highlights the disparity between the peace and solitude engendered by masculine rooms (such as, for example, the study or billiard room), and the 'more social and open' atmosphere of those rooms associated with women, such as the drawing room. Important as well is the amount of space allocated to men and women, with Rosner arguing that, typically, 'more rooms were given over to the gentleman of the house than to its mistress' (2005, p. 64). In the hotel, a similar gendering is at work in the demarcation of the public rooms, though the question of privacy within these rooms differs somewhat. None of these rooms can be understood as private in the same way that the spaces within the home are—indeed, quite the opposite is the case, with these rooms within the hotel forming some of its most public spaces. This is, then, one major way in which the public rooms of the hotel can only ever loosely echo, rather than directly replicate, the spaces within the home. While they may be engineered to reproduce the comfort and familiarity of the domestic sphere, the inherently exposing nature of these spaces lends them an inescapable air of inauthenticity.

It is, however, the very same public nature of these spaces within the hotel that makes them so ideal for authors seeking to bring characters together. In these public rooms, fellow guests are able to form relationships with one another, but the public rooms of the hotel are also frequently open to the public, creating a broader social spectrum in which hotel guests mix with visitors and with members of the hotel staff. In terms of narrative, these public rooms are therefore the primary spaces within the hotel in which authors are able to gather characters in one place, and to keep them in that place for sustained periods of time. In this sense, whereas the lobby might be the site of initial though brief meetings—such as the first meeting between Maria Gostrey and Lambert Strether in James's *The Ambassadors*—spaces such as the lounge, dining room, smoking room, or drawing room are those spaces in which characters are, due to the designated purpose of the rooms, and the nature of the furnishings within them, encouraged to spend increased amounts of time, thus enabling authors to establish the relationships between these characters. In *The Ambassadors*, for example, the friendship between Maria Gostrey and Lambert Strether evolves over the course of their breakfast together in the coffee room of their hotel, during which Strether begs her to 'teach him at all events [...] to order breakfast as breakfast was ordered in Europe', a task which Maria Gostrey takes up readily, having previously 'weaned the expatriated from traditions compared with which the matutinal beefsteak was but the creature of an hour' (James 2008 [1903], p. 24). In instances such as this, the public rooms of the hotel provide a crucial narrative opportunity for the development of connections between characters.

In the public rooms of the Santa Marina hotel in Woolf's *The Voyage Out*, the guests gather together in various different groupings, depending on the type of room. Moving along the outside of the hotel, Rachel Vinrace and Helen Ambrose, as I discuss in Chap. 2, observe the occupants of each room through the windows, at times pausing to make judgements about the nature of these groupings. For example, the first room that they encounter which is occupied by guests (the dining room having been lately vacated following the end of dinner) is the drawing room, 'where the ladies and gentlemen, having dined well, lay back in deep armchairs, occasionally speaking or turning over the pages of magazines. A thin woman was flourishing up and down the piano' (Woolf 2009 [1915], p. 109). While the layout of the furniture in this room is not described in any real detail, the fact that the guests only speak to each other 'occasionally' suggests either that the chairs are placed at some distance apart, and that the space is therefore not conducive to conversation, or that this room—the drawing room—has a certain formality to it that attracts a certain type of guest not prone to excessive conversation. At the 'general clearing of throats and tapping of knees' that accompanies the end of the piano piece, Rachel whispers to Helen, '"They're all old in this room"', thus confirming that the room attracts—and is designed for—a particular demographic. Very different is the scene in the billiard room, the next space into which Rachel and Helen peer, in which 'two men in shirt sleeves [were] playing billiards with two young ladies' (Woolf 2009 [1915], p. 109). In this room, a casual and flirtatious atmosphere pervades, as 'the plump young woman' protests loudly at having had her arm pinched by one of the men, causing her to miss her shot, and the men are reproved by another young man with a 'red face' for 'ragging', or making fun of, their female companions (Woolf 2009 [1915], p. 109). That the designated purpose of this room is for playing a game of billiards, rather than for sitting quietly, as in the drawing room, leads to the space being occupied by a different kind of guest, and being used in a very different kind of way. Again, the space itself here dictates not just the behaviour of those within it, but who enters, occupies, and feels comfortable in that space.

The same is true of the final public room in the hotel observed by Rachel and Helen, the lounge, of which more intricate detail is given than any of the other rooms:

> Hung with armour and native embroideries, furnished with divans and screens, which shut off convenient corners, the room was less formal than the others, and was evidently the haunt of youth. Signor Rodriguez, whom they knew to be the manager of the hotel, stood quite near them in the doorway surveying the scene. (Woolf 2009 [1915], p. 110)

Foregrounded in this description are the room's furniture and décor, which seem designed both to situate the hotel firmly with the local culture of Santa Marina, through the 'native embroideries', and, seemingly conversely, to draw consciously on the English country house tradition of using armour as decoration in a 'revival of the old Baronial Hall' (von Spreckelsen 1997, p. 544). This tradition witnessed a resurgence in the Victorian period and signalled, as Marieke von Spreckelsen suggests, 'a romantic nostalgia for "old English hospitality"' (1997, p. 544),[2] laying bare the aims of the hotel manager, Signor Rodriguez, to create an environment which will both allow his primarily English clientele to feel at home and satisfy their desire for an authentic South American experience. This blending of cultures in the public rooms echoes that witnessed in the Hotel Excelsior in Ford's *The Good Soldier*, and is indeed a quality replicated in the majority of hotels found in literature of this period.

[2] On the use of armour as decoration, see also: Mark Girouard, *Life in the English Country House: A Social and Architectural History* (New Haven: Yale University Press, 1978), p. 136.

That the lounge is 'less formal' than the other rooms is, however, significant, particularly given the rather ostentatious décor. This lack of formality is achieved through the particular arrangement of furniture, the 'divans and screens' which are placed around the room to 'shut off convenient corners', making it conducive to conversations which are both more private and more relaxed. While the 'deep armchairs' of the drawing room also promote relaxation, in the lounge, the divan is not only designed to encourage its user(s) to assume a more reclined, rather than upright, position, but its length also permits more than one person to sit on it at any one time, thereby engendering a potentially far more intimate seating arrangement. These increased opportunities for intimacy and seclusion in the lounge are what construct this space as 'the haunt of youth', as opposed to attracting those older guests, who are more likely to be married or established in their unattached lifestyle, and who are therefore perhaps less likely to be looking to establish new relationships, sexual or otherwise. Furniture here again dictates the way in which this particular public room of the hotel is used—as Sara Ahmed reflects, furniture '"invites" one to inhabit spaces' in a certain way, depending on how it is arranged in space (2006, p. 168). In this sense, Ahmed argues, furniture can be understood as 'an orientation device, a way of directing life by deciding what we do with what and where, in the very gesture toward comfort' (2006, p. 168). Once they have entered the hotel lounge, the younger guests are oriented towards conversation with each other by the furniture and its arrangement, a grouping which has been considered and planned by the hotel management to slow or stall people in their movement through this space.

Indeed, this careful engineering on the part of the hotel management is clearly successful, and is an example of what Robbie Moore refers to as 'the deeper logic of hotel architecture: the domestic commercialised, or rather, the domestic simulated for commercial ends' (2012, p. 257). In this instance, the domestic space of the lounge is replicated, or rather 'simulated', in order to drive the business and profitability of the hotel. Signor Rodriguez notes with pleasure 'the gentlemen lounging in chairs, the couples leaning over coffee-cups, the game of cards in the centre under profuse clusters of electric light', and, through the window, Rachel and Helen observe the way in which the guests 'were scattered about in couples or parties of four, and either they were actually better acquainted, or the informal room made their manners easier' (Woolf 2009 [1915], p. 110). The informality of the room, itself constructed through the type of furniture, and its precise arrangement in space, here explicitly shapes the behaviour of the guests within, making 'their manners easier', and encouraging them to pause and spend time here. Recognising his success, Signor Rodriguez 'congratulat[es] himself on the enterprise which had turned the refectory, a cold stone room [...], into the most comfortable room in the house. The hotel was very full, and proved his wisdom in decreeing that no hotel can flourish without a lounge' (Woolf 2009 [1915], p. 110). This purposeful manipulation of space by the hotel management demonstrates the way in which the hotel can be regarded as 'a social technology', the 'driving force' of which stems, according to Sandoval-Strausz, 'from a new way of organizing people' (2007, p. 48). The furnishings and décor of the public rooms in Woolf's Santa Marina hotel are thereby precisely choreographed to influence and determine the behaviour and movements of particular types of people in and through these spaces.

The bar of the Ormond Hotel, Dublin, in James Joyce's *Ulysses* (1922) is similarly designed to attract and engage—or, more appropriately in this instance, to entice and ensnare—hotel guests and members of the public. Appearing in the 'Sirens' episode, the bar plays second fiddle to the sirens of the title, the barmaids Lydia Douce and Mina Kennedy, but while descriptions of the interior are scarce, key information about this space can nevertheless be gleaned from the details given. Focus is directed, for example, to the mirror behind the bar: 'Miss Douce halfstood to see her skin askance in the barmirror gildedlettered where hock and claret glasses shimmered and in their midst a shell' (Joyce 2008 [1922], p. 248). A few pages later, Miss Douce again, '[w]ith grace of alacrity towards the mirror gilt Cantrell and Cochrane's [...] turned herself' (Joyce 2008 [1922], p. 250). The mirror itself is emblazoned in gilt letters with the name of the Irish drinks company Cantrell and Cochrane, and is thus, like many other mirrors in bars and public houses of the period, effectively an advertisement. But it advertises more than just the business whose name adorns it. Firstly, the placement of the mirror behind the bar greatly enhances the view of the selection of bottles of spirits, drawing the customer's attention to these, as well as to the 'shimmering' hock and claret glasses. More crucially, however, the mirror serves to foreground the barmaids themselves, and particularly Miss Douce, as spectacle.

Sitting at the bar, Simon Dedalus watches Miss Douce turn to pour a glass of whisky, and is able to gaze on her reflection in the mirror as she does so. In this sense, the mirror becomes a magnet for the male gaze, one of which the barmaids are acutely aware. Yet the sexuality of the barmaids, and the extent to which they retain control in and over this environment, is inevitably complicated by their commodification in the space of the Ormond Hotel bar. While the majority of criticism has tended to focus on Joyce's formal and stylistic experimentation in this episode of *Ulysses*, 'Sirens' is, according to Katherine Mullin, 'also intimately engaged with at least one contentious ideological struggle: the contest over the morality and meaning of bar work for women' (2004, pp. 475–6). Abolitionist reformers at the beginning of the twentieth century mounted a moral campaign against the position of barmaid, figuring them as passive victims of a ruthless pub and hotel trade who capitalised on their appearance and implicit sexuality in order to sell alcohol. And indeed, advertisements for barmaid positions often 'bluntly required them to be pretty', with Mullin citing the words of hotel chain Spiers and Pond that their barmaids were 'the pick of the basket' (2004, p. 477).[3] In this sense, the 'gildedlettered' mirror of the Ormond Hotel bar advertises not just the company whose name is emblazoned upon it, or simply the drinks lined up on the bar that it reflects—rather, it advertises the sexuality of Miss Douce and Miss Kennedy. The barmaids and the alcohol may well be the means by which the Ormond Hotel entices its wholly male clientele into its bar, but the careful positioning of the mirror behind the bar magnifies the spectacle, and by sustaining their gaze, this crucial item of décor successfully holds the hotel's customers in place.

However, to abandon the reading of the mirror here would be to over-look its more positive and subversive potential, and to relegate the bar-maids to passive victims within the space of the hotel bar. There is undoubtedly, as Mullin suggests, a complexity and an ambiguity in Joyce's depiction of Miss Douce and Miss Kennedy, and of the male clientele in this episode, which prevents a decisive reading as to whether or not the two women are 'concealing their victimhood behind a veneer of good-humoured availability, or vice versa' (Mullin 2004, p. 489). Certainly, the attention of the men in the hotel bar is almost wholly focused upon the physicality of the barmaids, with Lenehan in particular overcome as 'Miss Douce reached high to take a flagon, stretching her satin arm, her bust, that all but burst, so high.—O! O! jerked Lenehan, gasping at each stretch. O!' (Joyce 2008 [1922], p. 254). And yet, the agency of the barmaids is also made apparent throughout the episode, such as the moment at which

---

[3] See also: Diane Kirkby, *Barmaids: A History of Women's Work in Pubs* (Cambridge: Cambridge University Press, 1997), p. 46.

Miss Kennedy, smiling at Blazes Boylan in response to him tipping his hat to her, is 'out smiled' by Miss Douce, 'sister bronze', who 'preen[ed] for him her richer hair, a bosom and a rose' (Joyce 2008 [1922], p. 254). Read alongside this instance, the earlier appearance of Miss Douce's reflection in the mirror behind the bar, gazed so longingly upon by Simon Dedalus, can be read as a conscious and careful positioning on the part of the barmaid herself, as opposed to simply the exploitation of her form by the Ormond Hotel management. As Mullin suggests, while '[t]he barmaids of abolitionist fantasy are abject, pitiable damsels in distress, [...] Joyce's barmaids are adept at manipulating their sexuality for their own advantage' (2004, p. 483). On this understanding, while the Ormond Hotel bar might well be read as a distinctly masculine space of community, in which men, tempted and held fast by the promise of both alcohol and the spectacle of the barmaids employed therein, congregate together to converse and sustain friendships, it can also simultaneously be understood as a space which is largely controlled by the 'contained and carefully managed' agential feminine sexuality of Miss Douce and Miss Kennedy.

Episodes such as this from Joyce's *Ulysses* emphasise the extent to which gender plays a key role in the public rooms of a hotel, with certain rooms designed to attract men, and certain rooms designed to attract women. However, these divisions are often not quite as clear-cut as they may first appear. The Ormond Hotel bar is, for example, certainly a masculine space, geared towards enticing a predominantly male clientele, but as the discussion thus far has revealed, it can also be read as a space of 'carefully managed' feminine sexuality, and one which is therefore largely controlled by the barmaids, Miss Douce and Miss Kennedy (Mullin 2004, p. 487). This tension between a feminine presence in an otherwise masculine space is also evident in Bennett's *The Grand Babylon Hotel*. As discussed in the previous chapter on the lobby, the bureau of the Grand Babylon overlooks both the lobby of the hotel and the smoking room, a space which is marked from the outset as distinctly masculine in its direct comparison to a gentlemen's club: 'The Grand Babylon Hotel was a hotel in whose smoking-room one behaved as though one was at one's club' (Bennett [1902] 2016, p. 43). As Amy Milne-Smith points out, with their origins in 'the political coffeehouses of the seventeenth century', the gentlemen's club reached its 'peak of popularity in the late nineteenth century' (2011, p. 2). The embodiment of a certain kind of middle- to upper-class masculinity, these clubs were highly regarded by some, and provoked anger in other areas of society in the late nineteenth century, with Milne-Smith arguing that they could in one moment be 'praised for their embodiment of quiet, comfortable exclusivity', while in the next, they 'could be critiqued for the exact same traits: cozy community or exclusive clique, architectural masterpiece or ostentatious display, site of male bonding or misogynistic enclave, all that was best or all that was worst of late-Victorian society' (2011, pp. 1–2). Whether the reactions towards them were positive or negative, however, one certainty was that, due to the extent to which they were embedded in 'Victorian popular culture, […] even those who had never seen a gentlemen's club would have had some idea of that they were like' (Milne-Smith 2011, p. 4). As such, Bennett's knowing comparison of the gentlemen's club to the smoking room of the Grand Babylon Hotel instantly encapsulates and conveys to his contemporary readership the precise nature of that space. Just like the gentlemen's club that was, as Milne-Smith maintains, 'at the heart of late-nineteenth and early twentieth-century ideas about gender, domesticity, power, class, and urban space' (2011, p. 2), so too does the smoking room of the Grand Babylon evoke the debates surrounding these ideas.

Yet like the other public rooms of hotels, the smoking room of the Grand Babylon is decidedly not a gentlemen's club, but is instead a mere replica of this space. While it is indeed a space populated solely by men, and undoubtedly predominantly by men of a certain class, it has none of the exclusivity of the gentlemen's club, as guests and members of the public are allowed to come and go more or less as they please. The closest its occupants come to any kind of membership is their financial circumstances, which dictate whether or not they will have the funds to pay for the privilege of pausing in this space, to pay the bill either for their drinks or for their hotel room. Similarly, while the hotel smoking room might at first glance seem to be a solely masculine space, whether this be read as a 'site of male bonding or misogynistic enclave', it is significant that, in Bennett's novel, this space is overseen by Miss Spencer—and later by Nella Racksole—from the hotel bureau. In this way, while the feminine presence is perhaps not as clearly evident or noticeable here as it is in the Ormond Hotel bar, and while it is perhaps not used in the same way to entice and entrance the male occupants, it is no less pervasive, and reveals this seemingly masculine space to be largely controlled by women.

An 'Unbroken Front of Matronhood': Femininity, Community, and Exclusion

Gender is thus a powerful organising tool in the structure of the hotel's public rooms. Adhering to Victorian and Edwardian conventions regarding the division of space within the home, the hotel enacts and reinforces gendered boundaries of morality and propriety, determining appropriate behaviours for both men and women through the allocation of space. While certain spaces within the hotel, such as the lounge and the dining room, are designed to accommodate guests of both sexes, others, such as the smoking room or drawing room, are implicitly gendered masculine or feminine. In this distinction, the hotel thereby creates homosocial spaces of community, in which its guests might feel more comfortable and at ease than they would in the company of members of the opposite sex. A sense of masculine community is, for example, evident in the bar of the Ormond Hotel in Joyce's *Ulysses*, and in the smoking room of Bennett's Grand Babylon Hotel, and in the same way a powerful atmosphere of feminine community is in evidence in the hotel drawing rooms in both Elizabeth Bowen's *The Hotel* (1927), and May Sinclair's *Kitty Tailleur* (1908). However, just as these public rooms work to include and support certain occupants, they also, by that same token, operate to exclude not just those of the opposite sex, but anyone who does not adhere to a precise set of gendered norms according to which these spaces are constructed.

In many of these hotel narratives, it is typically spaces of femininity—specifically, those public rooms more closely aligned with femininity, such as the drawing room—that hold the most significance, and this disparity has much to do with the question of mobility and its specific relation to gender in the late nineteenth and early twentieth centuries. As the figure of the *flâneur* evinces, men were able to move about the urban space freely and in relative safety, while women's navigation of the cityscape (and beyond) tended not only to be bound up with moral codes of respectability and decency, but could also be fraught with danger. The hotel, and more specifically its bedrooms and its public rooms, offers female characters in many of the narratives explored here a vital respite or refuge from the public sphere. Crucially, however, it also enables them to escape the isolation of the domestic sphere.[4]

---

[4] For further discussion of the hotel as an escape from domesticity, see Chaps. 5 and 6.

This sense of isolation and alienation is powerfully conveyed through the conversation of the ladies who inhabit the drawing room in Bowen's *The Hotel*, and through the remarks of one in particular who comments:

As winter comes on with these long evenings one begins to feel hardly human, sitting evening after evening in an empty room [...] it feels so unnatural shutting oneself in with nobody [...] I really begin to feel [...] as if I didn't exist. (Bowen 2003 [1927], p. 61)

The loneliness of the homemaker is depicted here as both devastating and inevitable, and 'shutting oneself in with nobody' seems a foregone conclusion. Indeed, her comment suggests that the detachment felt by a woman within the home is so intense, so severe that it corrodes any sense of identity to the extent that it seems to threaten one's very existence. This sentiment evokes a Hegelian approach to the power and importance of the look of the Other to confirm and support one's existence (Hegel 1977 [1807]). For Hegel, self-consciousness is reached through the Other's recognition of oneself, an affirmative process through which the self is confirmed and the Other negated. As Stephen Houlgate reflects,

I find my identity *recognized* by something other than and independent of me. This moment of recognition is built into the act of independent self-negation performed by the other self-consciousness: for by negating itself the other declares itself to be nothing in and for itself—it 'posits its otherness ... as a nothingness'—and so *makes way for me*. The other thus allows me to relate wholly to *myself* in relating to another, because all I see in the other is his or her recognition of my identity. (2003, p. 15; Hegel 1977 [1807], p. 110)

According to Hegel, the look of the Other is positive and necessary to the solidification of one's own subjectivity. Alone in a house, the homemaker thus finds her very existence threatened, as there is no one else in whose look they might see themselves reflected to find confirmation of their being. Yet any possibility that the presence of a man might counteract or prevent this isolation is sharply dismissed by the acknowledgement of one of the ladies in Bowen's hotel drawing room that 'if one does make a home for anybody one is still very much alone. The best type of man is no companion' (Bowen 2003 [1927], p. 62). Here, the look of the man proves inadequate. He is 'no companion' as, in his look, woman is reflected as a wife and mother, as an object to his subject. Instead, these particular women seek refuge from the loneliness of the home in the community of women they find in the hotel, a community of equals in whose looks their subjectivity is sustained, supported, and, crucially, recognised. In this sense, those more feminine public rooms of the hotel, such as the drawing room, come to function in these narratives as crucial spaces of community, providing a refuge from the home, and a space in which women can come together in a supportive network.

Yet just as those rooms such as the drawing room can afford certain women with a vital space of community, so too can they work to exclude other characters, and particularly women who do not adhere to a particular kind of femininity, one which is bound up with class, age, and social standing. The potentially exclusionary nature of these spaces is explored at length in Bowen's *The Hotel*, in which the first reference to the drawing room, on the opening page of the novel, is not to the interior of the room itself, but instead to its 'veiled glass doors', over which 'not a shadow crossed […] to interrupt ∴he glitter from the sea' (Bowen 2003 [1927], p. 7). Focalised at this moment through Miss Pym, the narrative here depicts the drawing room as a somewhat impenetrable (and undisturbed) space, one that resists the efforts of characters such as Miss Pym to find a space of belonging there, its doors instead, reflecting the 'glitter from the sea', functioning as a barrier, rather than an invitation. This sense of exclusion is furthered in Chap. 7 of the novel, in which no fewer than three characters—Miss Fitzgerald (the close friend, or more likely partner, of the aforementioned Miss Pym), Colonel Duperrier, and Joan Lawrence—are to some extent intimidated by the drawing room and are consequently unwilling to enter. In an episode that begins with an encounter between Miss Fitzgerald and Mrs Hillier regarding the lift of the hotel being out of order, the social divisions between these characters are made increasingly clear through their respective mobility in relation to the drawing room. The chapter opens with the indignation of Mrs Hillier at the lift being broken, as she is depicted, after having pressed all the buttons 'unavailingly', stepping 'out into the lounge so suddenly and so angrily that Miss Fitzgerald, who had been watching sympathetically, was quite frightened' (Bowen 2003 [1927], p. 51). Mrs Hillier is very much a part of what Joan Lawrence later refers to as 'the drawing-room set', and as such, Miss Fitzgerald's sudden fear at her anger can be attributed just as much to Miss Fitzgerald's social position in relation to Mrs Hillier as it can be to a mere nervous temperament (Bowen 2003 [1927], p. 54). This is emphasised primarily through the comparative ease with which they move through the various spaces of the hotel, and particularly their respective ability to occupy spaces like the drawing room.

Within the hotel, Miss Fitzgerald's mobility is limited in a way that Mrs Hillier's is not. Feeling unable to cross the threshold of the drawing room, Miss Fitzgerald instead, 'standing on tiptoe, peeped over the lace blind through the glass of the drawing-room doors, sighed and shook her head. The room presented a too unbroken front of matronhood' (Bowen 2003 [1927], p. 53). As a spinster—and, crucially, as a spinster with a close female companion in Miss Pym, the quarrel between whom at the beginning of the novel is referred to by Rau as 'a sapphic disruption' (2006, p. 225)—Miss Fitzgerald is too much daunted by the 'unbroken front' of upper-middle-class married women, a mode of femininity into which she does not fit, to enter the drawing room, a space which is itself closely aligned and indeed defined here by this notion of 'matronhood'. Further, with a bedroom 'on the highest floor', Miss Fitzgerald's class position is likely lower middle class at best, falling distinctly beneath that of the women in the drawing room.[5] Unlike Miss Fitzgerald, Mrs Hillier—a married 'Anglo-Indian woman', albeit one whose husband is not mentioned once throughout the novel—is accepted without question into the drawing room (Bowen 2003 [1927], p. 51). Her marital and class status—as the likely upper-middle-class wife of a British colonial officer—enables her to return, after the lift incident, into 'a kind of gasp of feminine conversation' and a palpable sense of community (Bowen 2003 [1927], p. 52). Colonel Duperrier's observation of Mrs Hillier's return to the drawing room serves to further foreground that space's simultaneous inclusivity and exclusivity, as he reflects that '[s]he seemed, from the desolation, dusk, and excludedness of the lounge, to return at least to *something*' (Bowen 2003 [1927], p. 52; emphasis in original). While his own wife is very much a part of the community within the drawing room, as a man Colonel Duperrier is decidedly 'shut off' from the 'staccato indignation' following Mrs Hillier's entrance, and her news that the lift was out of order, leaving him in the lounge/lobby which, 'with its grouped furniture was of an isolating vastness' (Bowen 2003 [1927], p. 53). As Colonel Duperrier wanders 'sadly' and aimlessly amongst the chairs, 'long[ing] for

[5] See Chap. 5 of this book for further discussion of the relationship between class and the hotel bedroom.

the disorder of firelight among the orderly shadows', the acknowledgement that '[t]here was one open fireplace in the Hotel and it was in the drawing-room' once more underlines the coldness of the lounge in comparison to the drawing room, and the exclusionary nature of the latter space (Bowen 2003 [1927], pp. 52–3).

Despite his self-acknowledged ostracism from the drawing room, however, Colonel Duperrier does nevertheless enter this space a little later in the chapter, under the exhortation of Joan Lawrence. One of three sisters who attract the attention of several men in the hotel throughout the novel (including Colonel Duperrier), Joan's age is never specified, though her youth is conveyed through the 1920s colloquialisms she uses in the letter Colonel Duperrier spies her writing in the lounge: 'watching her absently he could not help seeing "the very limit", "macaroni" and "torn it"' (Bowen 2003 [1927], p. 53).[6] Following her exclamation that her 'Pen's the limit', Joan decisively rebuffs Colonel Duperrier's suggestion that she should look for another in the drawing room, retorting, 'Thanks very much, but I'm not going into the drawing-room' (Bowen 2003 [1927], p. 53). Then, emboldened by a brief moment of flirtation between them, Colonel Duperrier responds to Joan's challenge to find her a new pen in the drawing room:

> 'Go on, I dare you to!' repeated Joan.
> He stood a moment longer, tugging his short moustache, then braced himself, magnificently squaring his shoulders. 'Oh, very well,' said he. He hesitated in front of the lace-hung doors, whose appearance seemed to appal him.
> 'Funk!' called Joan excitedly, and he pushed the doors open and went in. She heard wave after wave of exclamations arising. (Bowen 2003 [1927], p. 54)

That Colonel Duperrier only finds the courage to enter the drawing room to do the bidding of an attractive young woman is no doubt significant, and his physical preparations before eventually crossing the threshold denote his continued reluctance to enter this space of hallowed femininity. However, importantly, he feels able to enter the space on account of his

---

[6] While Joan Lawrence's age may never be specifically referred to, it might be deduced that she is in her early twenties from Colonel Duperrier's subsequent rumination, as he gazes 'at the back of Joan's neck [...] with uncovetous appreciation', that if his 'wife were to die, he would marry some girl of twenty-three who would be very much in love with him and with whom he would be very happy' (Bowen 2003 [1927], p. 55).

own masculinity, and his increased mobility as an upper-middle-class man in the early twentieth century ought not to be overlooked here. Unlike Miss Fitzgerald who seemingly longs for acceptance within the drawing room—a longing hinted at by her impression of the 'narrow seat' in the hotel lift, on which she sits briefly with Mrs Hillier, as 'the most comfortable, intimate and exclusive corner of the Hotel and [she] dreamily desired it' (Bowen 2003 [1927], p. 51), and Joan Lawrence, who is, despite her bravado, 'a little daunted by the habitués of the drawing-room, who played bridge crushingly well, were impeccably manicured and had a hardish eye that negatived one's importance', Colonel Duperrier is able to cross the threshold of the drawing room with relative ease and confidence, thus providing an insight into the disparity between masculine and feminine mobility within the hotel (Bowen 2003 [1927], p. 54).

As in Joyce's *Ulysses*, the element of the gaze is again of considerable significance here, though in this instance it is the gaze of other women—rather than of men—that threatens to discompose characters like Miss Fitzgerald and Joan Lawrence. Joan's allusion to the collective 'hardish eye' of the drawing-room ladies, an eye which, crucially, 'negatived one's importance', explicitly announces the disturbing and unsettling nature of the gaze in this context. This departs somewhat from Hegel's more positive conception of the look of the Other as a vital means of support for one's sense of self. In a Hegelian reading, Bowen's hotel drawing room, and the feminine gaze that dominates it, would provide the otherwise isolated women who occupy that space with a strength and foundation for the self that can only be found in this kind of community. However, in *Being and Nothingness* (1943), Jean-Paul Sartre questions the validity of Hegel's argument, suggesting instead that he is 'guilty of an epistemological optimism' (2003 [1943], p. 264). For Sartre, the look of the Other is inherently hostile, not least because one's existence might come to depend entirely on that look: '*my* being as the condition of my selfness confronting the Other and of the Other's selfness confronting me' (2003 [1943], p. 309). Rather than functioning as the object that confirms my subjectivity, it is through the look that the Other can instead objectify me. In Bowen's *The Hotel*, the gaze of the drawing-room ladies is arguably closer to this Sartrean conception of the objectifying look of the Other than it is to the more positive Hegelian understanding.

It may well be that, for the women who are unquestioningly accepted into the drawing room—women of a certain age, class, and marital status—the returned gaze of the other women in that space offers what can be a life-sustaining sense of community, and a relief from the isolation of their lives outside this space, whether this be a confinement to the domestic sphere, or conversely a constant state of travel and movement that prevents and precludes meaningful connections with others. Indeed, a number of the women in the drawing room agree that community is one of the principal reasons for coming to a hotel in the first place. When Tessa Bellamy, Sydney's convalescent cousin (who has brought Sydney to the Italian Riviera on the advice of other relatives who considered this trip 'an inspired solution to the Sydney problem' (Bowen 2003 [1927], p. 20), tells the gathering of women in the drawing room that Mrs Kerr, Sydney's close but older friend, 'likes to be a great deal alone', one of the women exclaims: 'Then why should she want to come out to a hotel?' (Bowen 2003 [1927], p. 61). This notion of a hotel as a site of community and connection with others is furthered by a remark made by another of the women: 'It is so broadening to the mind, isn't it? to travel and meet people; we have been so fortunate in the hotels that were recommended to us, and we have been passed on from introduction to introduction so that we have always got to know people at once' (Bowen 2003 [1927], p. 62). This sense of community is, however, only available to those who can afford it, and more specifically, to those who adhere to a very particular kind of femininity.

Characters such as Miss Fitzgerald, Miss Pym, and Joan Lawrence all feel intimidated by the feminine, 'matronly' space of the drawing room to the extent that they feel unable to enter. The community within this space is therefore not only cut off to them, but actively excludes them on account of their age, class, marital status, and, in the case of Misses Fitzgerald and Pym, their sexuality. And yet throughout the novel, Bowen frequently undermines the power of this space. First and foremost, the notion of community portrayed within the drawing room is implicitly unstable, with the unnamed lady's remark about having 'been passed on from introduction to introduction' in hotels hinting at the illusory and transitory nature of the connections that are made. In other instances, characters are depicted as finding the community of the drawing-room repellent. Mrs Kerr rarely enters the drawing room, and her lack of familiarity with the space is indicated in a conversation with her son, Ronald, in which she answers his question of 'What is this room, anyway?' with the rather vague assumption, 'I think quite a number of women sit here' (Bowen 2003 [1927], p. 106). In addition to Mrs Kerr, 'The Honourable Mrs and Miss Pinkerton', hotel guests whose wealth is indicated by the positioning and size of their rooms on the first floor, 'never sat for more than a minute or two in the drawing-room where the other ladies forgathered. They withdrew to their own rooms where they would embroider, eat little pastries and drink coffee' (Bowen 2003 [1927], p. 27). The sisters-in-law are evidently wealthy, and come from a distinctly upper-middle-class background, meaning that they are welcomed by 'the drawing-room set'. However, their preference for privacy over the type of community offered within this space is clearly marked by their refusal to spend any length of time there.

Sydney Warren, the young protagonist of the novel, is also nonplussed by the drawing room. Feeling no qualms about entering this space, she goes in only to look for—and ultimately find—her cousin Tessa. Interrupting the flow of gossip in the drawing room—gossip which has, until her entrance, centred on the unsuitability of her relationship with Mrs Kerr—Sydney opens the door and looks 'in nonchalantly, as though she hardly expected to find whoever she was looking for' (Bowen 2003 [1927], p. 63). Her nonchalant attitude persists, as she is asked by the ladies within the drawing room to 'come right in, if she did not mind, and shut the door after her', a request with which 'she complied absently' (Bowen 2003 [1927], p. 63). Undaunted by the space and the unrelenting gaze of the community found within, she instead 'remained indifferent to their presence and made no effort to speak to them. Once she put her hand out and patted Tessa's hair idly' (Bowen 2003 [1927], p. 63). Sydney's 'nonchalance', 'absent' nature, and 'idle' actions convey a character who is both unimpressed and unintimidated by the 'matronly' feminine community in the drawing room, which other characters have found so threatening. Her unperturbed response to this space might well be attributed in part to her distinctive personality, which Bowen constructs as curiously passive—as Jessica Gildersleeve points out, 'Sydney suffers from an inability to engage in life, a kind of nothingness of the self' (2014, p. 28). Yet Sydney's ambivalence towards the drawing room might more fruitfully be read as a form of queer resistance to the boundaries that exist within the hotel, boundaries that are predicated on gender and class, as well as on age, marital status, and sexuality. Despite being a young woman for whom, as Rau suggests, 'reality is circumscribed by her lesbian desire', Sydney's mobility throughout the space of the hotel is significantly greater, and more unconstrained, than even upper-middle-class male characters such as Colonel Duperrier (2006, p. 225). In this way, Bowen reveals the boundaries of the hotel's public rooms to be inherently unstable and permeable, particularly for those characters who, like Sydney, refuse to recognise the ideologies on which they are built.

Yet more often than not in fiction of the late nineteenth and early twentieth centuries, the scrutiny of the hotel's public rooms is seemingly inescapable, as it proves to be in May Sinclair's 1908 novel, *Kitty Tailleur*, in which 'the intolerable impudence of the public gaze' is consistently foregrounded (1908, p. 8). Set almost entirely in the Cliff Hotel in Southbourne—a modest establishment which promised its guests 'a gay seclusion, a refined publicity', or rather, the perfect blend of privacy and community—the novel's eponymous protagonist is brought into focus through the eyes of Jane and Robert Lucy, siblings who have recently arrived at the hotel (Sinclair 1908, p. 3). The novel opens on the Lucys's entrance into the hotel dining room, a movement which is framed both as an exploratory and anticipatory:

> They came into the hotel dining-room like young persons making their first entry into life. They carried themselves with an air of subdued audacity, of innocent inquiry. When the great doors opened to them they stood still on the threshold, charmed, expectant. There was the magic of quest, of pure, unspoiled adventure in their very efforts to catch the head-waiter's eye. (Sinclair 1908, p. 1)

The excitement engendered by the space of the dining room within both Jane and Robert Lucy is made evident here, 'the great doors' implying a sense of grandeur not necessarily expected from a rather unassuming seaside hotel. For Jane and Robert, it is precisely the exposed and public nature of the dining room that creates and fuels their expectation, their feeling 'of pure, unspoiled adventure' derived from being able to observe freely the actions and behaviours of other guests.

Jane and Robert Lucy are therefore situated very clearly here as observers, as opposed to those who are themselves observed. Or rather, they situate themselves as such—in actual fact, the narration endeavours to undermine their assumed spectatorial role by drawing the reader in through direct address: 'You could never have guessed how old they were. [...] You might have taken them for bride and bridegroom' (Sinclair 1908, pp. 1–2). Effectively transplanting the reader into the hotel dining room, this narratorial technique works to implicate her/him in a voyeuristic position, almost as one of the crowd of hotel guests closely observing the Lucys' entrance into this space. Yet while the Lucys are indeed both the subject and object of the gaze in these opening pages, the principal target of such voyeurism within the hotel's public rooms is Kitty Tailleur herself, who enters the dining room shortly after the Lucys, accompanied by her companion, Miss Keating. The subject of swirling rumours in the hotel regarding her past affairs and sexual promiscuity, Kitty is perhaps best defined, as Suzanne Raitt suggests, as a 'courtesan' rather than as a prostitute, and this is a novel which certainly engages with—and complicates— the Victorian figure of the fallen woman. The observation of Kitty by the other hotel guests has a relentless quality, and, as Raitt notes, she 'is continually stared at as she moves around [the hotel's] reception rooms' (2000, p. 105). In the text's first encounter with Kitty, she enters the dining room 'slowly, with the irresistible motion of creatures that divide and trouble the medium in which they move. The white, painted wainscot behind her showed her small, eager head, its waving rolls and crowing heights of hair, black as her gown' (Sinclair 1908, p. 7). The description of her very movement into the room as 'irresistible' suggests a magnetic quality to Kitty's appearance, which is itself magnified and enhanced by the plain background of the white walls. There is thus a contiguity or indeed synthesis between Kitty, who is, Raitt points out, '[l]ike an article in a department store', and the dining room, a space which is inescapably public and in which the gaze of others works to objectify those who enter (Raitt 2000, p. 105).

This objectification of Kitty proves horrifying to Robert Lucy, who perceives 'the large, white room, half empty at this season' as giving Kitty 'up bodily to [...] the intolerable impudence of the public gaze' (Sinclair 1908, p. 8). Robert regards the exposed space of the dining room as threatening to Kitty, and locates himself in the position of her saviour, directing her to the 'secluded' table beside he and his sister after she looks round the room, 'it seemed to him, for her refuge' (Sinclair 1908, p. 9). Yet while Robert may well consider his actions to be based purely in a chivalric sense of duty to a lady in peril, he is himself implicated to the same degree as the hotel guests whom he perceives to threaten Kitty with their gaze. From the moment of Kitty's entrance into the room, the narrative is focalised through Robert, and the detailed account of her appearance is therefore from his perspective. It is Robert who observes 'her sweet face', and notes that '[i]t was white with the same whiteness as her neck, her shoulders, her arms—a whiteness pure and profound' (Sinclair 1908, pp. 7–8). As Robert's gaze travels over Kitty, the resultant fragmentation of her body parts—face, neck, shoulders, arms—works at once to objectify her, far more so than the room itself does, the plainness of which merely serves to complement her appearance. While Robert is distinctly irritated by the reactions of the other men in the room to Kitty—the young man with the 'furtive, objectionable smile', the 'severe' clergyman, and the 'obsequious waiter'—he is unable to recognise his own role in this process of objectification, and the fact that his own gaze never leaves her (Sinclair 1908, pp. 9–10).

The novel thus begins to reveal itself as one that is concerned, at least on one level, with people's impressions of each other, and specifically with the frequency with which inaccuracies creep into these impressions. Crucially, the public rooms of the hotel play a central role in this process of misperception and misunderstanding. It is in these spaces that characters feel as if they get to know one another, and in the Cliff Hotel—a smaller, cosier, and more modest establishment than 'its superb rival, the Métropole'—a period of bad weather enables what seems to be an increased intimacy between guests, whereby 'persons not otherwise incompatible became acquainted with extraordinary rapidity' (Sinclair 1908, p. 47). Yet this familiarity is ultimately revealed to be illusory, as despite this apparent intimacy, impressions of Kitty Tailleur vary wildly throughout the initial chapters of the novel depending on the character perceiving her. While Robert is drawn towards this woman whom he regards as a 'hurt thing' who has to 'bear' the '[p]ursuit and observation, perpetual, implacable' of other guests within the public rooms, Miss Keating—Kitty's companion—sees Kitty as one who purposefully seeks out the gaze of others, and who in fact finds pleasure in being the object of that gaze (Sinclair 1908, p. 39). Reflecting on her companion, Miss Keating notes that she

> had seen that there was something deliberate and perpetual in Kitty's challenge of the public eye. The public eye, so far from pursuing Kitty, was itself pursued, tracked down and captured. Kitty couldn't let it go. Publicity was what Kitty coveted. (Sinclair 1908, p. 29)

As far as Miss Keating is concerned, Kitty relishes and actively seeks out the attention of others, and the public rooms of the hotel provide her with the ideal backdrop for doing this. Of the dining-room scene in the opening chapter, Miss Keating thinks that

> small as it was, [it] had room for the perfect exhibition of Mrs Tailleur. It gave her wide, polished spaces and clean, brilliant backgrounds, yards of parquetry for the gliding of her feet, and monstrous mirrors for reflecting her face at unexpected angles. (Sinclair 1908, pp. 18–9)

To Miss Keating, Kitty's relationship with the space of the dining room is therefore mutually constitutive. A space engineered towards encouraging observation of its occupants, it here fulfils its function to enhance and attract attention towards Kitty. That Kitty supposedly desires the attention that the dining room engenders is, for Miss Keating, inherently problematic and immoral, and indeed she endeavours to warn Jane Lucy of her past indiscretions before leaving the hotel, and Kitty, in protest at her behaviour. As Raitt notes, for Miss Keating, '[p]art of the problem with Kitty [...] is that she has so internalised her own commodification that she seems deliberately to court the gaze of others' (2000, p. 105). Important, however, is the fact that this perception of Kitty is just that, a perception from Miss Keating's perspective. It is not until Chap. 8 that the narrative is focalised through Kitty herself—up until this point, all impressions of her are filtered through other characters, primarily Robert and Miss Keating, who function, respectively, as self-appointed male guardian or protector, and moral arbiter. But as Kitty herself warns Robert, 'The people [...] who are sure of *me*; who think I'm so easy to know. They don't know me' (Sinclair 1908, p. 56). In their echoing of the social spaces of the home, the public rooms may well bestow on hotel guests the illusion of intimacy and familiarity with one another, but in reality, the novel reveals these spaces to be instrumental in constructing mistaken impressions and misperceptions.

These mistaken impressions are grounded in a moral framework that is effectively reified within the space of the hotel. As in Bowen's eponymous hotel, many of the Cliff Hotel's public rooms are distinctly gendered in nature, again replicating the division of space within the Victorian and Edwardian home. In Sinclair's novel, while the dining room, lounge, and veranda are used by both male and female hotel guests, the drawing room is an almost exclusively feminine space, while the smoking and billiard rooms are more masculine spaces. Yet as Robert observes, correctly, in this instance, '[t]he women had driven [Kitty] from the drawing-room' (Sinclair 1908, p. 39). Throughout the novel, Kitty is decisively excluded from the drawing room, even though she is discussed at length within this space. It is in this room that Miss Keating decides to approach Jane Lucy to reveal the truth about Kitty's past, and thereby warn her off the developing attachment between Jane and Robert Lucy and Kitty. While description of the room itself is sparse, it is nevertheless clearly delineated as a feminine space by its occupants, and by the activities carried out within. Jane, who goes 'into the drawing-room to write letters', finds that '[t]here was nobody there but the old lady who sat in the bay of the window, everlastingly knitting, and Miss Keating isolated on a sofa near the door' (Sinclair 1908, p. 64). A constant presence, the elderly lady, Mrs Jurd, and her traditionally gendered pursuit of knitting, functions here as an unambiguous marker of femininity, and more specifically, of a very particular kind of feminine propriety. As in Bowen's novel, this space is only accessible to a certain type of woman, in this case one who adheres to turn-of-the century moral codes of gender and respectability.

Kitty Tailleur interrogates such notions of gendered propriety, notions which Sinclair consistently explores throughout the novel in spatial terms. For example, when Miss Keating attempts to talk to Colonel Hankin about her plans to leave Kitty and the hotel, and suggests that 'she had been sufficiently compromised already', Colonel Hankin, taken aback by her choice of words, reflects that 'by putting it that way Miss Keating had brought them a little too near what he called the verge, the verge they were all so dextrously avoiding' (Sinclair 1908, p. 89). Here, the limit of respectability and social convention is explicitly spatialised as 'the verge', and Colonel Hankin regards himself as solely responsible for the maintenance of this boundary. Sinclair's use of spatial terms to delineate questions of decency follows the tendency, identified by Suzanne Keen, of Victorian novelists to employ 'a moral vocabulary that expressed possibilities and impossibilities in geographical terms ("latitude"; "over the line")' (1998, p. 2). More specifically, Sinclair's 'verge' functions as one of the 'boundaries, borders, and lines of demarcation', which, Keen maintains, 'evoke not only the long tradition of traversing an ever-altering imaginary terrain, but also the censorious language of the Victorian cultural watchdog' (1998, p. 3). As Miss Keating, however, continues to move 'perilously' towards this verge, this metaphorical movement has a corresponding physical effect on Colonel Hankin: 'when Miss Keating, in her unsteadiness, declared that there must not be a moment's doubt as to her attitude, the Colonel himself was seized with a slight vertigo' (Sinclair 1908, pp. 90–1). In Colonel Hankin's palpable corporeal response to Miss Keating's proximity to early-twentieth-century boundaries of respectability, Sinclair traces a clear phenomenological link between morality, spatiality, and mobility. Miss Keating too has an embodied response to her own traversal of these boundaries as she cries out Kitty's name, shocking those around her:

> She had felt herself abandoned, left there, all alone on the verge, and before
> any of them knew where they were she was over it. Happily she was unaware
> of the violence with which she went. She seemed to herself to move, down-
> ward indeed, but with a sure and slow propulsion. (Sinclair 1908, pp. 91–2)

More than a mere metaphorical movement, Miss Keating's social transgression is accompanied by distinct physical sensations of moving 'down-
ward [...] with a sure and slow propulsion'. Figured in physical, bodily
terms, Miss Keating's infringement on the boundaries of moral decency is
in this way reified.

This spatialisation of social codes and conventions, and their reification
through embodied sensations, further reinforces the morality underpinning the gendered boundaries of the hotel's public rooms. As the threshold of the drawing room cannot be crossed by Kitty due to her past
indiscretions, so too must characters like Miss Keating and Colonel Hankin
take great care not to overstep social boundaries and cross 'the verge'.
This spatialisation of morality is also employed by Wilfrid Marston, Kitty's
former lover, who comes to the Cliff Hotel to reclaim her. Musing on his
relationships with women, and specifically with Kitty, Wilfrid identifies the
realm of social respectability as the 'upper-world', and distinguishes it
from the 'underworld' to which Kitty, as a courtesan, belongs (Sinclair
1908, p. 196). Crucially, however, unlike Kitty, Wilfrid is able to traverse
the boundary between the two, as he reflects that '[i]n the upper-world,
in a set that discussed its women freely, he had never used his knowledge
of a woman to harm her. He had carried this same scruple into that other
world where Kitty lived' (Sinclair 1908, p. 199). Confined to the underworld, Kitty's mobility in terms of these boundaries of respectability is
distinctly limited, just as her mobility in and around the public rooms of
the hotel is restricted. Wilfrid, however, is able to move freely across these
boundaries, to 'carry' his 'scruples into that other world', and his ability to
do so can be attributed not just to the fact that he is a man, but, more
importantly, to the fact that these (often gendered) moral boundaries are
distinctly patriarchal in nature.

Throughout Sinclair's novel, men sit in judgement on female behaviour—
indeed, Colonel Hankin regards his own attitude as one 'of judicial benev-
olence' (Sinclair 1908, p. 90), and holds himself solely responsible for
policing and maintaining 'the verge', reflecting that 'it was his business to
see that [the debate] was confined within the limits of comparative safety.

Goodness knew where they would be landed if the women lost their heads' (Sinclair 1908, p. 89). More often than not, this male judgement takes the form of the male gaze. This gaze is exemplified by the young man who, having picked up Kitty's fur tippet, 'stared into her face, and sleeked his little moustache above a furtive, objectionable smile'; by his companion, who 'fixed on the lady a pair of blood-shot eyes in a brutal, wine-dark face'; and by the clergyman, who 'looked severely at her' (Sinclair 1908, pp. 9–10). In all of these instances, however, Sinclair demonstrates adeptly the way in which society places the onus of the gaze, the responsibility for it, squarely on the shoulders of its female object, rather than on its male point of origin. Kitty is mistrusted by the hotel guests precisely because she is the object of the male gaze, and importantly, the novel charts the way in which men's judgements are frequently adopted and reinforced by women, like Mrs Jurd, who trust that 'they know more than we do' (Sinclair 1908, p. 81). Moral boundaries, like the boundaries of the public spaces within the hotel, may well be policed and controlled by both the male and female guests, but each of these thresholds is founded upon unmistakably patriarchal notions of feminine respectability and behaviour.

In this way, the hotel in Sinclair's novel must ultimately be read as a conspicuously patriarchal space, one in which Kitty's mobility is decisively restricted. As the novel progresses, Kitty feels increasingly unable to occupy the public rooms of the hotel due to the relentless nature of the gaze of other guests, preferring instead to engage a private sitting room in which to conduct her conversations. Even in this private room, however, there is a sense that Kitty is still confined, and indeed, throughout the novel, the only space in which Kitty seems truly free is the small alcove on the cliff's edge, just beyond the bounds of the hotel. Located at the edge of the cliff path, it is in this 'square recess, a small white chamber cut from the chalk and open to the sea and sky', that Kitty conducts her most intimate conversations with Robert, and it is here that he proposes marriage to her (Sinclair 1908, p. 54). It is only here, in this markedly liminal space hovering between land, sea, and sky that Kitty is momentarily liberated from the constraints of the patriarchal structures of morality and propriety, and it is only here that she can finally escape these constraints permanently by leaping to her death from the cliff's edge. Just as Jane Lucy reprimands Wilfrid Marston moments before Kitty's fate is discovered, telling him that 'You are responsible. It is you, and men like you, who have dragged her down' (Sinclair 1908, p. 311), so too does the novel place the blame for

Kitty's tragic demise, as Raitt points out, 'squarely on men's shoulders' (Raitt 2000, p. 107). Unable to extricate herself from those patriarchal discourses that are actualised in the space of the hotel, and which therefore surround and contain her, Kitty is left with no other option than death.

Both Bowen and Sinclair employ the public rooms of the hotel to explore the problematic and restrictive nature of early-twentieth-century ideologies of femininity. The feminine spaces of the hotel such as the drawing room can, as Bowen's novel suggests, function as vital spaces of community and support for those women who find themselves cut off by the isolating routines of housework and homemaking. However, as the 'unbroken front of matronhood' that so intimidates Miss Fitzgerald demonstrates, these spaces only offer such support to those women who adhere to specific codes of femininity, codes which take into account age, class, and marital status, and which combine these factors into a strict moral framework. As such, these feminine spaces work to actively exclude those who do not, or who indeed refuse to, conform to such codes. However, while this exclusion is often enacted and enforced by the female occupants of the drawing room as much as it is by the space itself, as Sinclair's novel reveals, the ideologies upon which these boundaries are built are decidedly patriarchal. In this way, both Sinclair and Bowen interrogate the insidious and pervasive nature of patriarchal restrictions upon all aspects of female existence—upon women's behaviour, upon the spaces they occupy, and above all, upon their relationships with other women— and both authors reify these restrictions through the walls of the public rooms in their respective fictional hotels.

'[W]HAT MUST THEY DO BUT GLANCE AND SNEER AND NUDGE ONE ANOTHER': SCRUTINY AND CLASS HIERARCHY

As demonstrated by the inability of Bowen's Miss Fitzgerald to enter the space of the drawing room in her eponymous hotel, class, as well as gender, can play a central role in the exclusionary nature of the hotel and its public rooms, and this is clearly demonstrated in H.G. Wells's 1905 novel, *Kipps*. While the fate of the eponymous protagonist of the novel is somewhat less dramatic than that of Sinclair's Kitty Tailleur, his experiences in the public rooms of the Royal Grand Hotel are no less painful to witness. Early on in the narrative, Arthur Kipps, a lower-middle-class draper's apprentice, unexpectedly inherits property and a large sum of money from his estranged paternal grandfather. As David Lodge notes, '[t]he unexpected legacy was a plot device often used by Victorian novelists to bring a story to a happy conclusion. In *Kipps*, however, it triggers the main action, giving the hero a chance to achieve happiness and fulfilment which he fails disastrously to seize' (Lodge 2005 [1905], p. xxi). Indeed, it is this sizeable inheritance that creates and sustains the central tension of the novel, that of a lower-middle-class man desperately trying, but failing, to behave like, and fit in with, those of a more elevated social class. Admiring the novel's comedy and its perceptive characterisation of Kipps, Henry James was moved to congratulate Wells on his depiction of the lower middle classes, writing to him following the novel's publication in 1905 that

> You have for the very 1st time treated the English 'lower middle' class, &c, without the picturesque, the grotesque, the fantastic & romantic interference, of which Dickens, e.g., is so misleadingly, of which even George Eliot is so deviatingly full. You have handled its vulgarity in so scientific & historic a spirit, & seen the whole thing all in its *own* strong light. (James 1999 [1905], p. 424; emphasis in original)

Through its focus on the trials and tribulations of its protagonist, the novel is concerned primarily with flaws and injustices of the English class system, and particularly with what Richard Higgins refers to as 'the persistence of class' (2008, p. 460). And nowhere in the novel is this persistence more starkly illustrated than in Kipps's brief sojourn in an upmarket London hotel.

The Royal Grand Hotel, next to Charing Cross Station, is the hotel in which Kipps 'endured splendour for three nights and three days', before 'retreat[ing] in disorder' (Wells 2005 [1905], p. 239). London itself is bewildering enough for Kipps, to whom the capital 'presented itself as a place of great, grey spaces and incredible multitudes of people, centring about Charing Cross station and the Royal Grand Hotel' (Wells 2005 [1905], p. 219). As the station into which Kipps's train arrives from New Romney in Kent, Charing Cross, and the Royal Grand, are for Kipps the very heart of London, corresponding with the nineteenth-century approximation of Charing Cross as the centre of the capital. While the Royal Grand is a fictional hotel, its counterpart in reality is likely the now-demolished Hotel Cecil.[7] Opened in 1896, the hotel was located on the Strand, roughly

---

[7] The Hotel Cecil was demolished, save for some of its façade, in 1930. The Shell Mex Building now stands in its place on the Strand.

a four-minute walk away from Charing Cross Station, a distance perhaps just far enough to justify the cab that Kipps takes from the station to the hotel, a cab he takes in an imitation of the manner of his middle-class friend, Walshingham.[8] The prestige of the Royal Grand, and the importance to Kipps of this prestige being recognised by others, is immediately made clear, as 'he was pleased to note the enhanced respect of the cabman when he mentioned the Royal Grand. He followed Walshingham's routine on their previous visit with perfect success' (Wells 2005 [1905], p. 220). Yet, as a lower-middle-class man, Kipps is only able to mimic the behaviour of the upper-middle-class Walshingham—he can 'follow his routine' to the letter, choosing the same hotel, and taking a cab 'in an entirely Walshingham manner', but he is unable to act on his own impetus. In addition to this, the significance that Kipps invests in the Royal Grand's renown as an expensive and high-class hotel serves to further indicate his own insecurity and desperation for others to recognise him as a wealthy member of the middle classes.

Almost immediately, however, the hotel itself threatens to undermine him. On his arrival at the Royal Grand, Kipps engages a room for 'fourteen shillings a night', reflecting that they had been 'very nice in the office', and that his room 'was a vast and splendid apartment, and cheap at fourteen shillings' (Wells 2005 [1905], p. 220). Kipps considers himself to have secured a bargain, but bedrooms at the Hotel Cecil would in fact have cost, according to the July 1900 edition of *The Official Hotel Directory*, anything from around five to eight shillings.[9] The engagement of an additional sitting room would have cost an extra ten shillings to one pound, but no mention is made of such a space in the brief description of Kipps's room, as he 'went up and spent a considerable time in examining the furniture of his room, scrutinising himself in its various mirrors and sitting on the edge of the bed whistling' (Wells 2005 [1905], p. 220). While the reference to the room's 'furniture' and 'various mirrors' might

---

[8] Further evidence to support the claim that the Royal Grand is based on the Hotel Cecil comes in the form of the gateway of the hotel, in which Kipps experiences 'a moment of elation [...]. He felt all the Strand must notice him as he emerged through the great gate of the Hotel' (Wells 2005 [1905], p. 221). Unlike the Savoy, whose entrance is set back from the Strand down a passageway, the Hotel Cecil did indeed have a grand gate opening out directly onto the Strand.

[9] The Hotel Cecil falls under tariff A (the most expensive tariff) of *The Official Hotel Directory* price guide (1898) and is defined as a family hotel. See Chap. 5 for further details of this tariff.

well suggest an additional private sitting room, the room itself is decisively referred to in the singular, hinting at the possibility that Kipps's evident naivety may well have been taken advantage of by unscrupulous hotel staff at reception.

That Kipps is under the illusion that he has secured a 'cheap' room betrays his credulity, yet this is somewhat countered elsewhere in his navigation of the hotel by his high levels of paranoia regarding the staff and other guests. Having left his room to explore the hotel, Kipps is immediately unsure of himself, 'descend[ing] by the staircase after a momentary hesitation before the lift' (Wells 2005 [1905], p. 221). Still, in the early twentieth century, a relatively new addition to hotels, the prospect of the lift here unsettles Kipps, who opts instead for the less technologically challenging staircase.[10] Reaching the ground floor of the hotel, Kipps 'drift[s] into the great drawing-room', the first of the public rooms that he has entered, and pauses here to read 'a guide to the Hotels of Europe for a space, until a doubt whether he was entitled to use this palatial apartment without extra charge arose in his mind' (Wells 2005 [1905], p. 221). Kipps's lack of experience in hotels is clearly marked by his anxious misunderstanding of the purpose of the public rooms of the hotel. His uncertainty regarding the freedom with which guests and members of the public can use the room stems directly from the grandeur of the space, which again intimidates and unnerves him to the extent that he quickly leaves the drawing room. The description of the space as 'palatial' conveys a sense not only of its size but of its opulent décor and furnishings, and photographs and descriptions of the drawing room of the Hotel Cecil certainly emphasise this luxury. An article in the Pall Mall Gazette from April 1896, previewing the opening of the Hotel Cecil in May of that year, highlights its 'magnificent suite of public rooms', and gives a detailed description of the décor of the drawing room in particular:

> Pale blue and gold are two of the leading colours in the decoration of the drawing-room, and much minute work has been lavished upon ceiling, cornice, frieze, and walls alike. Fluted pilasters adorn the sides of the room, and a conspicuous part of the fireplace decoration consists of a group of figures carved in marble representing the seasons from springtime to winter. (Anon 1896, p. 8)

---

[10] See Chap. 5 of this book for a more sustained discussion of the history and significance of lifts in hotels.

While the public rooms of the Hotel Cecil—and those of its fictional counterpart the Royal Grand Hotel—may well still be structured, like any other hotel, to follow the architectural layout of the home, the ostentatious splendour of their design and décor mean that they are anything but homely to many of the guests who pass through the hotel, and particularly to lower-middle-class guests such as Kipps. Distinctly unfamiliar in its grandeur, Kipps is unable to feel at ease in the hotel drawing room, and this unease stems from a quite literal sense of the Freudian *unheimlich* arising from the alien nature of the space.

Yet while the drawing room may inspire feelings of discomfort in Kipps, the dining room engenders absolute horror to the extent that, despite his hunger, he is unable to countenance eating in this space upon his arrival at the hotel. His initial attempts to enter the dining room fail 'at the sight of a number of waiters and tables, with remarkable complications of knives and glasses', at which point 'terror seized him, and he backed out again, with a mumbled remark to the waiter in the doorway about this not being the way' (Wells 2005 [1905], p. 221). In this instance, it is not so much the size of the room that intimidates Kipps, but the sheer number of tables— the *Pall Mall Gazette* noted that the dining room of the Hotel Cecil would 'accommodate some seventy tables' (Anon 1896, p. 8)—and, specifically, the 'complications of knives and glasses' on those tables, which fuel his 'inbred terror of the table' (Wells 2005 [1905], p. 221). As Kipps is all too aware, these intricate arrangements of cutlery and glassware require a firm and confident understanding of bourgeois dining etiquette, a knowledge that was typically gathered through sustained experience of middle to upper-class dining, experience in which the lower-middle-class Kipps is sorely lacking.[11] Kipps retreats from the dining room in this instance, intending to go to a restaurant instead for lunch, though after being similarly intimidated by the windows of various restaurants that 'demoralise' him, he eventually encounters his friend Sid on the street, and ends up dining at his home. It is here that Kipps meets the imposing character of Masterman, Sid's lodger, who attempts to convince Kipps of the merits of socialism. It is this encounter, and the burgeoning socialist ideas that it imbues within Kipps, that leads to the excruciating comedy of Kipps's experience in the dining room of the Royal Grand Hotel that evening.

---

[11] For further discussion of middle-class dining etiquette of the late nineteenth and early twentieth centuries, see: Rachel Rich, *Bourgeois Consumption: Food, Space, and Identity in London and Paris, 1850–1914* (Manchester: Manchester University Press, 2011).

The scene which takes place in the dining room of the Royal Grand Hotel is, perhaps, one of the most painfully humorous episodes in early-twentieth-century literature—humorous in its immaculately designed slapstick nature, and painful in what it reveals about the inescapability and cruelty of the English class system at the turn of the century. As Lodge points out, this scene

> constitute[s] the comic high-point of the novel. His prolonged and unsuccessful struggle to master the protocol of the luxury hotel where he is staying […] reinforces the moral of the story: that class and culture are stronger social forces than mere wealth. (Lodge 2005 [1905], pp. xxi–xxii)

In this episode, Kipps's failure to 'master the protocol' of the Royal Grand begins before he even reaches the intimidating space of the dining room when, in his bedroom, he makes a decision to wear purple slippers emblazoned with golden marigolds to dinner instead of boots. He immediately regrets this choice when he enters the dining room, whereupon 'he saw the porters and waiters and the other guests catch a sight of the slippers, [and] was sorry he had not chosen the boots. However, to make up for any want of style at that end, he had his crush hat under his arm' (Wells 2005 [1905], p. 239). The crush hat, or collapsible top hat, is another slight sartorial misstep on Kipps's part, as while this was a key part of evening dress for men, to wear a hat to dinner flouted the rules of Victorian dining etiquette. That Kipps keeps his hat under his arm denotes his faint awareness of this rule, but his loss at what to do with his hat once he has sat down, and his subsequent decision, 'after a moment of thought to rise slightly and sit on it', is yet another indication of his uncertainty in the face of middle- and upper-class table manners, which is only exacerbated by the grand space of the hotel dining room (Wells 2005 [1905], p. 240).

While the dining room itself, that 'vast and splendidly decorated place', is undoubtedly intimidating to Kipps, it is the public nature of this room, and specifically the gaze of the hotel staff and other diners, that steadily and decisively destabilises his ability to function here, and which destroys any shred of self-confidence he may have had (Wells 2005 [1905], p. 239).[12] As Rachel Rich observes, restaurants and hotel dining rooms in

---

[12] The aforementioned article in the *Pall Mall Gazette* features the following detailed description of the lavish décor in the Hotel Cecil dining room: 'The room measures about sixty feet by eighty, and will accommodate some seventy tables. The floor is of oak parquetry; a dozen highly decorated columns support the old-gold ceiling, and the fittings are of walnut.

the late nineteenth and early twentieth centuries were essentially spaces of performance, and partaking in a meal in these spaces 'afforded an opportunity to display cultural capital' (2011, p. 236). Apparently relentless, the gaze of other diners and staff unsettles Kipps, fuelling his paranoia regarding his right to occupy this space, and exacerbating his deep-seated awareness of his own lack of cultural capital. Alongside this paranoia, however, is Kipps's indignant and somewhat overblown sense of his own importance, which intensifies both the comedy and the discomfort of this scene, and makes it all the more painfully realistic. As Higgins argues, through characters like Kipps, Wells

> expresses the muted outbursts of anger, the veiled feelings of frustration and shame, as well as the small rebellions, the occasional bravado, and the flights of fantastic ambition and self-aggrandizing narcissism that he sees as characterizing the emotional lives of lower-middle-class men. (2008, p. 459)

In this dining-room scene, all of these emotions—anger, frustration, shame, bravado, ambition, and narcissism—are felt by Kipps, often simultaneously, as he struggles to blend in to the bourgeois society of the hotel dining room.

As he enters and crosses the dining room, Kipps feels himself watched by all, beginning with the 'band in the decorated recess', who 'looked collectively at the purple slippers, and so lost any chance they may have had of a collection, so far as Kipps was concerned' (Wells 2005 [1905], p. 240). Having sat down at a table, Kipps 'blushed deeply' upon finding a waiter 'regarding him' as Kipps was looking with interest at the bare-shouldered ladies in the dining room (Wells 2005 [1905], p. 241). Kipps's blush, this overtly physical reaction to the gaze of the other, reveals the distinction between the lived or subjective body, and corporeal body, or the body as object. As Thomas Fuchs observes, 'the corporeal body appears whenever a reaction or resistance arises to the primary performance of the lived-body', and in this case, the gaze of the waiter, perceived by Kipps, triggers at the moment of perception a separation between lived and corporeal body, which manifests in his blush of shame (Fuchs 2003, p. 225). Yet this shame, and the corporealised body in which it results, can in turn work to

Two fireplaces, set in white Sicilian marble, with red supporting columns, give the room an air of cosiness, in spite of its grandeur, and this effect is accentuated by the circumstances that these fireplaces are of the old English sort' (Anon 1896, p. 8).

cause further shame and embarrassment, with Fuchs pointing out that, in such instances, a 'vicious circle [can] arise' whereby shame can 'undermine spontaneous bodiliness so as to make one even more clumsy' (2003, p. 225). In this way, Kipps's feelings of embarrassment and shame lead him from one catastrophe to the next, each increasingly painful in their humiliation (or at least, in what Kipps perceives as their humiliation). The gaze of the waiter thus contributes substantially to Kipps's subsequent confusion over cutlery, and his resulting anger at 'the lady in pink' who 'glanc[ed] at him and then smil[ed] as she spoke to the man beside her' (Wells 2005 [1905], p. 241). The final straw comes when, having dropped most of a *vol-au-vent* down his shirt, Kipps, in his embarrassment, suddenly feels that

> everyone was watching him and making fun of him, and the injustice of this angered him. After all, they had every advantage he hadn't. And then, when they got him there doing his best, what must they do but glance and sneer and nudge one another. He tried to catch them at it, and then took refuge in a second glass of wine. (Wells 2005 [1905], p. 241)

The gaze of the other diners and hotel staff certainly discomposes Kipps, yet he nevertheless attempts to stand firm in the face of this gaze. Rather than retreating in shame at this point, he instead recognises the injustice inherent in the situation, in the fact that, by being born into a higher class than he, the other diners have been gifted an unearned privilege and experience that he cannot hope to emulate. It is at this point that the socialist ideas previously imparted to him by Masterman begin to take effect in Kipps, and intensify his resistance to the gaze and judgement of others. As '[e]choes of Masterman's burning rhetoric began to reverberate in his mind', Kipps 'discovered the eye of a diner fixed curiously upon his flushed face. He responded with a glare' (Wells 2005 [1905], p. 242). Here, the look of the other is perceived by Kipps to be inherently hostile, and thus, as in Bowen, follows a Sartrean rather that Heideggerian reading of the gaze. However, while the look of the other diner both alienates and disturbs Kipps, his countering of this look suggests an active and determined resistance to the threat that it poses to his sense of self.

Kipps's resistance to this threat is, however, only momentary, and is rendered somewhat futile by the ensuing events. Having refused a series of at least three dishes offered to him by the waiter, all of which he decides are 'fussed up food! Probably cooked by some foreigner', Kipps finally shows an interest in a green ice cream bombe. However, his attempts to eat the bombe prove disastrous:

> He seized a fork and spoon and assailed the bombe. It cut rather stiffly. 'Come up!' said Kipps, with concentrated bitterness, and the truncated summit of the bombe flew off suddenly, travelling eastward with remarkable velocity. Flop, it went upon the floor a yard away, and for a while time seemed empty. (Wells 2005 [1905], p. 242)

The intensity of Kipps's embarrassment is conveyed by the way in which, immediately following the incident, 'time seemed empty'. In this break in Kipps's perception of time, Wells draws, seemingly directly, on William James's concept of empty time, put forward in his 1890 work, *The Principles of Psychology*.[13] James argues that our perception of time is based upon an awareness of change, and that empty time is therefore almost impossible for us to perceive, as 'there exists no reason to suppose that empty time's own changes are sufficient for the awareness of change to be aroused. The change must be of some concrete sort' (1890, p. 620). On this understanding, we are unable to appreciate the passing of time which is truly empty as there are no changes—be they audible, visual, or tactile— for us to perceive, changes which typically mark for us the passage of time. These moments of empty time, then, are moments when time effectively stands still. Further, the way in which this experience is bound up with sensory and bodily perception means that these instances of empty time are most likely to arise when the distinction between the lived and corporeal body is most apparent. As Fuchs points out,

> lived bodiliness is a constant outward movement, directed to the environment from a hidden centre, and participating in the world. Corporeality appears whenever this movement is paralysed or stopped, when the lived body is thrown back on itself, reified or 'corporealized.' This is accompanied

[13] Sylvia Hardy has established the extent of William James's influence on Wells's writing, noting that Wells was not just familiar with James's arguments, but that he had read and was inspired by James's *Principles of Psychology*. See: Sylvia Hardy, "A Story of the Days to Come: H.G. Wells and the Language of Science Fiction", *Language & Literature* 12 (3) (2003): 199–212; and Hardy, "H.G. Wells and William James: A Pragmatic Approach", in *H.G. Wells: Interdisciplinary Essays*, ed. Steven McLean, 130–146 (Newcastle: Cambridge Scholars Publishing, 2008).

by an alteration in temporality: spontaneous life, always reaching out for the future, is interrupted, and the subject is suddenly fixed on the present moment or on a lost past. (2003, p. 225)

Kipps's clumsiness with the ice cream bombe, and his consequent embarrassment and shame under the gaze of the other diners in the hotel dining room, corporealises his body, halting the movement of the lived body towards the future, and fixing Kipps in the present in a moment of empty time. The impact of this incident is such that Kipps chooses to make 'a dignified withdrawal' from the dining room, leaving 'behind him a melting fragment of ice upon the floor, his gibus hat, warm and compressed in his chair, and in addition every social ambition he had ever entertained in the world' (Wells 2005 [1905], p. 243). In the grandeur of this hotel dining room, the pervasive and undeniable class hierarchy is brought to the fore and enacted to brutally undermine and exclude the lower-middle-class Kipps.

The public rooms of the Royal Grand Hotel are thus, for Kipps, spaces that exacerbate and intensify his latent but powerful anxieties regarding his own class identity. In their grandeur and opulence, these spaces are distinctly unfamiliar and unhomely to the lower-middle-class Kipps, and rather than setting him at ease, they instead work to intimidate and unsettle him. Without the experience of such places that has been unquestioningly granted to the other middle- and upper-class guests of the hotel, and the patterns of habit that this experience creates, at no point is Kipps able to feel comfortable in these public rooms. As Higgins emphasises, while Kipps may now be wealthy, it is the 'deeply ingrained habits of class [that] prevent him from becoming what his fortune ordinarily implies' (2008, pp. 460–1). Nowhere are these habits made more painfully apparent than in those spaces which actively preclude them, such as the public rooms of the Royal Grand Hotel, and it is in this way that Wells so skilfully employs the hotel to illustrate what Higgins refers to as 'the profound impact of social hierarchies on individual lives' (2008, p. 459). Already unsettled and overwhelmed by the lavish nature of the hotel, Kipps is increasingly susceptible to the scrutiny of others in the dining room, and it is here, under their gaze, that he experiences repeated instances of shame and embarrassment, until these feelings overpower him and he is effectively forcibly excluded from this space. While Kipps's sojourn in the Royal Grand Hotel is relatively brief within the context of the novel, lasting only one chapter, it is nevertheless one of the most

excruciating, and his humiliation in the public rooms of the hotel represents a crisis point in terms of his attempts, and failures, to emulate the
social codes and conventions of the middle classes.

*   *   *

In their design and architectural layout, the organisation of the public
rooms of the hotel follows the archetypal blueprint for the communal
spaces of the nineteenth-century home, and it is in this way that the hotel
perhaps most directly betrays its intention to echo the domestic sphere,
and to provide a 'home away from home'. And yet the hotel can only ever
offer a replica of the domestic, a faded copy that can never truly match the
authenticity of the home, if, indeed, there is such a thing. In their politics
of community and ostracism, what the public rooms perhaps in fact reveal
is the very way in which the home is itself based upon this same politics, a
'basic organizing principle' which is, as Rosemary Marangoly George
asserts, 'a pattern of select inclusions and exclusions' (1996, p. 2).
Certainly, the gendered boundaries of spaces such as the hotel drawing
room and smoking room function, in the same way as they do within the
home, to keep enforce gendered divides. And yet, due to the decidedly
more public nature of the hotel's communal rooms, these boundaries
function in the hotel in more varied and nuanced ways, working to exclude
not just those of the opposite sex, but also those who fail to conform to a
certain type of femininity or masculinity. As authors such as Bowen and
Sinclair demonstrate, class, age, sexuality, and marital status all feed into
the strict ideologies of femininity and masculinity that govern the public
rooms of the hotel, with those who fall short consequently finding themselves ostracised.

The process of exclusion is, however, often insidious and self-imposed.
Characters such as Miss Fitzgerald and Kitty Tailleur are not physically
barred from entering the drawing room of their respective hotels, that
space of feminine propriety and respectability, but an awareness of their
own shortcomings in relation to this ideology, combined with the penetrat-
ing and panoptic gaze of others in the public rooms of the hotel, works to
effectively preclude their movement into this space. The relentless quality
of the gaze of other hotel guests and staff is exemplified in Wells's *Kipps*, in
which this gaze coalesces with the lavish and opulent décor of the dining
room in the Royal Grand Hotel to unsettle, discompose, and ultimately
expel Kipps from the space. In these novels, the inherent and ingrained

insecurity of characters regarding their own identities—and, specifically, the extent to which these identities conform to late-nineteenth- and early-twentieth-century expectations of class, gender, and sexual propriety—makes them increasingly exposed to the exclusionary nature of the hotel's public rooms. The novels considered in this chapter explore and interrogate the way in which characters' subjectivities, already vulnerable, are further undermined and destabilised by the public rooms of the hotel, and the gaze of the Other contained within them. In this way, and through the hotel, these authors each offer an understanding of the significance of space and its impact on the modern subject that anticipates and prefigures later phenomenological understandings of this relationship.

References

Ahmed, Sara. 2006. *Queer Phenomenology: Orientations, Objects, Others.* Durham: Duke University Press.

Anon. 1882. Woods' Hotel, London. *Hotel World,* 1:24, 3, June 14.

———. 1896. The New Hotel Cecil: An Attempt to Attract Smart London. *Pall Mall Gazette,* 8, April 21.

Boer, Mary Cathcart. 1972. *The British Hotel Through the Ages.* London: Lutterworth Press.

Bowen, Elizabeth. 2003 [1927]. *The Hotel.* London: Vintage.

Ford, Ford Madox. 2002 [1915]. *The Good Soldier.* London: Penguin.

Fuchs, Thomas. 2003. The Phenomenology of Shame, Guilt and the Body in Body Dysmorphic Disorder and Depression. *Journal of Phenomenological Psychology* 33 (2): 223–243.

George, Rosemary Marangoly. 1996. *The Politics of Home: Postcolonial Relocations and Twentieth-Century Fiction.* Cambridge: Cambridge University Press.

Gildersleeve, Jessica. 2014. *Elizabeth Bowen and the Writing of Trauma: The Ethics of Survival.* Amsterdam: Rodopi.

Hegel, G.W.F. 1977 [1807]. *Phenomenology of Spirit.* Translated by A.V. Miller. Oxford: Oxford University Press.

Higgins, Richard. 2008. Feeling Like a Clerk in H.G. Wells. *Victorian Studies* 50 (3): 457–475.

Houlgate, Stephen. 2003. G. W. F. Hegel: The Phenomenology of Spirit. In *The Blackwell Guide to Continental Philosophy,* ed. Robert C. Solomon and David Sherman, 8–29. Oxford: Blackwell.

James, William. 1890. *The Principles of Psychology.* New York: Henry Holt & Co.

James, Henry. 1999 [1905]. Letter to H.G. Wells, 19 November 1905. In *Henry James: A Life in Letters,* ed. Philip Horne, 422–425. London: Allen Lane.

———. 2008 [1903]. *The Ambassadors.* Oxford: Oxford University Press.

Joyce, James. 2008 [1922]. *Ulysses*. Edited by Jeri Johnson. Oxford: Oxford University Press.

Keen, Suzanne. 1998. *Victorian Renovations of the Novel: Narrative Annexes and the Boundaries of Representation*. Cambridge: Cambridge University Press.

Lodge, David. 2005 [1905]. Introduction to H.G. Wells. In *Kipps*, ed. Simon J. James, xiii–xxxiii. London: Penguin.

Milne-Smith, Amy. 2011. *London Clubland: A Cultural History of Gender and Class in Late Victorian Britain*. New York: Palgrave.

Moore, Robbie. 2012. Henry James, Hotels, and the Invention of Disposable Space. *Modernist Cultures* 7 (2): 254–278.

Mullin, Katherine. 2004. 'The Essence of Vulgarity': The Barmaid Controversy in the 'Sirens' Episode of James Joyce's *Ulysses*. *Textual Practice* 18 (4): 475–495.

Muthesius, Stefan. 1982. *The English Terraced House*. New Haven, CT: Yale University Press.

Raitt, Suzanne. 2000. *May Sinclair: A Modern Victorian*. Oxford: Oxford University Press.

Rau, Petra. 2006. Telling It Straight: The Rhetorics of Conversion in Elizabeth Bowen's *The Hotel* and Freud's *Psychogenesis*. In *Sapphic Modernities: Sexuality, Women and National Culture*, ed. Laura Doan and Jane Garrity, 217–231. Basingstoke: Palgrave.

Rich, Rachel. 2011. *Bourgeois Consumption: Food, Space and Identity in London and Paris, 1850–1914*. Manchester: Manchester University Press.

Rosner, Victoria. 2005. *Modernism and the Architecture of Private Life*. New York: Columbia University Press.

Sandoval-Strausz, A.K. 2007. *Hotel: An American History*. New Haven: Yale University Press.

Sartre, Jean-Paul. 2003 [1943]. *Being and Nothingness: An Essay on Phenomenological Ontology*. Translated by Hazel E. Barnes. London: Routledge.

Sinclair, May. 1908. *Kitty Tailleur*. London: Archibald Constable & Co.

von Spreckelsen, Marieke. 1997. Halls and Vestibules. In *Encyclopedia of Interior Design*, ed. Joanna Banham, vol. 1–2, 541–544. London: Routledge.

Wells, H.G. 2005 [1905]. *Kipps*. Edited by Simon J. James. London: Penguin.

Wilson, Elizabeth. 1992. *The Sphinx in the City: Urban Life, the Control of Disorder, and Women*. Berkeley: University of California Press.

Woolf, Virginia. 2009 [1915]. *The Voyage Out*. Oxford: Oxford University Press.

CHAPTER 5

Space, Movement, and Inhabitation: Transgression in the Hotel Bedroom

.

Nowhere is a phenomenological approach to the hotel in literature more fruitful than in a consideration of the hotel bedroom. It is in the bedroom that the process of inhabiting space is at its most evident and most pronounced. It is both the anonymity of the hotel bedroom and its transitory, impermanent nature—the way in which we move *through* this space—that enable us to experience this process of inhabiting more directly and more acutely than anywhere else. As D.J. Van Lennep observes, this process of inhabiting is markedly different in a hotel bedroom than it is in a bedroom in one's own home: 'Nowhere can I experience the process of inhabiting as well as precisely in the hotel room because I am here in the midst of wall paper and furniture I did not choose myself, things which in no way are an expression of my personal preference or choice' (1987 [1969], p. 213). Exploring the hotel bedroom in the writing of Elizabeth Bowen, H.G. Wells, Jean Rhys, and Dorothy Richardson, this chapter explores the ambiguities and tensions inherent within this complexly signified space. Figured variously and often frustratingly simultaneously in the literature of this period as a space of respite, refuge, coercion, and threat, the hotel bedroom of modernity is a complex and multifarious space for those characters who inhabit it.

Precisely what this process of inhabiting involves, and how we come to inhabit space, is a more complex question. According to Maurice Merleau-Ponty, as an embodied subject, 'I am not in space and time, nor do I conceive

© The Author(s) 2019
E. Short, *Mobility and the Hotel in Modern Literature*,
Studies in Mobilities, Literature, and Culture,
https://doi.org/10.1007/978-3-030-22129-4_5

space and time; I belong to them, my body combines with them and includes them' (2002 [1945], p. 162). As embodied subjects we are not inert objects contained in space and time, nor are we able to remove ourselves from space and time to conceive of them objectively from a distance. Instead, we are always already part of space and time, necessarily bound up with them. In terms of how the body comes to inhabit space, action and movement are central to this process. Merleau-Ponty argues that 'it is clearly in action that the spatiality of our body is brought into being [...]. By considering the body in movement', he suggests, 'we can see better how it inhabits space' (2002 [1945], p. 117). It is in our very movement through space, then, that we come to inhabit that space, meaning that our actions within a particular space are a key part of the process of inhabiting it. This process of inhabiting is necessarily bound up in the mutually affective nature of the relationship between the body and space. Sara Ahmed argues, however, that the body is not an object in space, and space must therefore not be seen as a mere 'container for the body'. Rather, we must understand that 'bodies are submerged, such that they become the space they inhabit; in taking up space, bodies move through space and are affected by the "where" of that movement'. Through this movement, she maintains, 'the surface of spaces as well as bodies takes shape' (2006, p. 53). It is through our actions in and movements through spaces that we come to inhabit them, and that we come to be shaped and affected by those spaces. At the same time, however, our actions which make up this process of inhabiting shape those very spaces through which we move.

There are, however, factors that can work to constrain the actions and movements possible in any one space. Henri Lefebvre suggests that space itself decides what actions can and cannot take place within it, arguing that '[a]ctivity in space is restricted by that space' (1991, p. 143). One way in which to understand precisely how actions and movements are dictated by a particular space is in terms of Merleau-Ponty's theory of 'cultural environments', in which he posits that 'I experience a certain cultural environment along with behaviour corresponding to it' (2002 [1945], p. 406). For Merleau-Ponty, the 'cultural world' consists of human-made spaces and objects, examples of which he lists as 'roads, plantations, villages, streets, churches, implements, a bell, a spoon, a pipe' (2002 [1945], p. 405). Each of these, he argues, 'spreads around it an atmosphere of humanity, which may be determinate in a low degree in the case of a few footprints in the sand, or on the other hand highly determinate, if I go into every room from top to bottom of a house recently evacuated' (2002 [1945], p. 405). The concentration of this atmosphere of humanity is thus dependent on time and also on habit. Footsteps in the sand are transient, both in the amount of time it takes to create them, and in the amount of time they remain before they are eroded. A recently evacuated house that has been suddenly and abruptly left will retain all the markers of lived experience, of the movements, actions, habits, and routines that constituted the inhabitation of that space, all of which will have been ingrained and reinforced over a lengthy period of time.

The hotel bedroom exists somewhere between footprints in the sand and the recently evacuated house. Like a room in the house, there has been time and intention involved in its creation—décor has been decided upon, and furniture has been chosen and arranged in the space in a particular way. And all of these choices have been made in accordance with a wider idea and understanding of the hotel bedroom, and what this space is to be used for. As such, not only is the 'atmosphere of humanity' present in the knowledge that other guests have used the room beforehand—as van Lennep notes, on arrival in a hotel room we are aware that 'only a few hours before *my* room was someone else's room', and that this someone 'slept in this bed, washed himself [sic] in this sink, used this glass' (1987 [1969], p. 212)—but it is embedded in the space by the cultural significance of the hotel room. At the same time, however, like the footsteps in the sand, the hotel bedroom possesses an inherent transience and impermanence that the home does not. In order for a hotel room to be habitable it should not bear any traces of those previous guests. The 'atmosphere of humanity' in the hotel bedroom must be, to use Merleau-Ponty's words, 'determinate' in as low a degree as possible if the process of inhabitation is to be fully successful.

There are numerous ways in which hotel bedrooms vary, as I explore in this chapter. Some bedrooms in hotels are opulent and luxurious, some are merely functional, while others are dirty, run-down, and full of reminders of previous inhabitants. As the first section of this chapter demonstrates, the precise nature of the hotel bedroom can reveal a great deal about the socioeconomic background of the individual occupying it. Yet, in its aforementioned distance from the space of the house, and from the traditions, habits, and routines that construct that space, the hotel bedroom can, as I discuss in the second section, provide an escape from gendered alignments of femininity and domesticity. In the final section, I consider how this freedom also positions it as a space in which sexual desire can be explored and realised. However, this is complicated by the potential for it to be used as a space of sexual coercion and manipulation, and I demonstrate the various ways in which this space challenges the limits placed on women's sexual agency in the late nineteenth and early twentieth centuries. That the hotel bedroom can function, sometimes simultaneously, as all of these things renders it as a space that defies any attempt at straightforward categorisation. It is a space of sexual freedom that also functions, often simultaneously, as a space used by men in their attempts to coerce women. Similarly, it is a space in which certain characters find themselves trapped, but one in which those same characters seek refuge—a space in which women in particular are freed from the responsibilities of the domestic role, but also a space to which those who are *excluded* from the home are consigned. Characterised by impermanence, the hotel bedroom is a space through which the shifting and conflicting ideologies that construct the modern subject are negotiated and contested.

'THAT SORT OF HOTEL': CODIFYING CLASS THROUGH THE HOTEL BEDROOM

I have explored earlier, in Chaps. 2 and 4, the ways in which the travel and hotel guides of the late nineteenth and early twentieth centuries are vital to an understanding of the precise ways in which authors of this period use the space of the hotel. This is perhaps nowhere more the case than in a consideration of the hotel bedroom. Travel and hotel guides such as the popular *Baedeker*, along with *The Official Hotel Directory* (published by the *Hotel World* trade journal, beginning in 1892) provide significant insight into not only the various different types of hotel in existence, but also into the range of rooms available, the amenities on offer, and how the combination of these elements results in a room rate and tariff. These details can be used as a code through which to read the British hotel in fiction of the period. This code frequently reveals the centrality of the hotel in fiction to characterisation, to the network of relationships between characters, and to delineations of class and social status. In this section, I discuss how the hotel bedroom comes to function as an indication of class and social status in British fiction of the late nineteenth and early twentieth centuries. Beginning with this process of investigating travel and hotel guides published in this period, I then reveal the often-implicit codification of class in these texts. Finally, I consider the other primary reasons behind marginalisation in literature of this period—nationality, sexuality, and gender—which are similarly explored and interrogated in fiction of this period through the codification of the hotel bedroom.

Those seeking a hotel room in the late nineteenth and early twentieth centuries had recourse not only to a range of travel guides, such as the *Baedeker* and *Murray's Handbook for Travellers*, but also to hotel directories such as *The Official Hotel Directory*. While each publication provides slightly different types of information, they are useful to a study of the range and type of hotel bedrooms on offer throughout the period. As more general travel guides, the *Baedeker* and *Murray's Handbook* list a selection of recommended hotels, and offer advice to travellers (particularly foreign visitors) on what they might expect to find in terms of bedrooms, giving rough estimates of the prices they would likely be charged (although, often, these estimates are vague at best). The *Murray's Handbook to London As It Is* (1879) notes, for example, that prices of rooms

> vary exceedingly according to the position of the house and the season of the year. From Easter to September, the charge for apartments is nearly double what it is at other seasons. The charge for a suite of apartments ranges from 30s. To £30 per week, for a single bedroom from 2s. 6d to 10s. a night. (Anon 1879, p. 48)

Slightly more detail is given in the *Baedeker Guide to London and Its Environs* (1889), which, like the *Murray's*, observes that there is a variation in room prices, but specifies that this is 'according to the situation and the floor' of the room. There is a further difference made 'between a simple *Bed Room* and a bedroom fitted up like a *Sitting Room*, with writing-table, sofa, easy-chairs, etc., a higher charge being, of course, made for the latter' (Baedeker 1889, p. 6; emphasis in original). Here are distinctions between different types of room, and what will affect the price of a room: there is the indication in the *Baedeker* that the precise location of a room would have a direct impact on its rate. For example, rooms at the front of a hotel, with a better view and more light, tended to be more expensive than rooms at the back of a hotel.

There was also the question of which floor the room was on, and how the price was affected by this depended almost entirely upon whether or not the hotel had a lift. The invention of American industrialist Elisha A. Otis, passenger lifts were developed in the mid-nineteenth century, with the first one installed in New York in 1857. One of the first passenger lifts to be installed in Britain was in the newly opened Grosvenor Hotel at Victoria Station in 1861 (Carter 1990, p. 62). In an article of the previous year anticipating the opening of this hotel, *The Illustrated London News* commented on the likely importance of the arrival of this new invention, remarking that, despite the height of the building being 'upwards of 100 ft from the pavement, [...] a lifting room adjoining the staircase will diminish this internally to zero', and which would allow 'a possible mode of uniting moderate room rent with comfort, which cannot easily be much longer lost sight of in hotels abroad or at home' (Anon 1860, p. 17). The lift was thus quickly understood as a key amenity in the hotel, and one that had a direct impact on room rates. The absence of a lift in a hotel would mean that bedrooms on the lower floors were more expensive, with rooms on the upper floors often being reserved for the servants of wealthy guests.[1] As Andreas Bernard observes, 'the hierarchical structure of buildings is inseparable from the problem of access', and he notes that in 'the traditional grand hotels of Europe, [...] the reason the rooms became worse and worse the farther up they were was quite simply that only the most lowly guests and the hotel personnel could be expected to climb all those stairs' (2014, p. 69). The prices of bedrooms in hotels that did have a lift, however, were typically unaffected by floor. As the 1908 book advertising the Piccadilly Hotel in London exclaims:

> So perfect and so extensive is the scheme of elevators, or lifts, at the Piccadilly Hotel, that the choice of a floor becomes, comparatively speaking, a question of little moment. Some travellers and residents will doubtless prefer the apartments further removed from the constant echoes of London life, and affording advantages of air and prospect. (Anon 1908, pp. 56–7)

In hotels of the late nineteenth and early twentieth centuries, then, the lift has a kind of democratising function, levelling out the prices of rooms so that they were less dependent on the floor on which they are situated. However, especially in the late nineteenth century, when lifts were a relatively recent invention, those hotels that had a lift would necessarily have been at the more expensive end of the scale, catering for a certain class of guest, and indeed hotel guides of the period confirm this.

The lift is just one of many amenities with which hotels attempted to tempt their customers, and with which they justified their prices. When reading fiction of the period, therefore, the presence of these amenities

---

[1] As Derek Taylor and David Bush note, this 'explains the difference in [ceiling] height between the lower and upper floors, the difference in size and the small windows the higher up you went' (1974, p. 12).

can help us to discern the particular type of hotel in which the characters reside. Publications like *The Official Hotel Directory* are very helpful, featuring as they do a detailed tariff of hotels, and a key for the type of hotel, and for the amenities of each hotel listed. The August 1898 edition of the directory (vol. 37) provided this key:

> F., Family Hotel. F.C., Family and Commercial Hotel. C., Commercial. P., Private. T., Temperance. H., Hydropathic. B., Boarding. R., Rooms. Elec.L., Electric Light. Lft., Lift. Blds., Billiards. Stab., Stabling. C.C., Caters specially for Cyclists.

The seven categories of hotel or establishment, ranging from 'family' to 'boarding', give an indication not only of the variety of establishments available, but also of the tastes and requirements of the public who stayed in them. Read alongside *The Official Hotel Directory*'s tariff, this key becomes even more revealing about each category of hotel, as well as about their clientele.

From this wealth of information, it is possible to construct a code through which to read the various different hotel bedrooms encountered in the literature of the same period. This can, in turn, provide a significant account of how the space of the hotel bedroom can be read as a mode of characterisation, which authors employ to give vital clues about the backgrounds and identities of their characters. As Andrew Thacker observes, in modernist literature, 'the interiority of psychic space is often profoundly informed by exterior social spaces' (2003, p. 5), and this is particularly pertinent in considering the hotel bedroom, the specific type and location of which can reveal a great deal about a character's consciousness or state of mind, as well as about their socioeconomic background. The hotel bedroom, Lauren Elkin argues, functions 'as a barometer of our social standing' (2016, p. 248), and reading the hotel bedroom as a codification of class involves taking into consideration the amenities provided (the presence of a lift, for example, would suggest that the hotel is at the more expensive end of the scale), the location of the room (front or back facing, light or dark), the size of the room, and the design and quality of the furniture and décor.

The guide includes a comprehensive list of hotels in London, as well as a rather less exhaustive list of 'provincial hotels', covering all those located outside of the capital. Taking the list of London hotels, of the cheapest hotels in the price range, those falling under tariff *g* (Fig. 5.1), in which

	a	*b*	*c*	*d*
Bed Rooms	From 5/0 or 7/6 up	From 3/6 or 5/0 up	2/6 to 8/0	2/0 to 5/0
Sitting Rooms	From 10/0 or £1 up	From 10/0 up	From 5/0 up	From 5/0 up
Service	From 1/6 up	From 1/0 up	From 1/0 up	From 1/0 up
Breakfast	*a la carte*	2/6 to 4/0	2/0 to 4/0	1/0 to 2/6
Lunch	*a la carte*	2/6 to 5/0	2/0 to 4/0	1/0 to 2/6
Dinner	*a la carte*	4/0 to 10/0	3/6 to 7/6	2/6 to 5/0
	g	*p*	*it & bb*	
Bed Rooms	1/0 to 2/6	Pension or Boarding terms to be arranged.		
Sitting Rooms	From 2/6 up	If any of the	In order to provide for the peculiarity of	
Service	–	adjoining Tariffs suitable, add same.	some of the Hotel Tariffs, these are added; *it* representing Hotels which make inclusive	
Breakfast	1/0 to 2/0	Thus *pb* would represent Boarding	terms which remain a matter of negotiation, and *bb*, those Hotels which do not accept	
Lunch	1/0 to 2/0	in terms of about £3 3s. a week, *pc* £2 2s.,	guests without charging for Bed and Breakfast as a minimum.	
Dinner	2/0 to 4/0	and *pd* £1 10s. or £1.1s.		

Fig. 5.1   Hotel Tariff reproduced from *The Official Hotel Directory*, Volume 37 (August 1898)

bedrooms range in price from 1/0 to 2/6 (approximately £5.50 to £14 in 2017), seventeen are temperance and three are private hotels.[2] In the next tariff up, tariff *d*, bedrooms range in price from 2/0 to 5/0 (approximately £11 to £28 in 2017), and there is a relatively even distribution between commercial, private, and temperance hotels. In terms of amenities, of forty hotels in total in this tariff, only three feature electric lights, with no lifts. Tariff *c* is the most heavily populated, with a total of 117 hotels falling in this price range. The majority of these are private hotels (forty-two) followed by commercial hotels (thirty-eight), with sixteen family and commercial hotels, and the remainder spread relatively evenly

[2] Temperance hotels emerged in response to the temperance movement, which developed in Britain around 1830. As the majority of accommodation for travellers until the 1830s were inns and public houses, followers of the movement were often unable to find somewhere to stay that did not serve alcohol. The first temperance hotel opened in Preston in 1832, and other establishments quickly followed. However, as Andrew Davison notes, not all of these hotels 'offered a comfortable experience for their guests', and indeed many of the hotels established during the early years of the movement 'were owned and operated by individuals whose primary motivation was the opportunity to make money'. The situation improved somewhat with the establishment of the Temperance Hotels Company Ltd. in 1872, though the purpose-built hotels developed by this company still tended to be 'aimed at the more cost-conscious traveller, offering accommodation in dormitories rather than in individual rooms'. See: Andrew Davison, "'Try the alternative': The Built Heritage of the Temperance Movement", *Brewery History* 123 (2006): 92–109 (p. 101).

between family, temperance, and no specified type. Within this tariff, in which rooms range from 2/6 to 8/0 (approximately £14 to £45 in 2017), amenities are far more common, though the majority of hotels (twenty-four) offer electric lights, with only five featuring a lift. The upper price limit for bedrooms is removed in the two most expensive tariffs, *b* and *a*. Bedrooms in hotels in tariff *b* start at either 3/6 (approximately £20 in 2017) or 5/0 (approximately £28 in 2017), and of the sixty-seven hotels in this tariff, the majority are family (twenty-six), private (twenty-two), and family and commercial (fifteen), with three unspecified, one commercial, and no temperance hotels in this price range. Within tariff *b*, the number of hotels offering amenities is again increased, with thirty-three offering electric lights, and thirteen featuring lifts. It is, perhaps unsurprisingly, in the most expensive tariff, tariff *a*, that we find the highest frequency of amenities. The tariff covers hotels whose cheapest room is either 5/0 (approximately £28 in 2017) or 7/6 (approximately £42 in 2017). The majority of the sixty-three hotels in this tariff are family hotels (thirty-four), with the next highest number being private hotels (twenty-two), then two commercial, one temperance, and four whose type is not specified. Forty-eight of the hotels in this price range (and all of the family hotels) are fitted with electric lights, and twenty-eight hotels feature lifts, and again, the highest incidence of lifts is in family hotels in tariff *a* (twenty-four). This tariff is invaluable to an interpretation of the hotel bedroom in literature of this period. It not only offers information on the different price ranges of hotel bedrooms, which in turn gives crucial information about the relative wealth of characters (which can in turn inform a reading of their class background), but it also indicates the amenities typical to hotels within each price band. In this way, it is central to the development of a code of the hotel bedroom.

Elizabeth Bowen's *The Hotel* (1927) is a novel in which these class divisions within the hotel itself are significantly marked, despite the fact that the eponymous hotel is a prime holiday spot for the 'leisured classes'. Located on the Italian Riviera, the hotel is considered by its (predominantly British) guests as 'an ideal place to pass the winter' and that they are spending an entire season there highlights their affluence (Bowen 2003 [1927], p. 11). In their history of travel writing in the 1930s, Charles Burdett and Derek Duncan note the importance of class and wealth to the ability to travel during this period, stressing the necessity of 'wealth and access to travel networks' (2002, p. 6). In Bowen's novel there is nevertheless a definite distinction between the lower-middle and upper-middle classes, which is clearly marked by the types of room allocated to each character. Early on in the novel, it becomes apparent that, despite the presence of a lift (albeit one which is frequently out of order), the first floor of the hotel is the most prestigious floor. This is signified by an oblique reference, in the early chapters of the novel, to the second floor, 'where people could not afford to have baths so often' (Bowen 2003 [1927], p. 26).[3] The exclusive nature of the front-facing rooms of the hotel is indicated by the fact that they are highly sought after by (some) guests, being filled with light and looking out 'over the town into dazzling spaciousness, sky and sea' (Bowen 2003 [1927], p. 26). The back rooms, on the other hand, are 'smaller, never so bright, and looked out over the road', straight into the windows of the adjacent villas (Bowen 2003 [1927], p. 26). Reverend James Milton arrives to find himself in a tiny back-facing room, which offered 'no space for his baggage', and the size and position of this room decisively place him as lower-middle class (Bowen 2003 [1927], p. 27). Sydney Warren, the young protagonist of the novel, reflects on the way in which the hotel denies its occupants the chance to elude their identities: 'she knew how inexorably the Hotel would refuse to let [Milton] escape from all that he was, and had pity on his innocent holiday taste for incognito, foredoomed from its birth on the threshold of the Hotel' (Bowen 2003 [1927], p. 40). The location of his hotel room acts as a clear and inescapable indicator, both for the reader of the novel and for the other characters within it, of Milton's lower-middle-class identity. Sydney herself occupies a back room in the hotel, and while she seems perfectly content here, the room is judged to somehow suit her by some of the other guests, such as the materialistic Veronica Lawrence, who 'thought that it was just like Sydney to be at the back of the first floor instead of the front of the fourth, with a balcony and sunshine' (Bowen 2003 [1927], p. 111). A clear association is made here between Sydney and this particular type of room, suggesting a certain perceived obstinacy of character in choosing the prestige of the first floor over the pleasure of a view on the fourth. However, Veronica's bitterness, conveyed through the rather dismissive and petulant nature of the phrase 'just like Sydney', hints at a barely concealed jealousy, and a failing attempt to

---

[3] This reference to guests not being able to afford baths seems to suggest that this was a convenience that had to be paid for in the hotel. In a study of Grand Hotels it is noted that, in 1896, 'the new Palace Hotel at St Moritz [...] was only providing one bathroom per floor on the grounds that visitors would not wish to pay the necessary price'. See: Elaine Denby, *Grand Hotels: Reality and Illusion* (London: Reaktion Books, 1998), p. 122.

convince herself that a front room on the fourth floor is better than a back room on the front floor, the implicit irony here being that Sydney's bedroom is almost certainly more exclusive than Veronica's. Despite the fact that Bowen's eponymous hotel caters to a decidedly middle-class clientele, the subtle variation in rooms occupied by each character is nevertheless a clear indication of their specific class identity.

Through the inclusion of a wide range of different types of hotel, texts in this period reflected upon the exclusionary nature of the expensive, luxurious establishments, which are affordable only to a certain section of society. Bowen's eponymous Hotel is such an establishment, and it is clearly marked as a space of leisure and indulgence. As such, it is distinctly opposed to the more utilitarian spaces of many of the other hotels found in late-nineteenth- and early-twentieth-century literature, such as the dingy Karachi Hotel in Bowen's *The Death of the Heart* (1938), and the overwhelmingly gloomy hotel bedroom in which Sasha stays in Jean Rhys's *Good Morning, Midnight* (1939). The clear demarcation of these spaces reinforces the way in which the hotel bedroom can function as a code signifying the precise class, social standing, and financial position of the characters. It is vital to note that this code is used by other characters, as when Anna Quayne observes, in Bowen's *The Death of the Heart*, that Portia and her parents 'always had the back rooms in hotels, or dark flats in villas with no view' (Bowen 1998a [1938], p. 21). Exiled by Mr Quayne's adultery and struggling financially, Portia's family lived a marginalised existence, and were thus confined to a certain type of room, a factor Anna uses to denote their socioeconomic position. Anna makes a similar, seemingly offhand remark about Major Brutt's hotel, referring to it as 'that sort of hotel that he stays at', from which it is clear that she views the Karachi Hotel as a particular type of hotel that caters for a particular type of person (Bowen 1998a [1938], p. 303). While Anna's comment is perhaps more revealing about her personal opinion of Major Brutt, whom she regards as 'quite pathetic' (Bowen 1998a [1938], p. 288), it also speaks to this code, through which he, as an out-of-work exile, 'the man from back somewhere, out of touch with London', is relegated to a certain standard of room—a dark, cramped attic room with no view—in a certain type of hotel (Bowen 1998a [1938], p. 45).

The dark, back-facing rooms on the top floors of hotels inhabited by Bowen's marginalised characters are also the types of rooms occupied by protagonists in the writings of Rhys, most notably Sasha in *Good Morning, Midnight* and Julia Martin in *After Leaving Mr Mackenzie* (1931). In both these novels, it becomes apparent that these characters' socioeconomic position is not the only determining factor towards the spaces in which they find themselves. What is instead suggested by these texts is that the marginalisation of these women may have as much to do with gender as it does with class, and that they are excluded from certain types of places and included in others according to how well they 'fit' normalised gender identities. Julia, for example, is judged by her landlady to be an alcoholic spinster, and is thus given a dark room on the second floor. On her arrival at a cheap Bloomsbury hotel, she is assigned room number nine, which 'was small and very cold' (Rhys 1971 [1930], p. 47). Finally, on her return to Paris, she finds herself in a room 'which depressed her because it was so narrow, and because it was so horrible not to be able to open the windows without having several pairs of eyes glued upon you' (Rhys 1971 [1930], p. 130). The remarkable similarities between these three rooms, their dingy and depressing natures, reinforce the notion that she cannot escape from this particular type of space. More importantly, however, the persistence of this type of room in Julia's narrative, along with the condescending opinions of the hotel staff, suggests that she, as a slightly older, unmarried woman belonging to a lower social class, is not worthy of any other space. In a society in which youth and marriage are prized as the ultimate feminine attributes, she is relegated to the shabby 'backrooms of hotels'.[4] Sasha, meanwhile, remains in the same hotel room throughout *Good Morning, Midnight*, despite her attempt to escape her current situation. In desperation, she takes a taxi to a 'respectable' hotel, and asks for 'a light room' (Rhys 1969 [1939], pp. 31, 32). She is initially offered room 219, but it then transpires that the room is occupied, at which point Sasha becomes frantic and anxious: 'Suddenly I feel that I must have number 219. Just try me, just give me a chance' (Rhys 1969 [1939], p. 32). Her failure to secure room 219 leaves her both exhausted and accepting of her fate, seemingly aware that any room she is given will be the same as the one before, and that any idea of escape is a fantasy: 'All rooms are the same. All rooms have four walls, a door, a window or two, a bed, a chair and perhaps a bidet...Why should I worry about changing my room?' (Rhys 1969 [1939], p. 33). On returning to her old room, Sasha appears completely

---

[4] For more on this see: Katherine Holden, *The Shadow of Marriage: Singleness in England, 1914–1960* (Manchester: Manchester University Press, 2007); and Sheila Jeffreys, *The Spinster and her Enemies: Feminism and Sexuality, 1880–1930*, 2nd ed. (Melbourne: Spinifex Press, 1997).

resigned to her place in society—'Here I belong and here I'll stay' (Rhys 1969 [1939], p. 34)—a place which has been designated for her by a culture which marginalises single women over a certain age, and which deems them unworthy of other spaces and other opportunities.

Certain types of hotel bedroom—those that are run down, dirty, and dingy, and which speak to van Lennep's definition of the 'uninhabitable' hotel room—can be read as a space to which marginalised subjects are consigned. The ageing and penniless bachelor Major Brutt is doomed to eke out his existence in shabby hotels such as the Karachi, despite his longing for a stable, family home like that of the Quaynes. His 'almost unremitting solitude in his hotel' constructs the Quaynes's residence as 'the clearing-house for his dreams', a 'visionary place, round which all the rest of London was a desert' (Bowen 1998a [1938], p. 86). Yet both he and Portia—for whom Windsor Terrace is the first real home she has ever known—are excluded from the Quaynes's home on account of their class backgrounds and questionable, inconvenient histories.[5] Brutt's bedroom in the Karachi Hotel—an establishment in whose walls 'no intimate life can have flowered'—is one of the attic rooms which, it is noted, offers the 'most privacy, though least air' (Bowen 1998a [1938], p. 285). Invited up to his room to talk, Portia recognises that, in the Quaynes's home at Windsor Terrace, 'that floor close to the skylight was mysterious with the servants' bodily life', and thereby interprets the code of the hotel bedroom. Brutt makes this implicit reflection on his socioeconomic standing concrete when he tells her that 'they give me cut price terms' (Bowen 1998a [1938], p. 291). His bedroom is on the top floor (in a hotel without a lift), and in addition to this it is 'dark' and cramped, with a 'doll's house window' and a 'lumpy olive sateen eiderdown' (Bowen 1998a [1938], p. 291). Not only does this 'temporary little stale room' preclude movement (Bowen 1998a [1938], p. 293), but it also carries with it the markers of previous inhabitants, it is heavy with the 'atmosphere of humanity' (Merleau-Ponty 2002 [1945], p. 405). For van Lennep, rooms like this one 'have lost their habitableness' (1987 [1969], p. 215). On account of their socioeconomic background, and with no home, characters such as Brutt, unable to afford anything beyond a hotel bedroom such as this, are thus denied the possibility of fully inhabiting *any* space.

[5] Portia is the product of Thomas Quayne's father's extramarital affair, and Brutt is an old acquaintance of Anna and her ex-lover, Pidgeon. As such, their inconvenience stems from the embarrassment they cause the Quaynes as unwelcome reminders of a past they would rather forget.

For Portia, the ambiguity of her origins contributes further to a life of permanent displacement—having been brought up in hotels, boarding houses and pensions across Europe, she does not really belong anywhere, and is, as a result, effectively exiled from the 'normal, cheerful family life' of the Quaynes's home (Bowen 1998a [1938], p. 15). The end of the novel sees Portia finally displaced to Brutt's cramped and uninhabitable hotel room, in which 'she looked at once harsh and beaten, a refugee' (Bowen 1998a [1938], p. 293). Rhys's *Quartet* (1929) and *Voyage in the Dark* (1934) are similarly revealing about the reasons behind the confinement of certain characters to certain types of hotel bedroom, as the protagonists of both novels share a complex background of uncertain origins. Marya inspires confusion in those who meet her as to her background, and Heidler's question upon meeting her, 'But you are English—or aren't you?', implies that there is something in her appearance or manner that marks her as Other (Rhys 2000 [1929], p. 12). Anna's heritage is even less clear to her fellow characters. A Creole woman from the West Indies, she is taunted by her fellow chorus girls who call her 'the Hottentot' on account of her birthplace (Rhys 1969 [1939], p. 12), and is gently mocked by her lover Walter when she repeatedly protests her ancestry: 'I'm the fifth generation born out there, on my mother's side. "Are you really?" he said, still a bit as if he were laughing at me' (Rhys 1969 [1939], p. 45). These characters thus find themselves forced into the temporary, shabby spaces of dilapidated hotel bedrooms on account of their indiscernible origins. Shut out of more affluent establishments, and, perhaps more importantly, from the homes of other characters, and speaking to Rosemary Marangoly George's aforementioned suggestion that 'the basic organising principle around which the notion of "home" is built is a pattern of select inclusions and exclusions' (1996, p. 2), characters such as Portia, Anna, and Marya are ostracised from mainstream society as a result of their Otherness, and, as marginalised bodies, are placed in the distinctly marginal spaces of the run-down hotel bedroom.

Bowen's Brutt and Rhys's Marya and Julia are trapped in a hotel lifestyle from which they cannot escape. Brutt has become a permanent resident of the Hotel Karachi. The dilapidated nature of the hotel is hinted at in descriptions of the shoddy way in which it has been converted from two adjoining houses, and in depictions of bedrooms in which 'the floors creak, the beds creak; drawers only pull out of chests with violent convulsions; mirrors swing round and hit you one in the eye' (Bowen 1998a [1938], p. 285). Similarly, Rhys's Marya moves from a shabby hotel bedroom on one side of Paris—'A bedroom, balcony and *cabinet de toilette* in a cheap Montmartre hotel' (Rhys 2000 [1929], p. 10)—to another similarly run-down room on the other—the Hôtel du Bosphore in Montparnasse. Despite the distance between them there is little to distinguish one room from the other. This inability to escape is conveyed most strongly by the prevalence in these narratives of certain types of hotel, and characters often observe the similarities between their current room and those that they have previously stayed in. In Rhys's *After Leaving Mr Mackenzie*, Julia suddenly recognises that, 'predestined, she had returned to her starting-point in this little Bloomsbury bedroom that was so exactly like the little Bloomsbury bedroom she had left nearly ten years before' (Rhys 1971 [1930], p. 48). The startling similarity between the two bedrooms, in lay-out and décor, triggers within her the uncanny sensation that 'her life had moved in a circle', and that she has failed to move forwards (Rhys 1971 [1930], p. 48). In *Good Morning, Midnight*, Sasha also reflects on the pat-tern that has become her life: 'Walking in the night. Back to the hotel. Always the same hotel. You press the button. The door opens. You go up the stairs. Always the same stairs, always the same room...' (Rhys 1969 [1939], p. 28). Sasha is unable to escape a certain type of hotel bedroom—dingy, dark and cramped—and the rooms in which she stays have become indistinguishable from one another. Anna Snaith notes a similar tendency in Rhys's *Voyage in the Dark*, in which Anna 'loses the ability to chart her surroundings as they become invisible to her by being indistinguishable' (2005, p. 80). Even if these characters are able to escape one particular hotel, the next will be exactly the same, and they will never be able to break free of the monotonous cycle in which they are trapped. The fact that the majority of the characters facing such a predicament are women only serves to further emphasise the gendered nature of their marginalisation.

Class, therefore, is not the only factor that determines the type of hotel bedroom occupied by a character. Writers were alert to the many different types and varieties of hotel room, and used this variation to interrogate the ways in which class, national identity, and gender impact upon an indi-vidual's access to and ability to inhabit particular spaces. Ahmed maintains:

> Spaces are not only inhabited by bodies that 'do things,' but what bodies 'do' leads them to inhabit some spaces more than others. If spaces extend bodies, then we could say that spaces also extend the shape of the bodies that 'tend' to inhabit them. (2006, p. 58)

This position illuminates the phenomenological inability of certain characters to escape certain types of hotel bedroom, those who—like Bowen's Portia Quayne and *all* of Rhys's interwar protagonists—become seemingly trapped in a cycle of occupying the temporary, run down, and uninhabitable spaces of cheap hotel bedrooms. Ahmed's assertion raises the possibility that the bodies of these characters are in some way marked by these spaces through which they move, and that this demarcation is what prevents them from moving beyond such spaces. This notion is reinforced by the readings of the texts in this section, which suggest further that it is only those whose bodies are not so clearly marked by this impermanence—those who have a home, or at least a sense of stability brought about by financial security—who are thus able to occupy, and thereby inhabit, the more comfortable, habitable, and likely expensive hotel bedroom. However, while the hotel bedroom might therefore be read in novels of the period as a space in which characters become trapped, several of these same narratives depict, as I discuss next, the hotel bedroom as a space of refuge, both from the unrelenting gaze of the public space, and from the stifling drudgery of the domestic.

'A Good Sort of Place to Hide In': Privacy and Refuge in the Hotel Bedroom

The hotel bedroom frequently figures as a space of retreat and refuge. I consider here how the hotel bedroom provides respite for characters not only from the disorientating effects of modernity, but, more specifically, from the potentially debilitating and deconstructive effects of the look of the Other upon the subject. Reading these effects alongside the 'boundary crisis' typically associated with spatial phobias, I discuss the necessarily embodied aspect of these retreats from the public space of the city. Building on this notion of the hotel bedroom as refuge, I explore how it functions, particularly for female characters in British fiction of this period, as an escape from the space of the home: the hotel bedroom is a space that can restore a sense of agency to its female guests through enabling them to perform an active resistance to domestic routine and drudgery. Arguing that the hotel bedroom provides for female characters a level of privacy unavailable elsewhere, and which therefore has a distinctly liberatory potential.

The hotel room provides a refuge from the scrutiny of the public sphere: this scrutiny often focuses on the socioeconomic position of these characters, as well as, in the case of female characters, on their marital and sexual status. Hotel rooms are explicitly referred to as refuges or hiding places on numerous occasions across many novels published across this period. In H.G. Wells's *Kipps* (1905) the eponymous protagonist feels '[s]afe in his room' at the Royal Grand Hotel (Wells 2005 [1905], p. 239), while the notion of the hotel room as a safe space is perhaps most evident in the interwar novels of Rhys, in which the hotel bedroom is figured variously as 'a refuge' (Rhys 2000 [1929], p. 14), 'a good sort of place to hide in' (Rhys 1971 [1930], p. 9), and, in *Good Morning, Midnight*, as 'a place where you hide from the wolves outside' (Rhys 1969 [1939], p. 33). As this last example makes clear, while the hotel bedroom can, as I discussed in the previous section, act as a forbidding space of entrapment or stagnation to those characters unable to afford a cleaner, brighter, and more expensive room, this complex space also frequently functions, often simultaneously, as a much-needed space of safety in which characters feel able to conceal themselves from the city outside.

Cities—particularly European capitals such as London, Paris, and Berlin—have come to be regarded as central to the geographical mapping of modern literature (Parsons 2000; Wilson 1992; Dennis 2008; Harding 2003). As Malcolm Bradbury points out, '[w]hen we think of Modernism', in particular, 'we cannot avoid thinking of these urban climates and the ideas and campaigns, the new philosophies and politics, that ran through them' (1976, p. 96). The industrial developments and technological advances of the late nineteenth and early twentieth centuries elevated the urban experience, thereby feeding the 'metropolitan art' of modernism (1976, p. 101). Much of modernist literature has been read as inextricably linked to the space of the city and, as Thacker maintains, 'we can note the streets and buildings of the metropolis as the setting for many key modernist texts, such as the perambulations of Leopold Bloom in Dublin, or of Clarissa Dalloway in London' (2003, p. 6). But this preoccupation with the space of the city is not unique to modernism, and is in fact widespread across the literatures of modernity. What is particularly relevant to a discussion of the hotel bedroom as refuge in novels of the late nineteenth and early twentieth centuries, however, is the impact that these urban spaces have upon the subjectivity of their inhabitants. The quickening pace of modernity was perhaps most in evidence in its larger cities, and Michael Whitworth suggests that the modern self living in those cities was therefore 'overwhelmed with sensations: the city is full of signs drawn from various codes, and full of fast and unpredictable movement' (2007, p. 7). The acceleration of modern life was at its peak in the urban centres of industry and technology, whose inhabitants faced a relentless and dizzying sensory overload. The overwhelming character of the modern metropolis, and its disruptive potential, is noted by Wendy Gan, who maintains that 'spatially, the city becomes the site' for all the changes of modernity,

> for the renouncing of the old and the embracing of the new. But while the city represents the cutting edge of capitalism, technology and ideas, it is also a place of anomie and alienation. The rush of the new brings with it a break with old certainties and familiar modes of being with resultant anxieties. (2009, p. 11)

These anxieties contribute to or indeed produce the anomie of the modern metropolis. The debate on the disorienting effects of the modern city upon the subjectivities of its inhabitants are well rehearsed, but such observations are worth repeating in order to understand why authors writing in this period so frequently figure the hotel bedroom as a space of refuge from the city.

The urban experience presents a threat to the stability of the modern subject, and to that of the modern female subject in particular. Gan suggests that the need for a space of one's own in which one could escape the chaos of the modern city was therefore all the more important. This metropolitan chaos is more than evident in the novels and short stories explored here—it is apparent in the startlingly bright lights of Paris which 'wheeled in the artificial dusk' in Bowen's *The House in Paris* (Bowen 1998a [1938], p. 232), and in the disorienting urban sprawl depicted in Rhys's *Good Morning, Midnight*: 'North, south, east, west—they have no meaning for me' (Rhys 1969 [1939], p. 26). For Gan, it is from this bewildering tumult that the modern female subject must—if only occasionally—retreat, and she highlights the importance of privacy to the modern woman, positing it as a means for her 'to process the upheavals of modernity' (2009, p. 3). These moments of privacy are particularly important for the female subject, whose gender often acts against her as a marginalising factor in the modern metropolis. I argue that, while the hotel bedroom can, by its very nature, never be private in the same sense as the home or domestic sphere, it nevertheless provides 'a crucial respite to momentarily protect [themselves] from the impact of change, to pause and reconsider [their] place in modernity', and offers these characters a level of privacy unavailable elsewhere (Gan 2009, p. 3).

Specifically, it is from the overwhelming scrutiny of the city street, from the piercing looks and stares of passers-by, that many of these characters seek refuge. According to Hegel, the look of the Other is what solidifies one's existence in the world—to be looked at and recognised confirms one's status as (at the very least) an object for the Other. However, the existence which the look confirms is not necessarily an existence with which one is familiar or comfortable, and the lack of control possessed by the subject over how s/he is perceived by the Other within that look is potentially disturbing. As discussed in the previous chapter, from a Sartrean perspective the look threatens to destabilise and disrupt the subject, often at the same time as it confirms his or her existence. As Joyce Davidson suggests,

> Although the look brings us an awareness of our separate existence, it also threatens to erode the very space within which we create ourselves. Without the look I am nothing, or at least not properly human, but with the look I become aware of the tenuous grounds of my own existence. The same look that solidifies and objectifies me also alienates, disturbs and threatens to *discompose* me. (Davidson 2003, p. 76; emphasis in original)

The power of the look is such that it can disrupt, and potentially 'discompose' or completely destroy, the subjectivity of its object. The look of the Other can construct the subject as something other than that which s/he comprehends her or himself to be—as Sartre notes, '[t]o be looked at is to apprehend oneself as the unknown object of unknowable appraisals—in particular, of value judgements' (2003 [1943], p. 291). This is particularly so for the experiences of many of these characters, who frequently become the unwitting objects of the value judgements of others in the public sphere. Characters such as Rhys's Sasha are actively constructed by the judgemental gazes of others in the public sphere as marginalised beings who do not, or cannot, exist within society. Sasha reflects upon the unrelenting gaze to which she is regularly subjected in the streets of the city: 'That's the way they look when they are saying: "Why didn't you drown yourself in the Seine?" That's the way they look then they are saying: "Qu'est-ce qu'elle fout ici, la vieille?" That's the way they look when they are saying: "What's this story?" Peering at you. "Who are you, anyway?"'

(Rhys 1969 [1939], pp. 76–7). Her emphasis on the insistent, questioning gaze, on the 'looking' and 'peering', captures the essence of the look of the Other, and the destabilising effect it can have on the subject.

Not only does the look have the potential to alienate the subject, but crucially it also has the power to disrupt a sense of embodiment: 'The other's look can seem to rob the individual of *vital* aspects of their identity, reducing their sense of embodied selfhood to that of an object over which they have only limited control' (Davidson 2003, p. 79; emphasis in original). To be seen and judged by another, and to be aware that what is seen by that other is a perspective of one's body that is both unfamiliar and unexpected, is an experience that inevitably shocks and disturbs. Highlighting Anthony Vidler's (1993) arguments regarding the diminishing distance between subjects that accompanied the development of urban space, Davidson suggests that, 'when robbed of this "distance", the invasive proximity of others is perceived by sensitive individuals to weaken their boundaries' (2003, p. 23). Sasha's dread that she might burst into tears in front of others, and her determination to avoid this at all costs, clearly demonstrates this boundary crisis: 'Above all, no crying in public, no crying at all if you can help it' (Rhys 1969 [1939], p. 14). As a bodily fluid, public tears are abject in the Kristevan sense—that which has been expelled from the body and which can inspire fear and horror (Kristeva 1982). Tears and other excretions pose a threat to our sense of embodiment and to our bodily boundaries, 'attest[ing]', Elizabeth Grosz argues, 'to the permeability of the body, its necessary dependence on an outside, its liability to collapse into this outside (this is what death implies), to the perilous divisions between the body's inside and its outside' (1994, pp. 193–4). The act of crying, of shedding tears, decisively breaks these divisions, and the fear of the collapse of these bodily boundaries is intrinsically linked to a fear of death and dissolution, a link which is clearly demonstrated by the contemplation of suicide that Sasha's fear of crying in public inspires within her: 'My throat shuts up, my eyes sting. This is awful. Now I am going to cry. This is the worst … If I do that I shall really have to walk under a bus' (Rhys 1969 [1939], p. 44). Such a reaction is too strong and too powerful to be ascribed to mere embarrassment or humiliation. Her alarm is such that it is as if the dissolution of these bodily boundaries in public might undermine the integrity, the wholeness of her corporeality—'I must be solid as an oak. Except when I cry'—leaving her body vulnerable to invasion from anything and anyone in the public sphere (Rhys 1969 [1939], p. 37). For Rhys's protagonists, the debilitating panic caused by the presence of others in the public spaces of the city triggers their retreat into the hotel room. They can be read as assuming the 'protective boundaries' of the hotel room 'as reinforcement and extension of the psychocorporeal boundaries of the self' (Davidson 2003, p. 24). At such moments, the hotel can be read as a vital support to the corporeal subjectivity of these characters, offering a safe, secure space away from the potential threats of the public sphere.

While the hotel bedroom can provide in these novels an escape from the scrutiny of the city streets, it also offers an alternative space away from the domestic, and specifically from the tasks of housework and homemaking that typically fell to women in this period. As Victoria Rosner observes, '[n]o social institution is more closely tied to the construction and reproduction of gender and sexual identity than the home' (2005, p. 14). Reading the novels of modern authors alongside feminist histories of women and the domestic reveals that the hotel existences of female characters in these novels are not so much a retreat from the domestic sphere, but might rather be appreciated as an active resistance to it. Domestic work is, as Simone de Beauvoir observes, never complete:

> Few tasks are more like the torture of Sisyphus than housework, with its endless repetition: the clean becomes soiled, the soiled is made clean, over and over, day after day. [...] Eating, sleeping, cleaning—the years no longer rise up towards heaven, they lie spread out ahead, grey and identical. The battle against dust and dirt is never won. (2010 [1949], p. 470)

The cyclical and never-ending quality of housework is a reality of which many of the characters in these novels seem all too aware, and are eager to avoid. That very few of the female protagonists (or indeed, other female characters) who populate the novels explored here conform to the role of housewife is highly significant. Those that are in possession of a home and a marriage—such as Anna Quayne in Bowen's *The Death of the Heart*, and Lois Heidler in Rhys's *Quartet*—are invariably surrounded by housekeepers (such as the formidable Matchett in *The Death of the Heart*), maids, and other forms of household help who carry out the chores of housework for them. However, many of the women in the novels explored here reside instead in hotels, where the task of maintaining the bedroom is automatically undertaken by the chambermaids and other members of staff. Having the chores of housework and tidying done for them permits an escape from the drudgery of everyday existence for these women.

The temporary nature of the hotel room further contributes to the absence of responsibility felt by those characters residing in hotels in fiction of this period. The ownership involved in a booked hotel room is ephemeral at best, lacking the stability and security that accompanies homeownership. By that same token, however, the temporary inhabitation of a hotel room also requires none of the responsibility involved in homeownership. Not only do characters such as Julia Mackenzie in Rhys's *After Leaving Mr Mackenzie* and Karen Michaelis in Bowen's *The House in Paris* enjoy the luxury of not having to clean their bedroom, but their lack of connection to, and investment in, these spaces means that they feel no desire to clean or maintain them. The dearth of belongings necessitated by the hotel lifestyle further contributes to this, as the characters have relatively few items with which to decorate the bedroom. The possessions they do have often tend to be functional rather than frivolous, such as the 'bottle of Evian' and 'the two books' belonging to Sasha (Rhys 1969 [1939], p. 11), and the characters are relieved of the responsibility or inclination to clean, dust, and arrange such objects. Yet, as Iris Marion Young asserts, 'not all homemaking is housework' (2005, p. 138). Rather, she defines homemaking as that which 'consists in the activities of endowing things with living meaning, arranging them in space in order to facilitate the life activities of those to whom they belong, and preserving them, along with their meaning' (Young 2005, pp. 140–1). Homemaking, then, has more to do with the act of creation—of interior decoration and design, and of the careful arrangement of belongings—than with cleaning, maintenance and upkeep. Young's definition of homemaking is also distinctly gendered—her emphasis on the importance of 'endowing [...] with living meaning' and 'preserving' belongings in the home parallels the experiences of birth and childcare.[6] Read in the context of these narratives, this invocation of the maternal and its concomitant duties and obligations serves to explain the desire of many of these characters to seek refuge from the heavy responsibilities of the domestic in the relative freedom of the hotel.

In several of these novels, the hotel bedroom also offers female characters a crucial level of privacy unavailable within the domestic sphere. For these women, the domestic 'profession' taking place within the private

---

[6] This distinction between housework and homemaking forms part of Young's attempt to demonstrate the creative and fulfilling potential of the domestic space, and to rescue it from the damaging critiques of second-wave feminism.

space of the home lacked a corresponding space in which to recover from the chores undertaken during the day, leading Gan to question the whereabouts of 'the private sphere's equivalent to the public sphere's private sphere' (2009, p. 4). For Gan, this equivalent is only found outside of the home, in the temporary habitations of modernist women's writing in particular, such as with Miriam Henderson's garret room in Richardson's *Pilgrimage* (2009, p. 1). In this sense, the hotel bedroom offers an essential privacy for women in many of these narratives, and signifies 'a distinctly modern achievement' for the characters who inhabit them (Gan 2009, p. 1). Not only do such spaces offer privacy and respite from the demands of husband and family, but they become, more importantly, a 'room of one's own' in the Woolfian sense, allowing women to break free, if only momentarily, from the fixed identities of wife and homemaker. The anonymous nature of the hotel bedroom and the lack of possessions further enables this release, permitting an escape from the memories of a life together imbued within those belongings. Possessions, as 'the material markers of events and relationships that make the narrative of a person or group', act as a constant reminder of one's role in the family, of a life together, and of a sense of duty (Young 2005, p. 140). Their notable absence within the hotel rooms of many of these characters might thus be a conscious omission, as opposed to a mere requirement of the transient hotel existence.

In this sense, the hotel can be understood as a space that permits an escape from a culturally prescribed identity. Privacy provided the modern woman 'with the space to affirm an alternative identity apart from a traditional domestic role or even the seemingly more progressive role of a wage slave' (Gan 2009, p. 3). The combined factors of privacy, anonymity, transience, and liminality construct the hotel room as a unique space in which characters can explore and construct a range of identities, free from the constraints of the home. The glamour and grandeur of a number of the hotels featured in the texts explored here—such as the 'vivid glitter' of Bowen's eponymous Hotel on the Italian Riviera—construct a fantasy environment in which guests are encouraged to abandon the monotony of an everyday, domestic existence, and in which they are free to indulge in alternative identities (Bowen 2003 [1927], p. 154). This sense of freedom from the drudgery of the home is echoed in Julia's thoughts on those still trapped within the domestic sphere. In a dramatic switch of emphasis in Rhys's *After Leaving Mr Mackenzie*, the imagery of the prison cell, employed at the beginning of the novel to describe Julia's hotel room

(Rhys 1971 [1930], p. 14), is transposed in the final pages of the novel onto the bedrooms of women in their homes: 'The houses opposite had long windows, and it seemed to Julia that at each window a woman sat staring mournfully, like a prisoner, straight into her bedroom' (Rhys 1971 [1930], p. 129). This passage denotes a final recognition of the freedom inherent in a hotel existence, lending credence to a more positive reading of the hotel as a space that makes possible a level of independence, which was otherwise unattainable to the modern woman.

Sasha in Rhys's *Good Morning, Midnight* relishes the extravagance of having her bedding changed by someone else: 'That's my idea of luxury—to have the sheets changed every day and twice on Sundays. That's my idea of the power of money' (Rhys 1969 [1939], p. 68). The feeling of freedom from the responsibility of housework extends beyond the confines of the hotel room and into the hotel itself when Sasha observes the clutter on the hotel landing, the 'brooms, pails, piles of dirty sheets and so forth' (Rhys 1969 [1939], p. 13), but then appears to forget them in an instant, as she will not have the job of cleaning it up. This absence of responsibility is at the root of Sasha's lack of concern towards the 'black specks' on the wall of her room (Rhys 1969 [1939], p. 12), and the cockroaches in the communal bathroom which she calmly watches 'crawling from underneath the carpet and crawling back again' (Rhys 1969 [1939], p. 29). While these two examples might demonstrate Sasha's resignation to, and acceptance of, her lowly place in life, her relaxed attitude could also signal her acknowledgement that these things are not her responsibility. The combination of the presence of hotel staff whose job it is to clean the rooms with the lack of ownership inherent in this hotel lifestyle, means that the hotel becomes the ideal place in which to hide from the responsibilities of the home.

A more pronounced sense of freedom within the hotel bedroom is conveyed in Richardson's 1927 novel, *Oberland*. The ninth in the *Pilgrimage* series of novels, this novel immediately follows *The Trap*, first published in 1925, the title of which aptly conveys the feelings of *Pilgrimage*'s protagonist, Miriam Henderson, towards domestic confinement. In this previous novel, Miriam has been living in a cramped, one-room flat with a Miss Holland. The end of the novel sees Miriam fleeing in horror the 'dreadful little room' (Richardson 1979b [1925], p. 481), in which she feels herself existing with Miss Holland in a kind of 'marriage of convenience' (Richardson 1979b [1925], p. 428). Caught up and 'trapped' in domesticity, Miriam yearns for freedom, and significantly, in this earlier novel she envisions this freedom as being possible in the hotel bedroom. In the initial chapter of *The Trap*, Miriam reads and re-reads the first pages of Henry James's 1903 novel, *The Ambassadors*, which opens with Lambert Strether awaiting the arrival of his friend, Waymarsh, in a Chester hotel.[7] Utterly fascinated, Miriam wants 'the presentation of the two men, talking outside time and space in the hotel bedroom, to go on forever' (Richardson 1979b [1925], p. 408). This draws attention to Miriam's love of literature, and, in particular, her appreciation of the uniquely modern style of James, who has, she reflects, 'achieved the first completely satisfying way of writing a novel' (Richardson 1979b [1925], p. 410). However, it also plays another equally crucial function as the first indication—possibly even for Miriam herself—of her desire to escape to a hotel room, and of her dawning realisation of its liberatory potential. That Miriam focuses on the 'presentation of the two men, talking' serves to mark the hotel bedroom as a space that is more aligned with the masculine than the feminine in the independence it offers. Further, her conception of its existence 'outside of time and space' denotes how the hotel bedroom is, for Miriam, free from the constraints of everyday existence, offering an escape from the routine and drudgery of everyday life.

It is this routine and drudgery that Miriam seeks to leave behind when she travels, at the beginning of *Oberland*, to the Hotel Alpenstock in the Swiss Alps. Upon arrival at the hotel, Miriam, tired from her journey, is keen to get to her room, one of the cheaper rooms in the hotel—a fact which, she discovers during a frustrating conversation, has annoyed the proprietress. When she finally reaches her room, despite the sense of relief denoted by the description of the door being 'at last blessedly closed upon the narrow room', Miriam's first impressions of the bedroom itself are initially obscured by her disappointment that the air—which downstairs in the hotel she had found to be stuffy and dry—is no different, and that even near the window there is 'not only no lessening but an increase of the oppressive warmth' (Richardson 1979a [1927], p. 33). That the room is described as 'narrow' and 'oppressive' reveals Miriam's initial perception of the room as cramped and claustrophobic, living up (or down) to her expectations of it as a 'cheaper room'. Very quickly, however, her attitude towards the room changes, and she finds 'a new quality in her fast closed windows and the exaggerated warmth. Though still oppressive they were triumphant also, speaking a knowledge and a defiance of the uttermost

---

[7] See Chap. 3 for a more in-depth discussion of the opening pages of James's novel.

possibilities of cold' (Richardson 1979a [1927], p. 33). Importantly, this shift in perception is a result of Miriam's movement through the room, from the door to the 'cool light of the end window' (Richardson 1979a [1927], p. 33). It is through movement that Miriam begins to inhabit the hotel bedroom. By moving through the space, Miriam discovers other parts of the bedroom, discoveries that form part of this process of inhabitation. She sees first that the window is in fact 'a door giving on to a little balcony' and encounters the view that it offers of 'the great mountains across the way [...] now bleak white, patched and streaked with black' (Richardson 1979a [1927], p. 33). She then discovers the radiator, 'the source of the stable warmth', whose 'concentrated heat' is no longer unwanted, but which instead 'revive[s] her weary nerves' (Richardson 1979a [1927], p. 33). There is a synaesthetic quality to the description of 'the staunch metallic warmth' emitted by the radiator, combined with the 'flavour of timber added to it in this room whose walls and furniture were all of naked wood', which thereby roots Miriam's 'love' of the room in the sensory, emphasising the necessarily embodied experience of space.

Central to this experience, and to the novel's explication of the process of inhabitation, is the communication between Miriam and the room itself. When Miriam first enters the room, the narrator notes that the room's 'first statements miscarried' (Richardson 1979a [1927], p. 33). The room is not only personified here, but it is figured as participating in a dialogue with Miriam in which both are active, equal subjects. The dialogic nature of the relationship between Miriam and the hotel bedroom effectively establishes the mutual character of the relationship between the embodied subject and space. The 'miscarrying' of the room's 'first statements' conveys the way in which the process of inhabiting is, for Miriam, momentarily precluded by a combination of factors: the fatigue of her journey, the excessive warmth, and the frustrations of her conversation with the 'hostile and suspicious' proprietress immediately prior to entering the room (Richardson 1979a [1927], p. 32). However, her movement through the room alters her initial impressions of the room, enabling Miriam to turn to it 'in greeting' (Richardson 1979a [1927], p. 34). Her movement through the bedroom also increases her sense of its spaciousness—despite it being small, it seems to expand through her movement, and she finds, for example, that the way to a second window 'was endless across the short room from whose four quarters there streamed, as she moved, a joy so deep that she brought up opposite the window as if on another day of life' (Richardson 1979a [1927], p. 34).

Richardson depicts here a positive process of inhabitation, whereby Miriam's movement through the room engenders an explicit sense of *jouissance*, which is inextricably bound up in the rejuvenating effect of the room upon Miriam's sense of self. In this little hotel bedroom, Miriam is able to 'revel in freedom and renewal'. As she anticipated in her earlier reading of James, the hotel bedroom offers Miriam a vital space away from the routine and drudgery of modern everyday existence.

Positioned in between the public space of the city street and the private space of the home, the hotel—and specifically, the hotel bedroom—is uniquely placed to offer sanctuary from both. For those who are marginalised on account of their class, gender, age, and/or nationality, the hotel bedroom can, as the novels explored in this section demonstrate, offer respite from the unrelenting gaze of the other that is so endemic to the public, urban spaces of modernity. For women, however, the hotel bedroom also affords a different kind of freedom—an escape from domestic labour and drudgery, revelled in by characters like Rhys's Sasha Jansen. As Richardson's *Oberland* shows, the hotel can be a vitally important space for 'rejuvenation', for reflection, contemplation, and renewal. In this sense, the hotel bedroom offers a type of privacy unavailable elsewhere, and thereby provides a level of support for the female subject that is both crucial and unparalleled in the spaces of the late nineteenth and early twentieth centuries.

'An Atmosphere of Departed Ephemeral Loves': Sexuality in the Hotel Bedroom

Existing in between the public and the private, the hotel is located outside the moral boundaries of those more normative spaces. The powerful cultural association that exists between hotel rooms and illicit sexual activity is a persistent one, and in several of the novels explored here, the sexual connotations of the hotel bedroom are made strikingly apparent. This ideological association is reinforced in these narratives through descriptions of glamorous, luxurious, and occasionally overtly erotic décor and furniture, which often create a sense of luxury (or indeed the absence thereof). The anonymity of the hotel bedroom, discussed in the previous section, can offer not just an escape from domestic drudgery, but also the potential freedom to explore sexual desires that would elsewhere be morally impermissible. Yet for many female characters in novels of the late nineteenth and early twentieth centuries, the line between sexual freedom and sexual coercion is a fine one, and one that is frequently blurred or indistinguish-able. Novels like H.G. Wells's *Ann Veronica* (1909) and Rhys's *Voyage in the Dark*, for example, demonstrate the coercive potential of the hotel bedroom for men wishing to take advantage of the female protagonists.

Wells's *Ann Veronica* explores the New Woman question through the eponymous protagonist, who, in the opening chapters of the novel, leaves home for London in search of independence. His middle-class heroine finds herself in financial difficulties soon after her arrival in the capital, hav-ing been unable to find what she regards as suitable employment. On the verge of pawning her jewellery, Ann Veronica decides to visit Mr Ramage, a much older acquaintance and neighbour of her father. Ramage is the man with whom she had discussed her plans to leave home earlier in the novel, and who had encouraged her to 'strike out in the world' (Wells 1943 [1909], p. 65). By the time Ann Veronica goes to visit him in his offices in the City, Wells's narrator has made it abundantly clear that Ramage is only interested in Ann Veronica as a potential sexual conquest. He is established early on in the novel as a serial womaniser who, enabled by the wealth of his invalid wife, has had a string of 'disturbing, absorbing, interesting, memorable affairs' (Wells 1943 [1909], p. 64). Ramage is also depicted from the outset as a man who is experienced in flattering, manip-ulating, and coercing women. Ramage, finding Ann Veronica 'in a com-municative mood, […] had used the accumulated skills of years in turning that to account' (Wells 1943 [1909], p. 65). Thus, the novel foregrounds the events that are to come, events to which Ann Veronica herself is some-times wilfully ignorant. After reluctantly accepting Ramage's offer of forty pounds to enable her to support herself while studying Biology at Imperial College, Ann Veronica begins to see Ramage 'almost weekly, on a theory which she took very gravely, that they were exceptionally friends' (Wells 1943 [1909], p. 135). While the 'theoretical' nature of their friendship hints at the misgivings that lie buried in the depths of Ann Veronica's consciousness, she nevertheless continues to see Ramage, until eventually he declares his love for her during a highly symbolic performance of Wagner's *Tristan und Isolde*. Even after this, however, a moment which profoundly disturbs and upsets her, Ann Veronica agrees, at Ramage's insistence, to talk about the incident with him 'some other time. Somewhere, where we can talk without interruption' (Wells 1943 [1909], p. 160). And so it is that Ann Veronica finds herself, the following night, trapped and advanced upon by Ramage in a *cabinet particulier* in the Hotel Rococo in Jermyn Street.

Typically found in hotels, but also occasionally available in restaurants, a *cabinet particulier* is a private dining room with an adjoining bedroom. In the late nineteenth and early twentieth centuries, this type of room had its own very specific connotations. As Rachel Rich notes, the 'private nature' of *cabinet particuliers* meant that they were often 'associated with illicit encounters, especially sexual ones' (2011, p. 138). The *cabinet particulier* was frequently used in literature, plays, and art of the late nineteenth and early twentieth centuries to aid in the characterisation of women of low repute, often those who used their sexuality to gain financial advantage, such as in Edouard Gallier's Parisian comedy, 'La Belle Madame Hesselin' (1899), and in impressionist painter Jean-Louis Forain's etching, *En Cabinet Particulier* (c.1909). Forain's etching depicts a plump man sitting at a dining table, gazing at two topless women, and was one of at least two prints he produced during the late nineteenth and early twentieth centuries centred on this very specific type of room. This pervasive cultural association can also be found in accounts of legal proceedings, such as a Parisian 'matrimonial swindling case' reported in *The Standard*. In this case, men were duped by an agency into believing that they could win the hands of noblewomen. A Monsieur Mauser was presented to a woman purporting to be a Russian Countess, who had proposed that he take her 'to dine in a *cabinet particulier* in a fashionable restaurant', a request which, the Judge suggested, should have aroused Mauser's suspicion (Anon 1895, p. 5).

The space of the *cabinet particulier* here confirms not only the sexually predatory nature of Ramage's intentions towards Ann Veronica, but also indicates his perception of her as a woman who relies on her sexuality to get what she wants and/or needs—in this case money. That he regards his loan to her as being imbued with an unspoken yet mutual understanding bound up in sexual favours and gratification is made clear by the room itself. Ann Veronica, however, demonstrates very little, if any, awareness of Ramage's designs upon her, and seems largely ignorant of the cultural connotations of the *cabinet particulier*. Upon arrival at the Hotel Rococo, Ramage takes Ann Veronica 'upstairs to a landing on which stood a bald-headed waiter with whiskers like a French admiral and discretion beyond all limits in his manner. He seemed to have expected them' (Wells 1943 [1909], p. 162). The 'discretion' of the waiter, combined with the fact that their arrival appears to have been anticipated, signals the pre-meditated and sexually illicit nature of Ramage's intentions. The room into which the pair is shown is 'a minute apartment with a little gas-stove, a silk crimson-covered sofa, and a bright little table, gay with napery and hot-house flowers' (Wells 1943 [1909], p. 162). The 'hot-house flowers' are loaded with meaning, indicating luxury and expense alongside a palpable sensuality. In addition to this, the 'crimson' silk of the sofa is not only luxurious, but is heavy with erotic symbolism, connoting skin flushed with sexual excitement. While Ann Veronica merely comments that it is an 'Odd little room', she nevertheless 'dimly apprehend[s] that obtrusive sofa' (Wells 1943 [1909], p. 162). Her ignorance and innocence is at once highlighted and undermined here—her suspicions regarding Ramage's plans to seduce her, which have been present yet suppressed since their initial meeting in the opening chapters of the novel, are at this point, following Ramage's declaration of love the previous evening, justifiably strengthened. However, while she is wary of Ramage, and has an underlying awareness of the potential significance of the sofa, she nevertheless does not seem to appreciate the cultural connotations of the *cabinet particulier*, or indeed recognise this room as such. When, once they have finished eating, and the waiter has 'closed the door behind him with an almost ostentatious discretion', Ramage locks the door, Ann Veronica attempts to conceal her concern. She feels that she has 'stepped into a world of unknown usages' (Wells 1943 [1909], p. 162). Her lack of knowledge regarding the *cabinet particulier* and the behaviours with which this space is associated, combined with her misplaced (and often rather forced) trust in Ramage, is what has led to her dangerous predicament at this moment.

Rhys's *Voyage in the Dark* features a similar scene in a *cabinet particulier*, and reading this alongside Wells's novel proves particularly fruitful in a consideration of how the hotel bedroom is figured as a space of sexual coercion across middlebrow and modernist literature. In Rhys's novel, the protagonist, Anna Morgan, has been taken to a *cabinet particulier* in The Hoffner Hotel and Restaurant in London by Walter Jeffries, another older man. After meeting in Southsea in October, while Anna is on tour there as chorus girl, Anna agrees to dine with Walter upon her return to London in mid-November. The relatively recent nature of their acquaintance differentiates them from Ann Veronica and Ramage, whose relationship dates back at least several months to their conversation in the opening pages of Wells's novel (if not beyond, given that he and her father are neighbours). In terms of the opportunity for sexual manipulation and coercion, then, Ramage is at an advantage over Walter, and has had a longer period of time over which to ingratiate himself with and flatter Ann

Veronica. He has also, importantly for him, been able to craft a situation whereby she is in debt to him, putting her at a disadvantage that extends beyond the financial, and increasing her vulnerability in his eyes.

Yet the financial situation, and crucially class backgrounds, of both female protagonists is significant. While Ann Veronica is indeed in debt to Ramage by £40[8] her background is nevertheless decidedly middle class, as her father is 'a solicitor with a good deal of company business' (Wells 1943 [1909], p. 7). The class background of Rhys's Anna Morgan, however, is less clear. As detailed in the opening section to this chapter, Anna has travelled to London from the West Indies, and is eking out a poorly paid and precarious existence as a chorus girl, staying in a series of temporary rooms in boarding houses. As such, she has moved from her existence in Dominica to one much more economically unstable in England. It is her indeterminate national identity that results in this instability. As Anne Cunningham notes, 'Anna is not quite white—or certainly not properly British; rather, she is doubly excluded as a woman who appears white but is socially and economically disinherited from British colonial wealth when in the mother country' (2013, p. 377). Compared to the white, English, and middle-class Ann Veronica, Anna's class status is decidedly less certain, meaning that she is arguably more vulnerable to Walter's advances (or is at least regarded as such by him) than Ann Veronica is to Ramage's, despite there being no debt between Anna and Walter at this point.

Also different is the reaction of both female characters to the space of the *cabinet particulier*. While Ann Veronica is 'dimly' aware of the significance of the 'silk crimson covered-sofa', she realises the meaning of the room itself only after Ramage's assault upon her, at which point '[i]nterpretation came pouring down upon her almost blindingly; she understood now the room, the waiter, the whole situation' (Wells 1943 [1909], p. 165). In Rhys's novel, the décor of the *cabinet particulier* in the Hoffner Hotel in Rhys's novel is, like the sofa in *Ann Veronica*, rendered in erotic terms. Upon entering the room, Anna observes that 'there was a red-shaded lamp on the table, and heavy pink silk curtains over the windows. There was a hard, straight-backed sofa, and two chairs with curved legs against the wall—all upholstered in red' (Rhys 1969 [1934], p. 18). With

---

[8] This is a considerable sum in Edwardian England, equating to over £4000 in 2017. Source: 'Prices and Inflation Calculator', *This Is Money*. Available at: http://www.thisis-money.co.uk/money/bills/article-1633409/Historic-inflation-calculator-value-money-changed-1900.html (accessed 5 March 2017).

its emphasis on the curves of the chair legs, the red upholstery and the pink silk curtains evoking the female body and genitalia, and the phallic imagery of the 'hard, straight-backed sofa', this heavily sexualised description of the room's décor and furnishings clearly denotes what the room has been, and is intended to be used for. This is not an anonymous room, free of connotations, but one designed and created for a specific purpose, a 'cultural environment' that is, Merleau-Ponty argues, experienced 'along with behaviour corresponding to it' (2002 [1945], p. 406). In such cultural environments or 'objects', we 'feel the close presence of others beneath a veil of anonymity. *Someone* uses this pipe for smoking, the spoon for eating, the bell for summoning, and it is through the perception of a human act and another person that the perception of a cultural world could be verified' (Merleau-Ponty 2002 [1945], p. 405; emphasis in original). In the 'cultural environment' of the hotel room, Anna feels 'the close presence of others', and can perceive the 'human acts' that take place within the room, and for which it is designed.

This perception is strengthened by the nature of the room to which Walter has taken her, and by the cultural connotations of the *cabinet particulier*. In the private dining room, Anna's reaction upon her discovery of the half-hidden door to the adjoining bedroom—a mixture of surprise and resignation—suggests that she, unlike Ann Veronica, is well aware of these associations:

> There was a door behind the sofa, but I hadn't noticed it before because a curtain hung over it. I turned the handle. 'Oh,' I said, 'it's a bedroom.' My voice went high.
> 'So it is,' he said. He laughed. I laughed too, because I felt that was what I ought to do. *You can now and you can see what it's like, and why not?* (Rhys 1969 [1934], p. 20)

Anna's ability to interpret the meaning of the concealed bedroom is owing to the months she has spent touring England with a group of chorus girls, some of whom, like her friend Maudie, advise her throughout the novel on what to expect from men, and how to behave around them. In the opening pages of the novel, Anna is also depicted 'lying on the sofa, reading *Nana*' (Rhys 1969 [1934], p. 9), Émile Zola's 1880 novel centred around prostitution, an intertextual inclusion which, as Andrew Thacker notes, highlights the theme in *Voyage in the Dark* of 'commodified gender relations' (2012, p. 514). Intertextuality is also employed in Wells's novel, as Ann Veronica's daydreams about employment when she first arrives in London are 'based largely on the figure of Vivie Warren' in George Bernard Shaw's *Mrs Warren's Profession*, a play which she had seen 'furtively with Hettie Widgett from the gallery of a Stage Society performance one Monday afternoon' (Wells 1943 [1909], p. 80).[9] However, Ann Veronica finds most of this play 'incomprehensible', and she seems only to have fully appreciated the character of Vivie herself, and the way in which she is 'hard, capable, successful, and bullying' (Wells 1943 [1909], p. 80). Anna, on the other hand, seems to have a far deeper understanding of Zola's tale of prostitution, which gives her 'a curious feeling—sad, excited, frightened' (Rhys 1969 [1934], p. 9). Having had a decidedly less sheltered existence than that of Wells's middle-class heroine Ann Veronica, Anna is able to perceive the sexual implications of the *cabinet particulier*, and clearly understands the situation in which she finds herself.

Walter's choice of hotel room plainly demonstrates to Anna both what he expects of her, and the assumptions that he, like Ramage, has made regarding her willingness to use her sexuality for financial gain. Indeed, Anna's distinct financial *dis*advantage in comparison to Walter is emphasised throughout their dinner in the hotel room, with Walter quizzing Anna on her earnings and acting shocked at her answer: 'Thirty-five bob a week, and of course extra for extra matinées. "Good God," he said. "You surely can't manage on that, can you?"' (Rhys 1969 [1934], p. 19). In fact, as the scene demonstrates, Walter's attraction to Anna is based largely on the disparity between their respective socioeconomic backgrounds, and it is significant that he only kisses Anna immediately after he tells her how 'awfully pathetic' she looked when, on their initial meeting, she was 'choosing those horrible stockings so anxiously' (Rhys 1969 [1934], p. 20). Walter is drawn to Anna's financial instability, to what he perceives as her 'pathetic' and 'anxious' approach to spending money, because, as far as he is concerned, it is precisely this that affords him control over Anna and her sexual behaviour towards him. It is Anna's relative poverty that will, at least in his eyes, make it easier for him to coerce her through the hotel room.

---

[9] George Bernard Shaw's play, *Mrs Warren's Profession*, was written in 1893, but was censored by the Lord Chamberlain for its discussion of prostitution in England. First performed in London in 1902 at the New Lyric Club—a private, members-only club—it was not publicly performed in London until 1925. Vivie Warren, with whom Ann Veronica here feels such an affinity, is the well-educated daughter of Mrs Warren, and an archetype of the New Woman.

Anna follows her literary predecessor in her rejection of Walter's advances, and it is in this mutual refusal that the parallels between the two novels are most apparent. Both women are forcibly kissed against their will. In the case of Ann Veronica, Ramage's 'mouth sealed hers and his breath was mixed with her breath', and the narrator details the way in which she 'shut her lips hard, her jaw hardened, and she set herself to struggle with him' (Wells 1943 [1909], p. 164). In Rhys's novel, there is the same 'hardness' of mouth, though this time on the part of Walter (Rhys 1969 [1934], p. 20). In both novels, the female protagonists feel a strong hatred towards the men assaulting them—in *Ann Veronica*, the narrator observes that, 'If hate could kill, Ramage would have been killed by a flash of hate' (Wells 1943 [1909], p. 164), and in *Voyage in the Dark*, Anna describes how, as she is being kissed by Walter, she 'hated him' (Rhys 1969 [1934], p. 20). This hatred transmutes, in both texts, to a physical rejection of the male, and while there are varying degrees of strength involved—Ann Veronica mounts a defence which 'ceased rapidly to be in any sense ladylike, and became vigorous and effective' (Wells 1943 [1909], p. 164), while Anna pushes Walter away 'as hard as I could' (Rhys 1969 [1934], p. 20)—there is in both a decisive feminine repudiation of masculine attempts to manipulate and seduce. Though Wells and Rhys demonstrate the hotel room as a space that is used by men to attempt to coerce women whom they regard as vulnerable, the violent responses of their female protagonists to these attempts at coercion reveal a clear feminine agency.

In the late nineteenth and early twentieth centuries, there existed pervasive cultural associations between the hotel bedroom and illicit sexual activity. Drawing heavily on such associations, T.S. Eliot, for example, employs the hotel in a number of his poems to denote the sordid underbelly of the urban environments he depicted, and to evoke the 'air of sexual discomfort' that, as critics such as Gail McDonald observe, pervades much of his early poetry (2017, p. 165). In 'The Love Song of J. Alfred Prufrock' (1915), the 'restless nights in one-night cheap hotels' referred to in the poem's opening stanza imply not only a sense of impermanence, but hint at clandestine and unsettling sexual liaisons (Eliot 1961 [1922], p. 11, l. 6).[10] In 'The Fire Sermon', the third section of Eliot's *The Waste Land* (1922), a speaker recounts how

---

[10] That these hotels are themselves located in 'half-deserted streets, [...] that follow like a tedious argument/Of insidious intent' (Eliot 1961 [1922], p. 11, ll. 6–8) further insinuates

> Mr Eugenides, the Smyrna merchant
> Unshaven, with a pocket full of currants
> C.i.f. London: documents at sight,
> Asked me in demotic French
> To luncheon at the Cannon Street Hotel
> Followed by a weekend at the Metropole.
> (Eliot 1961 [1922]), p. 59, ll. 209–4)

The Smyrna merchant can, as critics such as David Roessel point out, be read as 'a symbol of the decay of Europe', and more specifically as embodying the conflict between Turkey and Greece over the allocation of Smyrna to Greece at the end of the First World War (1989, p. 175). His 'unshaven' appearance, together with his 'demotic French', marks him out as a somewhat unsavoury character, but this suggestion is wholeheartedly reinforced by his invitation 'to luncheon at the Cannon Street Hotel/Followed by a weekend at the Metropole'. The significance of the Cannon Street Hotel alone works on a number of levels—it can in one sense be read, as Roessel suggests, as an allusion to the death of Constantine XI, the last Byzantine emperor, at the Cannon Gate in 1453, and the consequent fall of Constantinople to the Turks (Roessel 1989, p. 175). However, as Roessel observes, 'Eliot deflates this great national dream by linking it to the fulfilment of a transient desire in a Brighton hotel' (1989, p. 175). Yet even discounting the added allusion to sexual impropriety in a seaside resort, the mere inclusion of the Cannon Street Hotel is itself arguably enough to 'deflate this national dream'. Opened in May 1867 as the City Terminus Hotel at Cannon Street Station, it was renamed the Cannon Street Hotel in 1879 after accumulating significant debt in its first decade. In *The Official Hotel Directory* of July 1900, the establishment was listed under tariff C as a mid-price family and commercial hotel, befitting a merchant like Mr Eugenides. Increasingly, however, the hotel became known for its affordability, and by 1923, just one year after the publication of *The Waste Land*, the *Baedeker* guide to London listed the Cannon Street Hotel as the most inexpensive of the railway hotels in London, 'at nineteen shillings and sixpence for bed, breakfast, lunch and dinner' (Carter 1990, p. 114). The choice of this particular second-rate hotel for an invitation to lunch thereby constructs Mr Eugenides as a frugal and even parsimonious character.

the same sense of circularity and entrapment that is, as previously discussed, explored in more depth by Jean Rhys in her novels of the same period. The poem's epigraph from Dante's *Inferno* only serves to reinforce this notion of inescapability.

The tawdry atmosphere developed throughout the stanza is sharpened and reiterated by the suggestion of 'a weekend at the Metropole' in its final line. The Metropole was, as Marjorie Perloff notes, 'one of the leading hotels in Brighton' at the time of the poem's conception (1981, pp. 11–2).[11] Opened by the Gordon Hotels Company on 12 July 1890, the hotel was, as a review in the *Illustrated London News* noted, 'designed to afford visitors the same well-ordered entertainment as is provided at the Hôtels Métropole, Grand, and First Avenue in London', establishments owned by the same company.[12] Yet, while the Metropole may have been a grand and well-respected hotel in its infancy, by the early twentieth century, it had, like so many other hotels, come to be associated with illicit sexual encounters.[13] Just as the protagonists of Rhys's and Wells's novels discover the sinister meaning of the hotel bedroom, the connotations of 'a weekend at the Metropole' are thus strikingly apparent for the speaker to whom the invitation is posed. Less clear, however, is the identity—and more specifically, the gender—of that speaker. There has been some debate on precisely who is being propositioned by Mr Eugenides in this stanza: a number of critics (including, but by no means limited to, Perloff 1981, p. 15; Koestenbaum 1988, pp. 128–9) have identified the speaker as male, and the invitation as homosexual in nature. Yet, while a queer reading of this moment in the poem is persuasive and welcome, there is little concrete evidence to suggest that the speaker in this stanza is definitely male. The Eugenides episode occurs directly before that featuring 'The typist home at teatime' (Eliot 1961 [1922]), p. 59, l. 222), which is narrated by Tiresias, the mythological figure who is both male and female, 'throbbing

---

[11] It is also worth noting here that Eliot wrote a significant amount of *The Waste Land* during a stay at the Albemarle Hotel in Margate, another seaside town that is, like Brighton, popular with Londoners due to its relatively close proximity (77 miles east of London, whereas Brighton is located 47 miles to the south). Eliot stayed at the hotel from 22 October to 12 November 1921 to recuperate following a nervous breakdown, and Elaine Borish notes that he 'completed a substantial portion of his long poem at the Albemarle, including the "Fire Sermon" section. When he left Margate on 12 November, he attached to the manuscript the hotel bill, which came to £16' (Borish 1995, p. 80).

[12] 'The Hotel Métropole, Brighton', *The Illustrated London News*, 26 July 1890, p. 118.

[13] Its reputation was not helped by its role in scandalous divorce cases that were heavily publicised in the press, such as that of Captain Samuel Loveridge, who in 1920, two years prior to the publication of *The Waste Land*, was granted a decree nisi on the grounds of the misconduct of his wife in the Hotel Metropole with a Major Christopher Lowther, M.P. (the son of the then Speaker of the House of Commons, the Right Hon. James Lowther). For further details of this case, see: 'Society Scandal', *The Western Times*, 14 July 1920, p. 4.

between two lives' (Eliot 1961 [1922], p. 59, l. 218). But it also occurs directly after the 'Twit twit twit/Jug jug jug jug jug jug' call of Philomel (Eliot 1961 [1922], p. 59, ll. 203–4). At the very least, then, there is a distinct ambiguity concerning the gender of the speaker propositioned by Mr Eugenides. This is an ambiguity to which, given the inherently multi-vocal nature of the poem, any reading should be alert, particularly as the tone and implication of the invitation varies significantly depending on the identity of the person to whom it is addressed. While the sexual connotations of a weekend at the Metropole are evident regardless of the speaker's gender, the shift in the power dynamic of that invitation can be charted from potentially slight, in the case of a male speaker, to moderate, in the case of the transgendered figure of Tiresias,[14] to extreme, in the case of Philomel, who, 'So rudely forc'd', is synonymous with sexual violence against women (Eliot 1961 [1922], p. 59, l. 205). If the speaker is taken to be the latter, a woman already rendered sexually vulnerable by brutal attacks, then the proposed 'weekend at the Metropole' assumes a far more coercive and predatory undertone.

As Rhys's Anna Morgan and Wells's Ann Veronica demonstrate, however, the successful use of the hotel by men to manipulate and coerce is by no means inevitable. The lack of response to Mr Eugenides's invitation—the poem moves directly from this to Tiresias's description of the end of the working day, 'the violet hour, when the eyes and back/Turn upward from the desk' (Eliot 1961 [1922], p. 59, l. 220)—suggests that the speaker has chosen to reject the sexual connotations of the hotel. The hotel in Eliot's *The Waste Land* might well, in this sense, be understood as integral to an exploration of feminine sexual agency. Within the space of the hotel bedroom specifically, female characters in the literature of this period enact such agency both through denying and refusing the advances of men, as well as through fulfilling their own desires. The unique position of the hotel in between and therefore apart from the more dominant social spaces of the public and the private marks the hotel bedroom (which is the most private of spaces within the hotel) as a space in which otherwise impermissible activities and behaviours become possible. Offering more privacy than the public space of the street or park, the hotel bedroom provided, in this period, a space in which couples might engage in sexual activity that was otherwise closely scrutinised in the more open, public

---

[14] For further discussion on the way in which Tiresias complicates conceptions of transgender and transsexual identity, as well as of hermaphroditism and bisexuality, see Madden (2008).

spaces of Britain. In the nation's capital, for example, the London Public Morality Council monitored and reported on what Jeffrey Weeks summarises as 'the observed sexual activities of couples in various open spaces (such as Hampstead Heath, Clapham Common and Parliament Hill Fields)' (1989, p. 214). The introduction of female police officers during the First World War led to an increased level of surveillance of female sexual behaviour in such spaces. Edith Smith was 'the UK's first attested policewoman', who 'cautioned 50 "prostitutes" and secured the conviction of 10 others in 1917 by way of warning' (Jackson 2006, p. 73). The increasing vigilance of the police force meant that acting upon these curiosities in public carried a far greater risk, an awareness of which is often demonstrated in the fictions of these authors. For many of the female characters encountered in novels of this period, public spaces are imbued with the threat of exposure and retribution. The enclosed space of the hotel bedroom, and its semi-privacy, offers a far more suitable location in which to explore their sexual desires.[15] Those same moral codes that triggered this increase in surveillance of sexual activity in public spaces also governed the more private space of the home during this period.

Though not necessarily enforced in precisely the same way as in the public sphere, the surveillance of family, friends, and neighbours played a significant role in encouraging people to adhere to the norm of the stable family home with a married couple at its heart. Young unmarried girls such as Karen Michaelis in Bowen's *The House in Paris* often lived with their parents in the family home. Engaged but not yet married, Karen's affair with Max—who is also engaged to someone else—falls just outside the legal boundaries of adultery, yet still clearly violates the moral boundaries of premarital sex in Britain during this period. Karen's transgressions are prompted, Neil Corcoran argues, 'at least in part, [...] by her desire to break free from the constrictions of her apparently amiable, decent,

---

[15] While the increasing interest in and popularity of sexology and psychoanalysis during the late nineteenth and early twentieth centuries may suggest a consequent loosening of debates surrounding sexuality and sexual behaviour, the reach of these new debates was nevertheless limited. Even the discourse of sexology itself had its limits—the frank discussions found within its texts, and within the sex manuals of writers such as Marie Stopes, were meant for a specific audience. The title of Stopes's most well-known publication, *Married Love* (1918) clearly demonstrates this, as the book addresses itself directly and solely to married heterosexual couples. The sexological discourse and marriage manuals of the period failed to acknowledge or accommodate the sexual desires of single (or non-heterosexual) people, instead serving to reinforce heterosexual marriage as the norm from which all other lifestyles could only deviate.

moneyed, liberal, Regent's Park-metropolitan family' (2004, p. 94). Yet the locatedness to which Corcoran refers—his firm placing of it as 'Regent's Park-metropolitan'—means that his description better suits her family *home*, rather than simply her family. The Michaelis's home at Chester Terrace is depicted in Bowen's novel as the archetypal upper-middle-class home in its stability and normality. Beyond its walls, the city pulses with life—'streets [...] full of light and echoes of barrel-organs playing the new tunes'—while 'indoors at Chester Terrace, Michaelis family life continued as ever; intelligent, kind, calm', the home standing in static opposition to the activity outside (Bowen 1998b [1935], p. 123). The realisation of Karen's desire for Max is impossible within this space, not least because it affords her no privacy, no escape from the all-encompassing gaze of her parents—'her family's powerful confidence was a searchlight that dipped into every valley, not letting you out of view' (Bowen 1998b [1935], p. 133). In order to be with Max there is, for Karen, 'nowhere left to go' but the hotel (Bowen 1998b [1935], p. 133).

A similar situation is faced by Emmeline Summers in Bowen's *To the North*, despite the fact that the home she shares with her sister-in-law Cecilia is, at first glance, a strikingly modern domestic arrangement. Without the moral standards and constantly prying eyes of parents, Emmeline's anxiety to conceal her relationship with Markie Linkwater might initially seem curious, though could be explained by her characteristic 'reserve' and 'profound shyness' (Bowen 1987 [1932], p. 50). Yet her reluctance to bring the relationship into her home betrays the powerful morality with which the very concept of home is imbued, regardless of whether or not the actual space in question is a typical family home. When Cecilia remarks to Emmeline that 'You really are very young [...]: I suppose I ought to take better care of you than I do. Do be sensible about Markie', her apparent concern stems from popular interwar doctrine regarding the damaging effect of premarital sex upon a woman's reputation (Bowen 1987 [1932], p. 98). It is a combination of an awareness of this concern for her, and of the truth underpinning it, that drives Emmeline away from the home to spend the night with Markie in the Hôtel du Padoue in Paris (Bowen 1987 [1932], p. 142). For Karen and Emmeline, both single women, the hotel bedroom offers a more private, sheltered space in which their affairs can exist, hidden from the gaze of others. The hotel bedroom figures across these novels as a space of potentialities in which individuals could and did transgress the codes and ideologies by which they are confined in everyday life.

Providing greater privacy and safety than the public street or park, and lacking the strict moral codes of the private domestic setting, the hotel bedroom instead exists in between the two spheres, offering a temporary no-man's-land, a seemingly lawless realm in which characters are aware of the possibility that they might transgress the strict moral boundaries of late-nineteenth- and early-twentieth-century British society. However, I have argued that the hotel bedroom is also often figured as a space used by male characters in their attempts to manipulate and coerce women into sex. As Wells's *Ann Veronica* and Rhys's *Voyage in the Dark* make clear, the hotel bedroom can, in its décor and furnishings, encapsulate Merleau-Ponty's notion of the 'atmosphere of humanity' that compels us into a particular mode of behaviour or action. Yet, as the examples from Wells, Rhys, and Eliot demonstrate, the success of this coercion is rarely inevitable, and the hotel bedroom can also be figured as a space of feminine sexual agency. That the hotel bedroom is so frequently used as a principal setting for romance and sexual transgression effectively foregrounds the impossibility of such behaviour outside the boundaries of the hotel bedroom through an explicit demonstration of the prohibitive nature of both public and private spaces. The palpable fear of discovery displayed by characters such as Karen in Bowen's *The House in Paris* confirms the threat of retribution present in public spaces for sexual misdeeds. The hotel bedroom thus functions as a crucial narrative space to think through and challenge the restrictions placed upon sexuality, and specifically female sexuality, during this period.

*   *   *

The hotel bedroom provides more of an insight into the intimacies of lived experience than any other space within the hotel. In novels of this period, it can provide what is perhaps the clearest indication of a character's socio-economic background or social status through its precise location, its décor, its furnishings, and its amenities. It is a space that is characterised primarily by transience and impermanence, and it is owing to these characteristics that the hotel bedroom so effectively lays bare precisely what is involved in the process inhabitation. It is through movement that we come to inhabit the space around us, and movement is inherent to the hotel bedroom—it is a space which characters like Miriam, Sydney, Sasha, and Karen move *through*. Yet it is also, crucially, a space of mobility, it is a space in which movement is, as Charlotte Mathieson notes, 'made meaningful through the interplay of subject, space and social relations' (2015, p. 13). Within the hotel bedroom a number of interactions and interplays take place, including social and sexual interactions between characters, and interactions between characters and the space itself. Just as significant, however, is the interplay that occurs within the hotel bedroom between movement, mobility, and the inhabitation of space. The hotel bedroom brings this web of relations to the fore, allowing authors writing in this period to interrogate the ways in which ideologies surrounding class, gender, race, and age come to bear on the capacity of the embodied subject to inhabit particular kinds of spaces.

The hotel bedroom also, in its figuration as a refuge, reveals the often threatening and destabilising nature of modernity for those subjects who find themselves scrutinised and marginalised on account of their class, gender, age, nationality, and/or sexuality. This notion of the hotel bedroom as a sanctuary is complicated, however, by the way in which it is frequently figured in British fiction of this period as a space of sexual coercion. Employing its connotations with illicit sexual behaviour to their advantage, male characters like Wells's Ramage and Rhys's Walter Jeffries use the space of the hotel bedroom in their attempts to manipulate and control women. However, these male attempts at sexual coercion in the hotel room can, as Ann Veronica and Anna demonstrate, be violently resisted, and I argue that this ability to resist comes from the potentialities of the hotel bedroom. These qualities are best exemplified by Miriam Henderson's experience of her hotel bedroom in Richardson's *Oberland*, whereby her dialogic relationship with this space rejuvenates and refreshes her, and offers her a vital freedom from the constraints of day-to-day existence. While the relationship between Wells's Ann Veronica and Rhys's Anna and the hotel bedrooms to which they are taken may not be anywhere near as positive (particularly as they have been taken to these rooms, rather than choosing them themselves), these are nevertheless still spaces which are not 'owned' by anyone, and which are thereby more neutral than the space of the home. Ramage and Walter may have paid for their respective hotel bedrooms, but the temporary nature of this ownership means that their authority in this space is less certain than it might be in their own home. Further, the not-quite-private nature of the hotel bedroom, and the constant presence of hotel staff beyond its walls, brings an element of safety to the hotel bedroom that is decidedly absent from the space of the home. Indeed, the threats made by both Ann Veronica and Anna to scream or, in Anna's case, 'make a hell of a row' are integral to their ability to extricate themselves from the potential danger (Rhys 1969 [1939], p. 20). While the hotel bedroom may be a complex and occasionally threatening space for women, it is, more than anything else, a space that affords them a level of agency and independence unlike that found anywhere else in modernity.

REFERENCES

Ahmed, Sara. 2006. *Queer Phenomenology: Orientations, Objects, Others*. Durham: Duke University Press.

Anon. 1860. *The Illustrated London News*, 17, July 7.

———. 1879. *Murray's Handbook to London As It Is*. London: John Murray.

———. 1895. Parisian Topics. *The Standard*, 5, Thursday, May 30.

———. 1908. *A Twentieth Century Palace: The Piccadilly Hotel*. London: The Piccadilly Hotel.

Baedeker, Karl. 1889. *Baedeker Guide to London and Its Environs*. London: Dulau & Co.

Beauvoir, Simone de. 2010 [1949]. *The Second Sex*. Translated by Constance Borde and Sheila Malovany-Chevalier. London: Vintage.

Bernard, Andreas. 2014. *Lifted: A Cultural History of the Elevator*. Translated by David Dollenmayer. New York: New York University Press.

Borish, Elaine. 1995. *Literary Lodgings: Historic Hotels in Britain Where Famous Writers Lived*. Boulder: Fidelio Press.

Bowen, Elizabeth. 1987 [1932]. *To the North*. London: Penguin.

———. 1998a [1938]. *The Death of the Heart*. London: Vintage.

———. 1998b [1935]. *The House in Paris*. London: Vintage.

———. 2003 [1927]. *The Hotel*. London: Vintage.

Bradbury, Malcolm. 1976. The Cities of Modernism. In *Modernism: A Guide to European Literature, 1890–1930*, ed. Malcolm Bradbury and James McFarlane, 96–104. London: Penguin.

Burdett, Charles, and Derek Duncan. 2002. Introduction. In *Cultural Encounters: European Travel Writing in the 1930s*, ed. Charles Burdett and Derek Duncan, 1–8. Oxford: Berghahn Books.

Carter, Oliver. 1990. *An Illustrated History of Railway Hotels, 1838–1983*. St Michael's: Silver Link Publishing.

Corcoran, Neil. 2004. *Elizabeth Bowen: The Enforced Return*. Oxford: Oxford University Press.

Cunningham, Anne. 2013. 'Get on or Get Out': Failure and Negative Femininity in Jean Rhys's *Voyage in the Dark*. *Modern Fiction Studies* 59 (2): 373–394.

Davidson, Joyce. 2003. *Phobic Geographies: The Phenomenology and Spatiality of Identity*. Aldershot: Ashgate.

Dennis, Richard. 2008. *Cities in Modernity: Representations and Productions of Metropolitan Space, 1840–1930.* Cambridge: Cambridge University Press.

Eliot, T.S. 1961 [1922]. *Selected Poems.* London: Faber and Faber.

Elkin, Lauren. 2016. The Room and the Street: Gwen John's and Jean Rhys's Insider/Outsider Modernism. *Women: A Cultural Review* 27 (3): 239–264.

Gan, Wendy. 2009. *Women, Privacy and Modernity in Early Twentieth-Century British Writing.* Basingstoke: Palgrave Macmillan.

George, Rosemary Marangoly. 1996. *The Politics of Home: Postcolonial Relocations and Twentieth-Century Fiction.* Cambridge: Cambridge University Press.

Grosz, Elizabeth. 1994. *Volatile Bodies: Toward a Corporeal Feminism.* Bloomington: Indiana University Press.

Harding, Desmond. 2003. *Writing the City: Urban Visions and Literary Modernism.* London: Routledge.

Jackson, Louise A. 2006. *Women Police: Gender, Welfare and Surveillance in the Twentieth Century.* Manchester: Manchester University Press.

Koestenbaum, Wayne. 1988. The Waste Land: T. S. Eliot's and Ezra Pound's Collaboration on Hysteria Winner of the 1988 TCL Prize in Literary Criticism. *Twentieth Century Literature* 34 (2): 113.

Kristeva, Julia. 1982. *Powers of Horror: An Essay on Abjection.* Translated by Leon S. Roudiez. New York: Columbia University Press.

Lefebvre, Henri. 1991. *The Production of Space.* Translated by Donald Nicholson-Smith. Oxford: Blackwell.

Madden, Ed. 2008. *Tiresian Poetics: Modernism, Sexuality, Voice, 1888–2001.* Madison: Fairleigh Dickinson University Press.

Mathieson, Charlotte. 2015. *Mobility in the Victorian Novel: Placing the Nation.* Basingstoke: Palgrave Macmillan.

McDonald, Gail. 2017. Gender and Sexuality. In *The New Cambridge Companion to T.S. Eliot*, ed. Jason Harding, 162–174. New York: Cambridge University Press.

Merleau-Ponty, Maurice. 2002 [1945]. *Phenomenology of Perception.* Translated by Colin Smith. Abingdon: Routledge.

Parsons, Deborah. 2000. *Streetwalking the Metropolis: Women, the City and Modernity.* Oxford: Oxford University Press.

Perloff, Marjorie. 1981. *The Poetics of Indeterminacy: Rimbaud to Cage.* Evanston: Northwestern University Press.

Rhys, Jean. 1969 [1934]. *Voyage in the Dark.* London: Penguin.

———. 1969 [1939]. *Good Morning, Midnight.* London: Penguin.

———. 1971 [1930]. *After Leaving Mr Mackenzie.* London: Penguin.

———. 2000 [1929]. *Quartet.* London: Penguin.

Rich, Rachel. 2011. *Bourgeois Consumption: Food, Space and Identity in London and Paris, 1850–1914.* Manchester: Manchester University Press.

Richardson, Dorothy. 1979a [1927]. *Oberland*. In *Pilgrimage*, 4 vols., IV, 9–127. London: Virago.

———. 1979b [1925]. *The Trap*. In *Pilgrimage*, 4 vols., III, 397–509. London: Virago.

Roessel, David. 1989. 'Mr Eugenides, the Smyrna Merchant,' and Post-War Politics in 'The Waste Land'. *Journal of Modern Literature* 16 (1): 171–176.

Rosner, Victoria. 2005. *Modernism and the Architecture of Private Life*. New York: Columbia University Press.

Sartre, Jean-Paul. 2003 [1943]. *Being and Nothingness: An Essay on Phenomenological Ontology*. Translated by Hazel E. Barnes. London: Routledge.

Snaith, Anna. 2005. A Savage from the Cannibal Islands: Jean Rhys and London. In *Geographies of Modernism: Literatures, Cultures, Spaces*, ed. Peter Brooker and Andrew Thacker, 76–85. Abingdon: Routledge.

Taylor, Derek, and David Bush. 1974. *The Golden Age of British Hotels*. London: Northwood.

Thacker, Andrew. 2003. *Moving Through Modernity: Space and Geography in Modernism*. Manchester: Manchester University Press.

———. 2012. Texts and Editions of Jean Rhys: Another Voyage in the Dark? *Women: A Cultural Review* 23 (4): 510–524.

van Lennep, D.J. 1987 [1969]. The Hotel Room. In *Phenomenological Psychology: The Dutch School*, ed. Joseph J. Kockelmans, 209–215. Dordrecht: Martinus Nijhoff.

Vidler, Anthony. 1993. The Explosion of Space: Architecture and the Filmic Imaginary. *Assemblage* 21: 44–59.

Weeks, Jeffrey. 1989. *Sex, Politics and Society: The Regulation of Sexuality Since 1800*. 2nd ed. Harlow: Longman.

Wells, H.G. 1943 [1909]. *Ann Veronica*. London: J.M. Dent & Sons.

———. 2005 [1905]. *Kipps*. Edited by Simon J. James. London: Penguin.

Whitworth, Michael, ed. 2007. *Modernism: Blackwell Guide to Criticism*. Oxford: Blackwell.

Wilson, Elizabeth. 1992. *The Sphinx in the City: Urban Life, the Control of Disorder, and Women*. Berkeley: University of California Press.

Young, Iris Marion. 2005. House and Home: Feminist Variations on a Theme. In *On Female Body Experience: 'Throwing Like a Girl' and Other Essays*, 123–154. Oxford: Oxford University Press.

CHAPTER 6

'The Bowels of the Hotel': The Laundry, Kitchen, and Back Areas

Behind the glamour and opulence of the grand hotel, or the comfort and convenience of a more modest establishment, lie those hidden areas accessible only to the hotel staff. The hotel, like the domestic sphere of nineteenth- and early-twentieth-century Britain, contains within it multiple types of spaces, rooms that are dedicated to any number of uses, from eating, sleeping, and conversing, to playing games and dancing. Yet there also exists within both the hotel and the home one very distinct division between the spaces of leisure and work. In the home, the spaces of leisure—the dining room, living and drawing rooms, and bedrooms— were occupied by the owners of the house and their family, while the spaces of work—primarily the kitchens—were occupied by their servants. Servants, as Alison Light points out, lived 'a parallel existence' to the families for whom they worked, '[r]elegated to the basements and the attics, using separate entrances and staircases [...], segregated in separate wings and outbuildings' (2008, p. 1). In the hotel, the same principle applies— while guests occupy the spaces of leisure, the spaces of work, more numerous and varied in the hotel than the home, are occupied solely by the hotel staff. Though the physical distance separating them may be minimal, the hotel of the guests and the hotel of the staff are two very different worlds.

 This final chapter turns from the public-facing spaces of the hotel toward those spaces that are concealed from view and occupied only by the hotel workers whose labour makes possible the leisure of their guests.

© The Author(s) 2019
E. Short, *Mobility and the Hotel in Modern Literature*,
Studies in Mobilities, Literature, and Culture,
https://doi.org/10.1007/978-3-030-22129-4_6

In a small hotel, these spaces are likely limited to a kitchen, an office or two, and possibly a dining room or mess hall for the few staff. In addition to this, there might well be concealed passageways, back staircases, and service lifts to aid staff in their navigations of the hotel. In larger hotels, not only are these hidden routes more extensive, but the number and type of staff areas inevitably increase to match the demands of its clientele. An 1895 article on the architecture of London's Hotel Cecil, for example (which, in 1900, boasted 1250 bedrooms), notes that 'the extent of the site made it quite impossible to have only one central kitchen', and that 'each block has, therefore, been provided with one or more' (Anon 1895, p. 33). As to the ideal location of staff areas, most architects favoured the basement of the hotel. In a lecture delivered to the Royal Association of British Architects in April 1907, Stanley Hamp (himself responsible, with partner Thomas Colcutt, for the remodelling of the Savoy Hotel Thames frontage in 1910) argued that, aside from the manager's office—which should be situated on the ground floor—'the kitchen department and offices; the staff dining-rooms; [and] servants hall' should be housed in the basement of a hotel (Anon 1907, p. 259). Frequently located below ground, the spaces occupied by the workers of the hotel existed at a marked remove from the guests they served.

Of all the spaces within the hotel, none have been more consistently overlooked and ignored in literature than those areas populated by its staff. On the one hand, the absence of such spaces from nineteenth- and twentieth-century fiction makes a degree of sense—the spaces that we, as readers, encounter in literature are, after all, typically those spaces that make up the known world of a narrative's central characters. But this in itself reveals a great deal about the subjects of literature during this period, or, more specifically, whose lives or stories were considered worth telling. In the modernist hotels of authors such as Woolf, Joyce, Rhys, and Bowen, the back areas and the staff who occupy them are fleetingly, if ever, mentioned. To embark on a search for the stories of kitchen staff, waiters, chambermaids, and porters is to repeatedly encounter a literary lacuna, one that is only really filled by the work of one author—Arnold Bennett. Published a year before his death, Bennett's *Imperial Palace* (1930) features the most detailed representation of the hotel back areas and of the staff that occupy them in literature, and as such this novel forms the primary focus of this chapter. Opening with a discussion that locates the hotel as a mainstay of nineteenth-century corporate capitalism, this chapter moves to consider the impact of this on employees through an analysis of the regimented staff areas found in Bennett's *Imperial Palace*. The focus of the second section shifts to an interrogation of the societal class structures that are replicated in miniature within the hotel staff hierarchies and a variety of ways in which the mobility of those staff at the bottom of such hierarchies is repeatedly restricted and curtailed.

'A Terrific and Ruthless Machine':[1] Managing the Profitable Hotel

While for its guests the hotel is typically a space of luxury and relaxation (although, as has been demonstrated throughout this book, this was by no means always the case), underpinning and facilitating the leisure and accommodation of its guests is the intricate structure of the hotel as a business. As observed in the Introduction, the hotel industry in Britain grew rapidly throughout the mid-to-late nineteenth century, a growth which saw a concomitant rise in the number of people employed in hotels, and in those venturing into the realm of hotel ownership and management. Towards the end of the nineteenth century, hotels represented for many a golden opportunity to make money, be that in the form of a living wage or a lucrative investment opportunity. The burgeoning hotel industry was thus inextricable from, and indeed formed a significant part of, what Paul Johnson refers to as 'the legislative, organisational and behavioural foundations of corporate capitalism which were laid in nineteenth-century Britain' (2010, p. 3). As Robbie Moore notes, '[h]otel history is entangled [...] with the history of corporate finance' (2012, p. 278). In its unique and complex structure, the hotel might well be read as a microcosm of those 'organisational and behavioural foundations of corporate capitalism' to which Johnson refers. Often owned by a frequently faceless company, hotels in the nineteenth century—and indeed still today—depended for their profit upon the satisfaction of their guests, and this in turn was dependent upon the effective management of services, staff, and space. More crucially, as novels such as Bennett's *Imperial Palace* make plain, such management took the form of the control and restriction of the movement and mobility of staff within the space of the hotel.

In part at least, the growth of the hotel industry during the nineteenth century was due to substantial changes in the law surrounding commercial organisations, and particularly to that concerning limited liability. In

---

[1] Arnold Bennett, *Imperial Palace* (London: Cassel & Co. [1930] 1969), p. 251.

essence, limited liability means 'that investors in a corporation are liable for no more than the amount they agree to invest' (Johnson 2010, p. 139). Johnson notes that,

> The most important institution of the modern market—the joint-stock limited liability company—was a disputed, legally suspect and morally dubious organisational form at the beginning of Victoria's reign, yet by the 1880s it had become the primary form of business organisation in Britain. In 1801, when the London Stock Exchange was founded, it was widely viewed as a locus for morally indefensible gambling, but by the end of the nineteenth century it had become the hub of a global investment market. (2010, p. 2)

Under the Bubble Act of 1720, companies not incorporated by Royal Charter or Act of Parliament were prevented from trading, and while this Act was repealed in 1825 due to the effect it had on British trade, the formation of companies and commercial organisations was still severely limited in terms of their size and the number of shareholders permitted, with a great deal of control exerted by the Crown and parliament. Exceptions to this were, as Derek Taylor notes, 'major industries such as canals and railways, which were specifically excluded by the government of the day because of their size' (1977, p. 1). As such, aside from individuals with significant private wealth, railway companies alone were able to raise the funds needed to build hotels, meaning that station hotels were the only kind to proliferate in the mid-nineteenth century. However, the Limited Liability Act of 1855 and the Companies Act of 1862 gave rise to the joint-stock limited-liability company, bringing together, as John Micklethwait and Adrian Wooldridge point out,

> the three big ideas behind the modern company: that it could be an 'artificial person,' with the same ability to do business as a real person; that it could issue tradeable shares to any number of investors; and that those investors could have limited liability (so they could lose only the money they had committed to the firm). (2005, p. 5)

Crucially, however, the 1862 Act meant that companies no longer had to limit their activities to, as Micklethwait and Wooldridge observe, 'a specific worthy aim (like building a railway between two cities)' (2005, p. 5). Rather, under the Act any group of at least seven people could set up a company for whatever purpose. This, combined with the unlimited number of investors, opened up the potential for hotel building and ownership to a much broader demographic, and did indeed lead to numerous new hotel companies being set up. The consequent substantial growth in and success of the hotel industry was further marked by the emergence of major new trade publications, such as *Caterer and Hotel Keeper* in 1878, and *The Hotel World* in 1882, evidencing the increasing significance of the hotel in late-nineteenth-century society.

The impact of these changes in corporate law—and in particular the introduction of limited liability—upon the hotel industry in Britain was, therefore, considerable. Yet even prior to these developments, commentators in the mid-nineteenth century had been calling for English hotels to be updated and brought in line with superior establishments on the continent and in America. An 1846 article in *Chambers's Edinburgh Journal*, for example, criticises the cramped facilities and poor service in English and Scottish hotels, comparing them unfavourably with hotels in Germany, Belgium, and Switzerland. Having given an account of the various ways in which continental hotels surpass those at home, the author stresses the need for 'the improvement of the inns in England and Scotland' and suggests that

> some enterprising men, having the command of large capital, [...] enter into the profession [...] with a view of extending to innkeeping the same improvement which has now been made in several other kinds of business, in which a small profit in each separate transaction, but large in the aggregate, from the great extent of the sale, is looked for, rather than a considerable profit on each of a few transactions. (Anon 1846, p. 190)

The language used here, that of 'transactions' and 'profit', 'aggregate' and 'sale', at once locates the hotel as a capitalist endeavour, and aims to entice those 'enterprising men' to invest their money in this line of business. With the advent of the Limited Liability Act of 1855, debates on the need for improvement to British hotels only increased in their urgency. Published in the same year as the aforementioned act, Albert Smith's pamphlet, *The English Hotel Nuisance*, criticises numerous aspects of British hotels, not least their typically high prices, whereby the accommodation that a guest is able to secure 'in return for his lavish expenditure is scarcely commensurate with the outlay' (Smith 1858, p. 12). For the lack of superior and more reasonably priced hotels in England, Smith notes that 'the excuse hitherto has been that the means of individuals are not sufficient to set an undertaking of this kind afoot' (1858, p. 14). However, citing the

Limited Liability Act of that same year, he argues that 'the recent alteration in the law of partnership will obviate every objection of this kind. There is no reason why a number of persons should not club their £1000 a-piece, place the affair under competent management, and command success' (Smith 1858, p. 14). In his call for the establishment of companies to build and oversee grand hotels, Smith was one of the first to recognise and articulate the potential contained within the Limited Liability Act for the future of the hotel industry in Britain.

The significance of the Limited Liability Act was referred to frequently in subsequent discussion of hotel development and reform throughout the latter half of the nineteenth century, though the initial positivity and hopefulness found in articles such as Smith's quickly dwindled. The potential that Smith had seen for the formation of hotel companies and the construction of grand hotels to rival those on the continent in America was indeed realised, but his modest projection of one or perhaps 'a dozen hotels of this kind' in London was almost immediately eclipsed (Smith 1858, p. 14). Instead, a mere decade after the publication of Smith's pamphlet, critics were writing of the rising number of 'monster hotels' in the capital and beyond. An 1866 article of the same name saw one of the first uses of the term 'monster hotels', and harked back directly to Smith's 'clever little book', noting that since its publication, 'English enterprise, whetted or encouraged by the "Limited Liability" Act, has been erecting in the capital and chief towns of our island structures like the "Charing Cross" [...], the Westminster Palace, the Langham, and the Grosvenor hotels' (Anon 1866, p. 689). But where previously commentators such as Smith had criticised the few London hotels in existence in the first half of the nineteenth century for their cramped conditions and unreasonable expense, it was now the spaciousness of these new 'monster hotels' that was cause for concern. An 1871 article in *The Sphinx* on the Crosier Hotel in Manchester acknowledged:

> Monster hotels, however gorgeously and elaborately got up, are not exactly the places where one may expect comfort. They partake too much of the character of a vast wilderness [...]. To our thinking it is the reverse of agreeable to have your bedroom several stories and corridors removed from the coffee-room [...]. Neither is going up to your bedroom in a hoist, whenever you may desire to visit that apartment, at all a pleasant alternative. (Anon 1871, p. 43)

For the author, the hotel guest in the newly built grand, or 'monster', hotels now suffered from an excess of space, which not only heightened the risk of fatigue due to the lengthy journey from bedroom to the public rooms (or indeed of injury, with the hotel lift characterised as a precarious 'hoist'), but which also impacted negatively on their emotional wellbeing. Referring to these new hotels as 'barrack-like', the article goes on to remark on their 'cold, freezing, and comfortless' atmosphere, and claims that the inevitable result will be a hotel guest who feels 'isolated, lonely, [and] dejected' (Anon 1871, p. 43). This 1871 article thus not only offers a phenomenological reflection on the potential alienation engendered by a hotel existence, but, perhaps unwittingly, reveals a distinct shortcoming of the capitalist ideology underpinning the grand hotel project, particularly during its infancy in the mid-to-late nineteenth century. The birth of the joint-stock limited-liability company enabled the development of hotels that far exceeded their predecessors in size and splendour, but with profit at the heart of this endeavour to fit in as many guests as possible in order to collect ever more revenue, the comfort of guests fell by the wayside seemingly all too easily.

The pitfalls of the Limited Liability Act upon the development of hotels were further discussed in an article of the following year on 'English Hotel Life', which acknowledges the impact of the act that, 'for good and evil, has immensely modified the character of English commercial transactions' (F.A. 1872, p. 256). Yet the author also makes the pertinent observation that this change in the law essentially made it possible for—and indeed encouraged—any group of individuals with the financial means to build and/or establish a hotel, and to therefore realise 'the tradesman's profits with something decidedly less than the tradesman's responsibilities' (F.A. 1872, p. 256). This was not, however, without its repercussions on the standard, and in particular on the management, of the resulting hotels:

Innkeeping was supposed to be a peculiarly prosperous business yielding immense returns. It became a famous investment, and limited-liability hotels arose on every side. Clergymen, country gentlemen, and spinster ladies, all became innkeepers so far as the taking of shares could make them such. But it soon became evident that you could not have the tradesman's profits, unless you also had his constant assiduity and keen interest in his daily takings. (F.A. 1872, pp. 256–7)

This extract gives some idea of the sheer extent of hotel development in the years following the Limited Liability Act of 1855, and the Companies Act of 1862, which, by the time this article was published, amounted to little more than a decade. Again, however, this author locates the drive for profit as being key to the lack of success enjoyed by many of these hotels, though in this instance it is the hotel management, rather than an excess of space, that is to blame. By necessity, hotel companies employed managers to oversee the running of their establishment, but these managers were, the author maintains, too often not invested enough in the success of the hotel, given that they had no stake or share in it themselves. This lack of enthusiasm frequently resulted in a lack of motivation in the staff who 'seemed to know that the manager's eyes, unquickened by the intense responsibility of a personal venture, had not its wonted terror and command' (F.A. 1872, p. 257). While hotels could, thanks to nineteenth-century changes in corporate law, be potentially very profitable ventures, contemporary commentary suggests that too much of a drive for profit, in the areas of hotel space and management at least, often in fact had the opposite result.

The manager of the hotel was, as the aforementioned article demonstrates, key to the success or failure of the establishment, and thus needed to be invested wholeheartedly in this endeavour. Whether they had been appointed by a hotel company or (more rarely due to the capital required) owned the hotel themselves, the hotel manager was the highest point of authority visible to guests. As such a presence, hotel managers frequently appear in literature of the mid-nineteenth and early twentieth centuries, though, barring a few exceptions, the role they play is typically small and often seemingly insignificant. In Virginia Woolf's *The Voyage Out* (1915), for example, Signor Rodriguez, the manager of the unnamed hotel in Santa Marina is mentioned a mere three times throughout the novel. In his first appearance, Rodriguez is shown standing in the doorway of the hotel lounge, 'surveying the scene' and 'congratulating himself' upon turning the old refectory of the hotel (itself a former monastery) into a lounge, and, watching the crowds of guests populating the space, reflecting upon the success of this enterprise (Woolf 2009 [1915], p. 110). Here, Rodriguez is located explicitly as being primarily invested in the business of the hotel, with his main concern being to increase the number of guests in the hotel, and to retain them while they are there. As is the case with Rodriguez, the hotel manager is perhaps most frequently depicted as a figure focused primarily on the profit and success of the hotel of which they are in charge.

In May Sinclair's *Kitty Tailleur* (1908), the manager of the Cliff Hotel is characterised as someone for whom profit and financial gain trump all other concerns. He appears only once in the novel in discussion with his wife as to whether or not Kitty Tailleur should be asked to leave the hotel on the basis of rumours regarding the suspected immorality of her past. While 'the manager's wife was for turning Mrs. Tailleur out on the bare suspicion of her impropriety', insistent that 'there should be no suspicion as to the reputation of the Cliff Hotel', the manager himself is reluctant to ask a paying guest to leave (Sinclair 1908, p. 131). Reflecting that 'the scandal of the ejection would be more damaging to the hotel than [Mrs. Tailleur's] present transparently innocent and peaceful occupation of the best room in it', the manager is concerned above all else with filling rooms and keeping them filled (Sinclair 1908, pp. 131–2). Occupying the best and therefore most expensive room, Kitty is thus the hotel's highest pay-ing guest, and for the hotel manager, whose 'intelligence was concen-trated in the small commercial eye which winked, absurdly, in the solitude of his solemn and enormous face', her custom is too valuable to risk on what amounts to little more than hearsay (Sinclair 1908, p. 132). Without concrete evidence, and 'in the absence of complaints, he didn't consider the question a profitable one for a manager to go into in the slack season' (Sinclair 1908, p. 132). In his sole appearance in the novel, the manager of the Cliff Hotel is characterised through the language of commerce and profit, locating him as a businessman driven by the capitalist ideology of the late nineteenth and early twentieth centuries that underpinned the hotel industry.

Nowhere in literature is this business of hotel management explored in more depth, however, than in Bennett's final work, *Imperial Palace*, which was published in 1930, a year before the author's death from typhoid. Like its early predecessor, *The Grand Babylon Hotel*, the inspiration for *Imperial Palace* was London's Savoy Hotel, an establishment at which Bennett himself frequently dined and stayed (indeed, he wrote the entire manuscript for *Imperial Palace* while staying at the hotel), and which famously created the Omelette Arnold Bennett in his honour.[2] Yet while *The Grand Babylon Hotel* was an adventure-filled crime novel of mystery and suspense, *Imperial Palace* is a far slower and more sedate affair, which follows the managing director of the hotel, Evelyn Orcham, in his daily

---

[2] The main ingredients of the Omelette Arnold Bennett are eggs, cheese, and smoked haddock.

running of the establishment. The plot of *Imperial Palace* very loosely charts the romance and eventual engagement of Evelyn and Violet Powler, staff manageress of the hotel's laundry room who rises through the ranks to become head-housekeeper. More accurately, however, the novel is a fictionalised account of the intricacies involved in the day-to-day operation of a grand hotel from the perspective of its managing director and staff. As noted in the introduction to this chapter, in his focus on the workings of the hotel, and in particular on its staff, Bennett is somewhat unique amongst authors of the late nineteenth and early twentieth centuries. Far more typical are novels that focus almost entirely on the experiences of hotel guests, showing minimal—if any—concern for the staff and the spaces they occupy. Even Bowen's *The Hotel,* rare in being set almost entirely within a hotel, contains only three references to the manager of the eponymous establishment, and these occur only in the discussions of guests, with the manager never once appearing directly.

In *Imperial Palace,* however, the staff, the systems of hotel management, and the back areas of the hotel take centre stage. Bennett dedicated the novel to and modelled its protagonist, Evelyn Orcham, on Sir George Reeves-Smith (1863–1941), a renowned hotelier who was the managing director of the Savoy Company from 1900 until his death in 1941. Bennett's portrayal of Evelyn as fastidious, focused, and skilled in his approach to managing the Imperial Palace Hotel tallies with accounts of the management style of Reeves-Smith which was, according to the *Oxford Dictionary of National Biography,* 'precise, for he was aware of the slightest derogation from high standards of housekeeping or service; yet he was innovative and capable of masterly delegation. [...] he had a shrewd business appreciation of practical detail and people's taste in leisure activities'.[3] The qualities attributed to Reeves-Smith, and immortalised by Bennett in Evelyn Orcham, encapsulate the spirit of capitalist endeavour that characterised the British hotel industry in the late nineteenth and early twentieth centuries. As managing director, Evelyn's role exists between the hotel and its board of directors as 'the medium of communication' between the two, and his dedication to his job is driven by a passion for the processes of running a large hotel, and for the authority it affords him, 'exult[ing] in the exercise of the function of management' (Bennett 1969 [1930], p. 47). In its grandeur and in its commercial stature, the Imperial Palace is

---

[3] 'Sir George Reeves-Smith', *Oxford Dictionary of National Biography* (2004). Available at: https://doi.org/10.1093/ref:odnb/37887 (accessed: 10 July 2018).

a 'religion' for its staff, and particularly for its department heads, the hotel's 'high-Priests' who are imbued, by Evelyn—'their God'—with 'the corporate spirit' (Bennett 1969 [1930], p. 50). The theological language here speaks not only to the devotion to profit and financial gain that is characteristic of capitalism, but also hints at the all-encompassing nature of the grand hotel as an organisation—a self-contained universe which replicates the outside world, and in particular its class hierarchies, in miniature.

The extent of this universe, and the precise nature of the hotel as a business and the practicalities of running it, does, of course, vary significantly depending on the size of the establishment in question. In a small hotel, such as, for example, those Parisian hotels found in the early novels of Jean Rhys, fewer rooms require minimal staff, with perhaps only one or two chambermaids employed throughout. In such establishments, the manager, or in the case of Rhys's hotels, the *patronne*, is occupied less by the management of staff, and is thus more focused on the guests themselves, leading in many instances to an increased level of surveillance of the guests' activities.[4] At the other end of the scale are the grand literary hotels, immense in size, such as the Royal Grand Hotel in H.G. Wells's *Kipps*, and Bennett's Grand Babylon Hotel and Imperial Palace. Of these, Bennett's Imperial Palace is perhaps the largest, at the very least in terms of the size of its workforce. The precise spatial dimensions of the hotel itself are never given, and there are instead only brief allusions to its eight floors, with over forty rooms on each, not including the laundry room and the 'bowels of the hotel' (Bennett 1969 [1930], p. 215). However, Evelyn proudly informs Gracie Savott— an American guest at the hotel whose millionaire father is interested in purchasing the Imperial Palace—of just how many staff work for the hotel: 'Thirteen hundred of 'em, not counting the Laundry and the works department' (Bennett 1969 [1930], p. 33). That the size of the Imperial Palace is denoted according to the number of its employees rather than by the number of guest rooms is significant. In its emphasis on staff rather than guests, the novel reveals a commitment to the voices of workers—and specifically of workers in the service industry—that are so often overlooked in nineteenth- and early-twentieth-century literature.[5]

---

[4] See Chap. 3 for further discussion of the surveillance of guests by hotel management.

[5] Although, as discussed later in this chapter, it is primarily those in positions of authority that are afforded a voice in Bennett's novel, meaning that it does not escape entirely from the class hierarchies that so firmly shaped late nineteenth and early twentieth-century Britain.

Throughout Bennett's *Imperial Palace*, the spaces within the hotel that are brought into the most detailed focus are those occupied by its staff. While the number and layout of guest rooms may not be afforded any importance, the novel pays close attention to those back areas of the hotel that usually remain unseen by the public, and which are typically omitted from fictional hotels elsewhere in this period. Fleeting descriptions of these areas can occasionally be found in novels such as Woolf's *The Voyage Out*, which affords one sentence to 'the kitchen, where they were washing up; white cooks were dipping their arms into cauldrons, while the waiters made their meal voraciously off broken meats, sopping up the gravy with bits of crumb' (Woolf 2009 [1915], p. 109). This brief account appears in a longer section in which Rachel Vinrace and her aunt, Helen Ambrose, crouch outside the hotel in Santa Marina, peering in at the windows of the ground floor rooms. That the kitchen is the only back area featured here is unsurprising, given the immediate nature of the responses from within this space to the needs of the guests, and its proximity to the dining room.[6] In terms of the unseen staff areas of the hotel, the kitchen is perhaps that which is most readily called to mind by the guests whose nourishment depends on it—as Molly Berger points out, while the kitchen 'may have been invisible to guests [it] was key to their satisfaction' (2011, p. 192). In Bennett's *Imperial Palace*, the extensive kitchens are the only back areas to be shown to a guest after Gracie Savott (daughter of millionaire Sir Henry and engaged in a brief affair with Hotel Director Evelyn) requests a tour of them during dinner with Evelyn and her father, asking 'couldn't we just go and see the kitchens? I've never seen a hotel kitchen' (Bennett 1969 [1930], p. 98). Her eagerness to see a real 'hotel kitchen', rather than the hotel laundry or any of the other numerous other back areas of the Imperial Palace, suggests that she regards (and is likely only aware or conscious of) this space and this space alone as integral to the

---

[6] Although, as Molly Berger points out, to have the kitchen located near or next to the hotel dining room was, at least in America, a development that only occurred in the early twentieth century. Prior to this, she notes, architects had typically 'placed the kitchen in the hotel's upper basement level, connected to the dining room floors by dumbwaiters, conveyors, and staircases. However, in 1910, the *Hotel Monthly* published a plan for Chicago's Blackstone Hotel that situated the kitchen adjacent to the main dining areas, a move considered to be a "daring departure."' See: Molly W. Berger, *Hotel Dreams: Luxury, Technology, and Urban Ambition in America, 1829–1929* (Baltimore: The Johns Hopkins University Press, 2011), p. 193.

hotel, and as that in which the most important work takes place. The ensuing tour of the kitchens becomes, unsurprisingly in a novel that is primarily
concerned with giving voice to the hotel staff rather than its guests, a
moment in which the privileges of the wealthy and leisured classes are
exposed and interrogated.

From the outset, Gracie's voyeuristic desire to be shown the hotel
kitchens is marked as frivolous by her youthful language, peppered with
slang such as 'sweetie' and 'crazy' (the latter of which is, she admits, a
'reminiscence of New York', the city in which she has spent much of her
life), and by Evelyn's somewhat cynical mental responses to this as he
'repeated' her phrases 'in his mind' (Bennett 1969 [1930], p. 98). As the
group enter the 'different world' of the kitchens, the 'world of frenzied
industry' and 'of racket', the 'shock of [...] the transition from indolent
luxury to feverish labour, was shown in Gracie's features' (Bennett 1969
[1930], p. 99). The division between the upper and working classes is reified in the passageway between the restaurant and the kitchens, the 'open
door, hidden like a guilty secret', and the 'very short corridor' beyond are
here a physical manifestation of the boundary between the classes. Having
crossed this boundary, Gracie's shock and her subsequent 'childlike'
request to witness the creation of her soufflé suggest an inherent ignorance regarding the origin of her culinary luxuries, and an ignorance of
'the realities of cooking' (Bennett 1969 [1930], pp. 99, 103). However,
by virtue of the narrative focalisation through Evelyn, the novel does not
offer a straightforward critique of Gracie. The sexual attraction Evelyn
feels towards Gracie colours his perspective, as he strives to render her a
naive young girl open and vulnerable to his advances, and his attitude
towards her is further shaped by his cynicism regarding the 'indolence' of
her upper-class background. Dismissive of her lack of knowledge and
experience, Evelyn's efforts at seduction effectively involve a reduction of
Gracie's personality, intelligence, and moral worth.

Yet after her initial shock, Gracie's response to 'the world of frenzied
industry' that is the hotel kitchen repeatedly confounds Evelyn's attempts
to undermine her. As he watches her make her way through the kitchens,
he attempts to read 'the changing expressions on Gracie's face', but finds
that he 'could not' (Bennett 1969 [1930], p. 102). Resistant to the pen-
etration of his gaze, Gracie instead 'confront[s]' Evelyn 'with a swift
movement', 'dazzling' him 'on the edge of his field of vision' (Bennett
1969 [1930], p. 103). Unable to catch sight of her, Evelyn is instead compelled to listen to her exclamation, 'I must *work!*' and her confession that

'This place makes me ashamed. Ashamed. I wish I could put a pinafore on, and work here, with all these men, instead of going back to that awful restaurant full of greedy rotters' (Bennett 1969 [1930], p. 103). In her evasion of his eye, Gracie momentarily escapes Evelyn's sexual objectification of her, affording her an opportunity to convey more directly her reaction to the space of the kitchens, a reaction that leaves Evelyn 'staggered' (Bennett 1969 [1930], p. 103). For rather than putting her off her food, as Evelyn 'half-expected' it would (Bennett 1969 [1930], p. 102), her traversal of the boundary between the luxury of the dining room and the world of industry contained within the kitchen in fact triggers within Gracie an affective response that is loaded with shame. Her physical movement between these two spaces marks a metaphorical one from the world of the upper class into that of the working class, resulting in a powerful sense of being out of place.

In its depiction of Gracie's consequent shame, this scene in the kitchens of the Imperial Palace Hotel is an inverse mirroring of that in Wells's *Kipps* (published twenty-five years prior to Bennett's *Imperial Palace* in 1905), in which the eponymous protagonist breaks down under the perceived scrutiny and judgement of his fellow diners and the waiting staff in the dining room of the Royal Grand Hotel.[7] As a lower middle-class man, Kipps is unable to feel at ease in the hotel dining room populated by the middle and upper classes, and as a wealthy member of the upper class, Gracie is similarly uncomfortable in the working environment of the hotel kitchen. But while the sensation of being out of place inspires in both characters feelings of shame, there are marked differences in their subsequent reactions to these feelings. Where Kipps stubbornly refuses to acknowledge his embarrassment, instead leaving the hotel dining room in an attempt at 'a dignified withdrawal' (Wells 2005 [1905], p. 243), Gracie clearly articulates her shame and its origins, acknowledging to Evelyn her disgust at what she now sees as an 'awful' and 'greedy' upper-class society. Her ability to publicly acknowledge her shame is linked to her gender, as the affective practice of articulating and displaying her emotions is aligned with early-twentieth-century ideals of femininity. Kipps, on the other hand, must attempt to embody the reserved stoicism and lack of emotion that was acceptable for men of the same period. Yet more crucially, the opposing reactions of Gracie and Kipps are bound up in questions of privilege and power. As a wealthy member of the upper class, Gracie risks nothing

[7] See Chap. 4 for a full discussion of this scene.

by making her feelings known, and indeed only gains further admiration from Evelyn and the head chef, Maître Planquet, both of whom, as working men, are situated below her in the class hierarchy. Kipps, however, does not have the option of voicing his feelings of shame and embarrassment to his fellow diners, as to do so would likely only lead to further and more explicit ridicule from those of a higher class position. In his reading of *Kipps*, Richard Higgins maintains that shame is a 'class-coded emotion' (2008, p. 459), though Bennett's novel complicates, to an extent, the suggestion that it is an emotion felt exclusively by the lower classes. However, through their interrogation of the public and private areas of the hotel, of the spaces of leisure and work, both novels ultimately reaffirm that the open acknowledgement and articulation of shame is an affective practice available only to those with the privilege of the middle and upper classes.

Gracie Savott's epiphanic experience in the kitchens of the Imperial Palace Hotel reveals the capacity of hotel back areas to engender moments of critical self-reflection in the middle- or upper-class hotel guest. Yet in Bennett's *Imperial Palace*, such moments are in fact fleeting and relatively rare, as the prioritisation of these non-public spaces over those inhabited by guests instead more typically emphasises the novel's concern with those who work in the hotel. The detailed depiction of the back areas of the Imperial Palace Hotel plays a key role in the characterisation of its staff, as well as in the novel's exploration of the hierarchical structure of hotel management, and particularly of the hidden workings of the hotel. Descriptions of the hotel laundry (located off-site) and, in particular, of the various departments located in the basement of the hotel, depict the Imperial Palace as an enormous machine, whose function depends upon the labour of hundreds of members of staff. The motif of mechanisation is one that develops in significance as the novel progresses, and is initiated in a discussion between Sir Henry Savott and Evelyn concerning the implications of the burgeoning 'new consumerism' of interwar Britain.[8] Described by Peter Gurney as 'a quantitatively and qualitatively distinct phase in the development of modern consumer capitalism', new consumerism was characterised as a period of 'buoyant consumer demand among those fortunate enough to be in work' (2012, p. 905). Like the nineteenth-century foundations of

---

[8] For further discussion of the rise in mass consumerism during this period, often referred to as the 'new consumerism', see: Sue Bowden, 'The New Consumerism', in *Twentieth-Century Britain: Economic, Social, and Cultural Change*, ed. Paul Johnson (London: Longman, 1994), pp. 242–262.

corporate capitalism from which it emerged, the impact of new consumerism was felt powerfully in the hotel industry, as the drive for profit, together with the escalating demands of guests, positioned them increasingly as consumers of the products and services offered by the hotel. In its detailed appraisal of the capitalist machinations that underpin the Imperial Palace Hotel, and particularly in its interrogation of the trend for corporate hotel mergers, Bennett's novel can in one way be read as a critique of the hotel's position at the forefront of the rise in consumer culture.

This critique is nowhere more apparent than in the aforementioned conversation between Sir Henry and Evelyn. As a millionaire businessman, Sir Henry's interests lie in the profits to be made from consumerism, and in the mass production that enables these profits to inflate. A true capitalist, industrialisation delights him, despite the catastrophic effects that it had on the lives of the working classes. As he explains to Evelyn, 'the soul-destroying monotony of organised labour' that resulted from the spread of mechanisation is merely 'part of the penalty of [the] cheap prices' enjoyed by those same workers (Bennett 1969 [1930], p. 167). Yet, while Sir Henry initially presents mechanical mass production as beneficial to 'the under-dog' whose 'purchasing power' is raised by the cheap prices occasioned by modern processes of mass production, this mask soon slips to reveal a far more ruthless attitude towards the livelihood of that same underdog. Calling for '[m]ore mass-production! And—more machinery!', Sir Henry moves from rationalising such developments on the underdog's behalf to callously acknowledging that 'machinery may at last put an end to the under-dog. It may wipe him off the earth by throwing him out of work. Well, somebody has to suffer. Anyhow, when he's dead he isn't an under-dog' (Bennett 1969 [1930], p. 167). Directing his argument towards the hotel, he refers to the glass and dishwashing machinery in use in larger establishments, telling Evelyn, 'with some excitement', that the 'miserable bottle-washers' replaced by such machines 'may have died of starvation, and their families with them', but that is 'all to the good. [...] There is a chance that mass-production and machinery will abolish the under-dog' (Bennett 1969 [1930], p. 168). Sir Henry's sentiments here represent the very apex of capitalism—as Karl Marx observed as early as 1867 in *Capital*, 'the capitalistic application of machinery' is not to lighten the load of the worker, but is instead 'intended to cheapen commodities [...]. In short, it is a means for producing surplus-value' (1909 [1867], p. 405). In his eagerness to supplant the labouring classes with machines in the sole interests of mass production and profit, Sir Henry embodies the very worst and cruellest aspects of capitalism and new consumerism.

As director of the Imperial Palace Hotel, with shares in the establishment and a seat on the board of directors, however, Evelyn's own position
on this question of mass production and consumption is by no means clear
cut, though he is depicted as being somewhat conflicted on the matter.
His unparalleled knowledge of and familiarity with every aspect of the
hotel means that he is well aware of the hierarchies in operation that range
from the wealthiest guests to the lowliest workers. As he tells Sir Henry,
'in a place like this you get some very melodramatic contrasts [...] when I
think for instance of you in your suite, or me here, and then of some of the
fellows and girls down in the basements, I get a sort of a notion that something must be wrong somewhere' (Bennett 1969 [1930], p. 167). His
uneasiness with the inequality that lies at the heart of the hotel originates
in part from his loyalty to his staff and his concern for their wellbeing, but
also from his own class background. As a man who has likely worked his
way up to his position as managing director,[9] Evelyn does not belong to
Sir Henry's upper-class world of the wealthy elite, and is as such attuned
and sympathetic to 'the plight of the under-dog'. Yet despite his protesta-
tions regarding this imbalance inherent to the hotel, Evelyn is nevertheless
responsible for maintaining the hierarchical structure on which it rests.
And despite initially balking at Sir Henry's desire for manual labour to be
outmoded, he is himself guilty of wishing, on occasion, for the compliance
of machines over the potential insubordination of his employees. Faced
with a missing housekeeper in the latter stages of the novel, for example,
Evelyn questions why 'hotel-employees [were] so cursedly human' and
reflects that '[t]he ideal was robots, mechanical, bloodless, tireless, without bowels and without human ties' (Bennett 1969 [1930], pp. 545–6).
In his (albeit fleeting) desire for the simplicity of machines over the human
complexity of his employees, Evelyn is himself complicit in a capitalist
system that prioritises profit over people.

   Alongside the machines referred to by Sir Henry, and those located in
the basement or 'bowels' of the hotel, around which Violet Powler—newly
appointed from the hotel laundry to the position of housekeeper—is given
a tour by Evelyn, metaphors of mechanisation abound throughout the

---

[9]While a detailed history of Evelyn Orcham's own background is not provided in the
novel, given that the character is based on hotelier George Reeves-Smith, it is safe to assume
that, like Reeves-Smith, who, according to the Oxford Dictionary of National Biography,
'was apprenticed to Bordeaux wine merchants, Jean Calvert & Co., before training in the
hotel industry', Evelyn worked his way up to his position via a similar route. See: 'Sir George
Reeves-Smith', *Oxford Dictionary of National Biography* (2004). Available at: https://doi.
org/10.1093/ref:odnb/37887 (accessed: 6 August 2018).

novel. That such imagery is most prevalent in those moments of the narrative focalised through Violet is significant, as these instances provide a hotel worker's perspective that reinforces the novel's critique of class hierarchies within the hotel. Having witnessed such sights in the basement as the engine room, with its 'clumps of machinery here and there, some moveless, some whizzing, clicking, sizzling', Violet soon comes to regard the hotel itself as one large machine (Bennett 1969 [1930], p. 222). On the first day of her new role as housekeeper, she remembers that she 'had meant to enquire from Beatrice', a chambermaid, 'about the machinery for getting flowers' (Bennett 1969 [1930], p. 235). Later, she is 'impressed by the reckless grandeur of the domestic machine' when she learns the ease with which she will be able to replace a ruined bedroom carpet, as 'every carpet in the Palace had its exact duplicate, in size and shape, at the Works Department in Craven Street' (Bennett 1969 [1930], p. 256). However, that same 'reckless grandeur' that spares no expense to ensure the comfort of its guests too often does not extend to the comfort or wellbeing of the hotel staff, as they themselves are subsumed into the machinery of the hotel. Pre-empting Evelyn's later thoughts about the inconvenient humanity of his staff, Violet's treatment as a member of staff in the hotel instils in her the idea that she is 'helplessly involved in a terrific and ruthless machine' (Bennett 1969 [1930], p. 251). The abrupt and unexplained instruction to move floors within days of starting her role as housekeeper on the eighth floor makes Violet feel undervalued: 'You weren't a human being. You were a robot. You had to exercise judgment, tact, take responsibilities, be smart, powder your face. But you were a robot' (Bennett 1969 [1930], p. 251). In this moment, the vast machine that is the hotel, with its anonymous operators and rigid structures of authority, overtakes and encompasses the hotel worker, and Violet is absorbed into its mechanics.

Bennett was certainly not alone in his employment of metaphors of machinery and automata to explore the human condition. Indeed, by 1930 there were numerous examples in literature of characters undergoing this same blurring of the lines between human and machine, from Mr Verloc in Joseph Conrad's *The Secret Agent* (1907), who obeyed his wife 'woodenly, stony-eyed, and like an automaton whose face had been painted red' (Conrad 2004 [1907], p. 144) to T.S. Eliot's typist in *The Waste Land* (1922), who 'smoothes her hair with automatic hand' (Eliot 1971 [1922], l. 225). Other examples are to be found in non-fiction writings of the late nineteenth and early twentieth centuries—in his 1901 work *Anticipations*, for example, Wells refers to the labouring class in precisely these terms, noting that this class 'has been, in fact—and to some extent still is—the multitudinous living machinery of the old social order; it carried, cropped, tilled, built, and made' (Wells 1902, p. 67). Most pertinent of all to Violet's experience, however, is Marx's discussion of the role of the machine in a capitalist society, and its impact upon the worker. Referring to machinery as 'the material embodiment of capital' (Marx 1909 [1867], p. 467), he argues that the worker becomes 'its mere living appendage' (Marx 1909 [1867], p. 462). Violet's sense that she is no longer human is due in part to the repetitive nature of her work as a housekeeper, and to the expectation that she will respond to orders as readily and unquestioningly as a cog to the switch of a lever. As a 'robot', she is not only one more part of the machinery of the hotel, but she is a commodity, an instrument of service to be bought and used. The impact of the back areas of the hotel—in the basement of which she witnesses the actual machines powering the hotel—and the endless corridors of her labour can be clearly traced upon her embodied subjectivity through this experience of mechanisation. The constrained nature of Violet's mobility within these spaces further contributes to her feelings of dehumanisation, as these feelings are triggered not simply by her movement between floors, but more specifically by her lack of choice in this movement. Her mobility is dictated and inhibited by what she calls 'the mysterious powers downstairs', the management who, like the enormous engine in the basement, drive the hotel forward in the interests of profit for its corporate shareholders.

The changes to corporate law that were implemented in the mid-nineteenth century played no small part in the subsequent boom in the hotel industry since referred to as 'the golden age of British hotels' (Taylor and Bush 1974), and situated the hotel at the forefront of capitalist endeavour for those wishing to make easy profit from their investments. For its guests, the hotel may well have been a space of leisure, but for its owners and shareholders, this leisure was a valuable commodity, albeit one which was almost entirely dependent upon the labour of the hotel staff. While these staff and their labour are largely overlooked in literature of the nineteenth and early twentieth centuries, novels such as Bennett's *Imperial Palace* attempt to provide an insight into their experiences. Through the greed and ruthlessness of characters like Sir Henry Savott, the novel interrogates the capitalist ideology upon which the hotel—and particularly the grand hotel—is built. The novel's prioritisation of the experiences of characters such as housekeeper Violet Powler, and its exploration of the impact

of the systems and spaces of hotel management upon her embodied subjectivity, adds to this critique of an industry driven by profit with little
regard for the human cost. However, the distinction between those who
own hotels and those who work in them is a broad one at best, and the
hierarchies of staff within the hotel are as extensive as, and often more
rigidly reinforced than, the class hierarchies in the world outside. As the
following section will show, even novels like Bennett's, which give voice to
a range of hotel workers like Violet, tend to neglect those who were
employed to carry out more menial labour and thus effectively reinforce
the hierarchies of class that they apparently seek to overcome.

The World in Miniature: Hierarchies in the Hotel

The success of a hotel has always been dependent on its ability to attract
guests, but this ability is in turn dependent on the quality and effective
management of its staff. Hotels, and in particular the grand hotels of the
late nineteenth and early twentieth centuries were, as A.K. Sandoval-Strausz
notes, 'sophisticated hospitality machines' (2007, p. 142), and the smooth
operation of these machines rested on the efficiency of members of staff
whose numbers could, in the case of very large hotels, extend into the
hundreds. As an 1882 editorial in *The Hotel World* pointed out, staff numbers were often so great that, 'in a large hotel the service department is an
establishment of itself, totally apart from the rest of the business, and
requiring as much consideration as any other item in managerial duties'
(Anon 1882, p. 4). These service departments could encompass a huge
breadth and variety of roles, as many grand hotels possessed their 'own
laundry, bakery, and many other departments where special labour [wa]s
required' (Anon 1882, p. 4). This variety in the types of employment
within the hotel, however, inevitably meant that not all staff were treated,
or paid, equally, and in fact hotel employees were organised according to
a hierarchical structure based on a range of factors. More often than not,
an individual's class, gender, and nationality tended to dictate their role
and experience within the hotel as a member of staff. Just as the hotel can,
as argued in this chapter's opening section, be read as a microcosm of the
structures of corporate capitalism, so can it be understood, by the same
token, as a microcosm of the social hierarchies of the late nineteenth and
early twentieth centuries.

While the focus of Bennett's *Imperial Palace* is upon the staff of the
hotel as opposed to its guests, the voices of the workers that feature

throughout the novel nevertheless belong predominantly to those in positions of authority. Even Violet Powler, who provides the novel's most sustained and rounded characterisation of a hotel worker, is a figure of some authority from the outset, being first introduced as the staff-manageress in the hotel laundry, before she is appointed housekeeper (in charge of chambermaids), and then quickly assuming the role of head housekeeper when the former head housekeeper, Miss Maclaren, is taken ill.[10] With the occasional exception of a figure such as Beatrice Noakes, 'the fat chambermaid on Eighth' (Bennett 1969 [1930], p. 321) included seemingly for light comic relief, only heads of department—those with authority over others—are afforded a voice and an identity. Much like domestic servants, their counterparts who form, as Alison Light points out, 'the greatest part of that already silent majority—the labouring poor', those staff whose labour was so essential to the running of a hotel are typically unknown and unheard (2008, p. 1). Those carrying out such menial labour have, Light argues, 'for so long lived in the twilight zone of historical record. Their voices are rarely heard and their features seldom distinguished' (2008, p. 1). Existing at the very edges of history, the documentation of individual hotel workers is patchy at best, thanks in part to their servant status, and in part to the inherently transient nature of hotel work, in which demand was often subject to seasonal fluctuations. For those in positions of relative authority within the hotel, such as housekeepers and clerks, the historical record is often more substantial. Minnie E. Albery, for example, worked in hotels for most of her life, with census records revealing that in 1881, by the age of twenty-five, she had already secured a position as a housekeeper in the West Cliff Hotel on Sandgate Road in Folkestone.[11] By 1891, she was working as a hotel clerk at the Lord Warden Hotel in Dover, but by 1901 she had returned to Sandgate

---

[10] Violet's own background is arguably significant here. As 'the daughter of a town-traveller in tinned comestibles', she occupies a class position markedly above that of the labouring class (Bennett 1969 [1930], p. 64).

[11] The previous record of 1871 documents Minnie, then aged 15, as living at home with her family. Her background is very similar to that of Bennett's Violet Powler—her father, Mark Albery, ran a stationer's/newsagent's shop, meaning that the family's finances would have been relatively comfortable, and that Minnie would likely not have been sent out to work at an early age. In terms of mobility, while Minnie remained in the South of England, she had nevertheless travelled the distance of 85 miles from her family home in Horsham, Sussex, to the West Cliff Hotel in Folkestone, Kent. The West Cliff Hotel opened in July 1861.

Road in Folkestone, ten miles away, to work as a housekeeper in the Bates's Hotel. She remained at the Bates's Hotel for at least another ten years, listed in the 1911 census as housekeeper, and her appearance in the record just below the names of the proprietors—George and Mary Pilcher—and just above that of the hotel clerk gives some sense of the importance of her position. However, many of those hotel workers employed in lower positions—such as boots, kitchenmaids, and chambermaids—are often much more difficult to follow, frequently appearing on one census and then disappearing from trace. The 1881 census gives details, for example, of workers such as Fanny Wilson, aged twenty, who worked as a general servant at the Neville Street Station Hotel in Newcastle upon Tyne; William T. Harrowsmith, aged twenty-two, who worked as a porter at the Royal Promenade Hotel in Ormskirk; and Sarah Ann Beston, aged just twelve, who was employed as a domestic servant in the Commercial Hotel in Tadcaster. For these and countless others who took on menial labour in hotels, the ephemerality of their marks in historical record reflects both the transient and impermanent nature of hotel work, and the precarity and anonymity of the labouring class.

The anonymity inherent to menial hotel labour is affirmed not simply by the absence of these workers from the historical record, but also by their absence from and/or silence within literature. Beyond the novels of Bennett, who can safely be regarded as the most prolific chronicler of the hotel and its staff in fiction of the late nineteenth and early twentieth centuries, rounded depictions of workers carrying out domestic or menial tasks are few and far between. Their omission can be attributed in part to their relative invisibility within the space of the hotel. Sandoval-Strausz observes that those who occupied the 'bottom of the hotel work hierarchy were people who labored in the back of the house, intentionally kept in the hotel's service areas and away from guests' (2007, pp. 179–80). As has already been established, aside from Bennett, representations of hotels in literature of this period focus primarily upon the experiences of guests, meaning that the back areas, those spaces unseen by guests, remain unexplored by the majority of authors of this period, and consequently, so too are those staff confined to these spaces. The working-class background of these employees, and the relative lack of opportunity and education available to them in the long nineteenth century, contributed to their lack of mobility within the hotel, not only keeping them out of sight of guests, but more often than not precluding them from climbing the hierarchy of hotel work.

In much the same way that the size and location of a fictional hotel bedroom can aid in the deduction of a character's status, the hierarchy of hotel workers is clearly mapped onto the spaces to which they are assigned. In Bennett's *Imperial Palace*, the detailed and thorough depiction of these hotel staff areas, and the notable distinctions between them, denotes the hierarchical location of the employees housed within. The vast space beneath the hotel, for example, those 'bowels of the hotel' which accommodates many of the hotel's workers, and which encompasses their dining areas, is set in opposition to the luxurious spaces above. As she is led down into the basement by Evelyn, Violet observes that '[t]hey were in the Imperial Palace, but it was another Imperial Palace: no bright paint, no gilt, no decorations, no attempt to please the eye, little or no daylight, electric lamps but no lampshades; another world in which appearances had no importance and were indeed neglected' (Bennett 1969 [1930], p. 215). The lack of attention paid to décor or comfort throughout the many rooms of the basement not only marks this as a purely functional space of work—or, in the case of the dining hall, the brief respite from it—but also emphasises the relative unimportance, in the eyes of the hotel management, of the employees for whom this space is designated. In drawing attention to the 'neglected' nature of this space, Bennett's novel highlights the way in which those hotel staff who occupy it are similarly neglected and undervalued. Their lowly status is reinforced by contrasting depictions of the spaces occupied by those in positions of authority, higher up the staff hierarchy. Managers and heads of department have their own offices. Ceria the grill-room manager, for example, has such an office, and while '[t]he room was less than small; it was tiny; [...] it was [...] a piece of private territory' (Bennett 1969 [1930], p. 325). Ceria's occupation of this space is solely attributable to his managerial position, revealing that privacy for staff members within the hotel is a privilege afforded only to those with authority over others. Yet the relatively low importance of Ceria's role within the hotel is indicated by the emphasis placed upon the 'tiny' dimensions of the room, which stand in stark contrast to those of the office occupied by Evelyn, the hotel director. Evelyn's room is, above all, 'spacious' and has numerous decorative touches, such as the 'two vases of flowers, and [...] plants in a box on the window-sill' (Bennett 1969 [1930], p. 47). In addition to the room's generous proportions, the room is, thanks to the similarly 'spacious window' (Bennett 1969 [1930], p. 47), flooded with natural light, a luxury denied those working in 'the bowels of the hotel' who are granted 'little or no daylight' (Bennett 1969 [1930], p. 215). Like the bedrooms of guests, the hierarchy of hotel staff is clearly delineated by the size and décor of the spaces they occupy.

Yet while their position within the hotel, and in its hierarchy, may well have remained fairly static, many of those engaged in menial work in hotels were, much like their counterparts in domestic service, obliged to move from their homes in order to find employment. In her study of domestic servants, Light draws attention to just 'how temporary and mobile a form of employment service actually was', and notes that a large number of servants were 'migrant[s], travelling hundreds of miles to the city to live and work in a stranger's house' (2008, pp. 13–4). Like these servants, actual hotel workers like those listed above—Fanny Wilson, William T. Harrowsmith, and Sarah Ann Beston—would likely have travelled to the city from rural areas to seek domestic employment in hotels. This transience, however, was not limited to those engaged in menial and domestic labour within hotels—it was also the experience of semi-skilled workers, such as waiters, many of whom travelled much further, coming from abroad to work in British hotels. In an 1892 article on 'Work and Wages in Hotels and Restaurants', C.H. d'E Leppington notes the frequency with which foreign waiters secured employment in British hotels by undercutting the wages expected by English waiters. According to Leppington, the foreign waiter 'arrives here almost ignorant of the language, and accepts a low wage to secure a situation where he will have the opportunity of learning it' (1892, p. 754). Not only did foreign waiters accept lower wages, but they were also, Leppington argues, 'generally the superior of [their] English comrade[s]' (1892, p. 756). Receiving less payment while exceeding their English colleagues in skill, these foreign waiters—who largely travelled from European countries such as Italy, France, Germany, and Switzerland—emblematised the poor working conditions of waiters more generally. While Leppington notes that low wages were generally supplemented by tips, in the case of foreign waiters 'a percentage on [these] gains' were frequently given up to their employer (1892, p. 754). Alongside the paltry remuneration for their work, the security of their employment was typically non-existent, and Leppington highlights the brevity of their contracts, observing that '[w]aiters are engaged by the month, week, or day, and in some establishments they can leave or be discharged without notice' (1892, p. 755). And in addition to the low wages and precarity of their position, the long hours worked by waiters also meant, as Brenda Assael points out, 'that they often suffered varicose veins and swollen feet, as well as ill health more generally' (2018, p. 87). The reasons behind these health problems extended beyond the dining room into the waiters' accommodation, with Assael citing a 'claim by the *Waiters' Record*, the official publication of the Amalgamated Waiters' Society, 'that the bedrooms of waiters, who had been offered accommodation by their employers, were often badly ventilated', and confirms that this claim 'was endorsed by London County Council inspectors' reports' (2018, p. 87), a statistic echoed in the depictions of cramped and dingy staff quarters in novels such as Bennett's *Imperial Palace*. Yet though the rates of unfair and dangerous treatment of waiters in London in the late nineteenth and early twentieth century were high, there was equally, thanks to the burgeoning hotel and restaurant trade, a continuous high demand for waiting staff. This demand meant that waiters were, unlike those engaged in menial hotel labour, usually able to secure employment elsewhere with relative ease, Assael noting that, '[g]iven their mobility compared to domestic workers, waiters were in a more privileged position' (2018, p. 95). Crucially, while the poor working conditions they frequently faced are undeniable, the mobility of hotel waiters throughout this period was more often a matter of choice than absolute necessity, as was so often the case for their domestic counterparts.

Of the semi-skilled workers such as waiters whose position afforded them an increased level of mobility to those employed in the more menial roles in the hotel, very few of these were women. Indeed, the allocation of roles to hotel staff in the nineteenth and twentieth centuries (and still today) was heavily based on gendered divisions of labour. The term 'waitress' may well have been, as Assael notes, 'in widespread use by the 1840s and 1850s', but it was nevertheless 'used loosely and inconsistently, being applied to women who undertook a number of service functions in a variety of hostelries, and even to domestic servants' (2018, p. 113). In literature of the same period, waiting staff were depicted as overwhelmingly male, with the possible exceptions of the two barmaids in James Joyce's *Ulysses*. However, the mobility of Miss Douce and Miss Kennedy is itself questionable—throughout the 'Sirens' episode in which they appear, both women remain trapped behind the bar of the Ormond Hotel, the 'barmirror gildedlettered' endlessly reflecting them back into that confined space (Joyce 2008 [1922], p. 248). A lack of mobility is typical of fictional representations of female hotel workers in the late nineteenth and early twentieth centuries, though this more commonly takes the form of the type of employment to which they are restricted. Aside from the occasional hotel clerk, such as Miss Spencer in Bennett's *The Grand Babylon Hotel* (who during her employment remains, after all, more or less confined to her bureau), semi-skilled women in positions of authority are largely limited to the role of housekeeper, a job bound up entirely with domestic labour and its management.

The hotel housekeeper was responsible for overseeing the duties of the chambermaids who are, for all intents and purposes, in her employ. In very large hotels, as depicted in Bennett's Imperial Palace, there was likely to be one housekeeper assigned to each floor, with one head housekeeper in charge overall. The authority involved in this position was, as is evidenced by figures such as the aforementioned Minnie E. Albery, conducive to an increased level of mobility between establishments. Writing in 1908, hotel housekeeper Mary E. Palmer affirms that 'few hotels retain their heads of departments any great length of time, while the inferior working class remains in one hotel for many years, and often for a lifetime' (1908, p. 32). While Palmer here offers an American perspective, the same principle might well be applied to British hotels, whereby mobility is a privilege afforded only to semi-skilled and skilled workers. The skills required of a hotel housekeeper are numerous, ranging far beyond the menial labour of cleaning to managing a team of chambermaids, ensuring stocks of linen, cleaning supplies, and other sundries are replenished, hiring staff, and inspecting rooms down to the smallest detail several times a day. For Palmer, the profession of hotel housekeeper is both 'a science' and 'an artistic achievement in which everything is in its right place, is of the proper grade, shade, quality, and cleanliness, harmonizing in every particular' (1908, p. 34). Palmer's blending here of scientific and artistic attributes in her account of the work of the hotel housekeeper prefigures the rhetoric that became so popular in the British women's magazines of the interwar period, which emphasised the very same qualities in the work of the housewife in an attempt to professionalise this role. An article in the first issue of *Wife and Home*, for example, attested to the satisfaction to be gained from being the perfect housewife, declaring 'the career of the home-maker' to be 'the finest in the world' (Anon 1929, p. 35).[12] Indeed, the work of the professional housekeeper (either working in a hotel or a home) and that of the housewife differs only in its financial remuneration and in the accompanying acknowledgement that it is, in fact, work. The tasks themselves remain the same, and much like her counterparts in the

---

[12] 'Keeping House for Him', *Wife and Home*, October 1929, p. 35.

private home—the professional housekeeper and the housewife—the hotel housekeeper carries out the countless daily requirements of domestic management, only on a grander scale.

This kind of work is, of course, inherently gendered in the way that is has been historically aligned with and assigned to women, and its distribution within the hotel conforms to this domestic ideology. In literary representations of hotels in the nineteenth and twentieth centuries, the roles of housekeepers and chambermaids are exclusively filled by female characters. Though their work frequently remains unmentioned or glossed over, it is in Bennett's *Imperial Palace*, once again, that an account of their labour can be found. When, for example, Mrs O'Riordan, the longstanding head housekeeper of the Imperial Palace, succumbs to an attack of pleurisy, Evelyn finally recognises the extent of her role, and the demands placed upon her:

> He appreciated, now, the tremendous effort which it must have entailed for her: keeping the peace among a pack of women and girls; mollifying and kowtowing to a pack of hypercritical visitors; trying to prevent the unscrupulous visitors from stealing coat-hangers and ashtrays and even electroplate—for the Palace, like all hotels, was no better than a den of well-dressed thieves; watching over the sewing-repairs; placating the Works Department, especially when trouble arose between the Works carpenters and her own private carpenters who carpentered exclusively within the hotel; pestering and being pestered by the electricians; dictating her wordy letters; passing on complaints about room-meals to the grill-room chef; dashing herself against the insensate rock which was Mr. Cousin; getting up early and going to bed late; always, always being sweetly diplomatic with the panjandrum; and always, always pretending that she allowed nothing to worry her or ever would! (Bennett 1969 [1930], p. 187)

Not only are the tasks listed here numerous and varied, calling for exacting management and organisational skills, but the majority involve a significant degree of emotional labour. Mrs O'Riordan must 'keep the peace' between her own staff, among whom the potential for unruliness and infighting is denoted by the (somewhat problematic) description of them as 'a pack'. She must 'mollify' the guests, and, in her dealings with male staff, she must 'placate' those in the Works Department, and patiently put up with 'being pestered by the electricians'. Her interactions with those above her (also male) are similarly emotionally draining. Evelyn's deputy, the hotel manager Mr Cousin, is described as an 'insensate rock', an immovable, stoic presence against which Mrs O'Riordan must 'dash herself'. This strikingly violent sacrificial imagery reveals not only the way in which the gendered division of labour extends beyond the menial hotel workers to those in positions of authority, but also hints at the devastating impact of this upon female members of staff such as Mrs O'Riordan, who are forced by uncooperative male colleagues to shoulder the burden of the necessary emotional work within the hotel.

Though the nature of the hotel as a business requires that the majority of its employees are engaged in catering to and looking after its guests, it is the work of its female employees—its housekeepers and chambermaids—that is most deeply rooted in practices of care. Their domestic labour involves caring for a space and those within it—maintaining and sustaining spaces and people in a day-to-day, cyclical fashion. This is also work that is resolutely bound up with corporeality. The body is present in the undeniably physical aspect of domestic labour, in the repetitive and often strenuous bodily actions of cleaning that, as it removes traces of dirt and wear from the hotel (or home) and its furnishings, simultaneously leaves its trace on the hands, feet, and knees in the form of callouses, bruises, and dry, cracked skin.[13] It is present in the dirt and mess to be cleaned that is itself the product of bodies, and, in a hotel, exclusively of bodies other than one's own. The very gendering of this work—the tendency, overwhelming in hotels like Bennett's Imperial Palace, for it to be carried out by women—is itself also haunted by the body, originating as it does from the deep-seated alliance within much western philosophical thought of femininity with corporeality. This is an alliance that stems from the opposition between mind and body that is articulated in the dualism of the Cartesian *cogito*. As Elizabeth Grosz maintains, 'the correlation and association of the mind/body opposition with the opposition between male and female, where man and mind, woman and body, become representationally aligned' (1994, p. 4). This mind/body dualism so prevalent in Western thought and culture is therefore of particular interest to feminist theorists, many of whom maintain that it reveals significant truths about, and even the reasons behind, the position of women in society. Many such thinkers have argued that it is the supposed link to embodiment that has resulted in women being excluded from the public sphere of

---

[13] I here follow Ahmed (2006) in calling for a philosophy, or more specifically a phenomenology, of housework.

social and political freedoms, instead relegated to the domestic sphere of housework, child-rearing, and general day-to-day maintenance and support of the lives of their male counterparts.[14] As Simone de Beauvoir so succinctly maintains, '[w]oman is destined to maintain the species and care for the home' (2010 [1949], p. 455). Just as in the domestic space of the home, the rigid and pronounced gendered division of labour within the hotel of the nineteenth and twentieth centuries is produced and sustained by the patriarchal alliance of femininity with corporeality.

Of course, for those women with the means and mobility to stay in the hotel, the space acts as a respite from such gendered labour. As discussed in the previous chapter, in literature of this period, female guests frequently find in the hotel an escape from domestic drudgery. The hotel allows them to relinquish the physical, intellectual, and emotional work involved in running a home. In Elizabeth Bowen's *The Hotel*, for example, the group of women gathered in the hotel drawing room agree that the domesticity that 'they had all escaped was terrible', with one woman adding that the effort required to 'make a home [...] nearly kills one' (Bowen 2003 [1927], p. 62). Unwilling to commit to a lifetime of housework and homemaking, this same woman adds that she has chosen instead 'to travel and meet people', moving from one hotel to the next to avoid the cyclical routine of the housewife. Similarly, for Sasha, the protagonist of Rhys's *Good Morning, Midnight*, having one's bedding changed by a hotel chambermaid is the ultimate extravagance, as she reflects 'That's my idea of luxury—to have the sheets changed every day and twice on Sundays. That's my idea of the power of money' (Rhys 1969 [1939], p. 68). This allusion to 'the power of money', however, is a reminder of the shadowy presence of the staff who are paid to carry out this work. While the figure of the chambermaid appears fairly frequently in novels of the nineteenth and twentieth centuries, her work does not, and she is rarely if ever depicted in literature carrying out the routine domestic tasks that constitute her role.

In her account of the lives of hotel staff in the early twentieth century, former hotel receptionist Dorothy Gray outlines the typical working day of the chambermaid in this period:

---

[14] For further discussion of the impact of women's embodiment upon their situation and oppression, see Moira Gatens, *Imaginary Bodies: Ethics, Power, and Corporeality* (London: Routledge, 1996); Young, *On Female Body Experience*; and Beauvoir, *The Second Sex*.

A list of arrivals and departures will have been given out from the office, and they go to the linen-room for their clean sheets and pillow-cases, having first collected the soiled ones. Then they make the beds and tidy up the wash-stands (if any) in each room before beginning again on a second round, this time to sweep, dust, and fill up water jugs and bottles. (1945, p. 164)

Recalling the day of the housewife in its repetitive nature, the cyclical nature of her work confers a level of immobility upon the hotel chamber-maid. Unlikely to progress beyond this menial role within the hierarchy of hotel employment, she remains caught in the unvarying, routine existence of domestic labour. The freedom, however brief, of the female hotel guest from this cycle is only made possible by the entrapment of another woman within it. Contemplating the work of the chambermaid in Bennett's *Imperial Palace*, Evelyn reflects that while the 'women-guests are fast asleep on their private embroidered pillows upstairs, all in silk pyjamas and nighties', the chambermaids 'have cleaned their homes and got breakfasts and washed children and been sworn at probably, some of them, and walked a mile or two through the streets, and put on their overalls, and here they are swilling and dusting like the devil!' (Bennett 1969 [1930], p. 34). The burden of domestic labour is thus merely transferred onto other women, and onto those whose class background precludes their own evasion of that labour, an exchange which remains unavoidably prob-lematic from a feminist perspective. In escaping the drudgery of the domestic realm, female hotel guests effectively trap other women in the same 'battle against dust and dirt' (Beauvoir 2010 [1949], p. 470). Their mobility is thus predicated upon the immobility of the chambermaid.

To consign the chambermaid to absolute immobility is, however, to oversimplify the nature of her role, and to ignore the potential for agency that lies within it. While the chambermaid may well be trapped in that cycli-cal 'battle against dust and dirt', her role necessitates her movement—typi-cally unseen—through the rooms of guests to clean them, thus imbuing her with a unique kind of mobility within the hotel. This was, however, a mobil-ity that frequently inspired uneasiness in hotel guests of the nineteenth and twentieth centuries. The fears of hotel guests regarding chambermaids usu-ally, as Sandoval-Strausz points out, 'sprang from what they could not see them doing' and ranged from worrying about the safety and security of their personal belongings, to more deep-seated anxieties 'that centred on more primal, personal, bodily concerns' (2007, p. 181). In her specific tasks of stripping bed sheets and cleaning rooms, the chambermaid was able to gain access to and scrutinise the bodily functions of the hotel guests in a way that no other member of hotel staff could. Like their domestic counterparts, who were, Light argues, 'the body's keepers, protecting its entrances and exits', the hotel chambermaid was 'privy to its secrets and its chambers' (2008, p. 4). The fears of hotel guests that the chambermaid might discover their most intimate secrets were not entirely without precedent. As Joseph Bristow notes, during the Oscar Wilde trials of 1895, two chambermaids at the Savoy Hotel, Jane Margaret Cotter and Emily Becca, gave damning evidence that they had 'discovered faecal stains on the bed linens in Wilde's room', along with 'comparable stains on towels, [...] face powder on one of the pillows and excrement on a utensil in the room' (2016, p. 49). Similarly, in her brief appearances in literature of this period, the uneasiness that the chambermaid inspires in the hotel guest is inextricably linked to sexuality, to the fear that she might uncover the closely guarded secrets of bodily intimacies. In fiction, such anxieties are often reified by the constant presence of the chambermaids who continue to watch guests within the supposed privacy of their rooms. The maid who shows Karen and Max to their room in the Ram's Head Inn in Bowen's *The House in Paris*, for example, at first refuses to leave: 'the maid who would not go refolded a towel over a jug; Number Nine shuffled with servants staring into your back' (Bowen 1998 [1935], p. 150). In *To the North*, the chambermaid of Emmeline and Markie's Parisian hotel attempts to engage Emmeline in conversation in her room, seemingly wishing to find out if they are married by enquiring if she and her 'husband' are enjoying their stay (Bowen 1987 [1932], p. 147). In these and other examples, the anxieties of the guests in question prove unfounded, and the chambermaid never reveals her secrets.[15] Nevertheless, the palpable suspicion engendered by chambermaids is bound up with issues of class, gender, and surveillance, wherein she who literally cleans up the dirt of these characters, knows in detail the personal behaviours and secrets of the guests who dismiss her. She may well, in one sense, be trapped in a cycle of domestic labour, but the unsupervised nature of the chambermaid's mobility throughout the bedrooms of the hotel endows her with a unique potential for agency.

*   *   *

---

[15] The exceptions to this were to be found in divorce cases. Under the Matrimonial Causes Act of 1923, adultery by either husband or wife was the sole acceptable ground for divorce. Hotels were used frequently by those seeking divorce so that chambermaids could 'discover' the adultery taking place, and later provide evidence in the divorce proceedings. In Evelyn Waugh's 1934 novel, *A Handful of Dust*, protagonist Tony Last spends a weekend in a Brighton hotel with a prostitute (albeit without engaging in sexual activity) in order to provide evidence for the divorce requested by his wife.

Despite their notable absence throughout much nineteenth- and twentieth-century literature, the hidden back areas of the hotel reveal as much as, if not more than, any other space within the hotel about the intricacies of the class divisions and the ideologies that sustained and perpetuated these during this period. The rigid, hierarchical organisation of these spaces exposes the processes of management and the drive for profit that underpinned the hotel as a business, and situates the hotel firmly within the rapid developments in corporate capitalism that gripped Britain in the mid-nineteenth century. Typically depicted in literature as a figure concerned first and foremost with financial gain, the hotel manager is often the embodiment of this corporate endeavour, overseeing the strict organisation of the staff areas according to capitalist principles of maximising the production of the workforce. As this chapter has shown, these principles frequently demanded the restriction of staff mobility to certain areas within the hotel, and often, in the case of those engaged in more domestic and menial labour, the limitation of their visibility.

The relative invisibility of hotel staff is matched by their absence in literature, and the infrequency with which they and the spaces they occupy appear across the literature of this period betrays a great deal about the exclusionary nature of the work of a large proportion of writers. In the majority of novels set in or featuring hotels, the spatiality featured is predominantly that of the front of house, public corridors, and bedrooms—those areas that are occupied by the hotel guest. Hidden from its guests, the hotel's back areas are, on the whole, hidden from the reader, and so too, consequently, are the narratives of the staff who populate them. The stories of hotel workers thus remain largely untold and unimagined, perhaps because many writers were unable to imagine the lives of those engaged in domestic and menial labour. This inability was at least acknowledged by some—in her diaries of 1940, for example, Woolf contemplated the history of her cook and housekeeper, Mabel Haskins, reflecting, 'Could I write it, how profoundly succulent it [would] be' (Woolf 1984). However, as Light notes, Woolf acknowledged that 'she couldn't write it. Faced with Mabel's deference she saw only "the bloodless servitude of the domestic poor." [...] when she cast her portrait of Mabel it became' (Light 2008, p. 264), in Woolf's words, 'something like an Arnold Bennett novel' (1984). Like so many others of her class, despite having lived alongside domestic servants for her entire life, Woolf was unable to see beyond their role and their work to the lives that lay beyond. That she is anxious not to replicate the work of Arnold Bennett is particularly telling. Woolf's disdain for Bennett's work had, of course, by this point been long established, but as this chapter has conclusively demonstrated, Bennett was one of the few writers—if not the only—to engage with and depict the characters of hotel staff in any real detail. As Light so pertinently observes, '[r]eading Arnold Bennett was the nearest [Woolf] had come to such lives' (2008, p. 264), and the same might well be said for many other modernist writers within whose novels the domestic worker is a conspicuous absence.

In this, however, as in so many other instances concerning the literary hotel, the boundaries between modernism and the middlebrow are by no means clear-cut. While Bennett may well have devoted an entire novel to the staff of the Imperial Palace Hotel, the characters who take centre stage are those middle and lower-middle-class characters in positions of authority. In this focus, Bennett does not differ hugely from canonical modernist writers such as Joyce, whose protagonist Leopold Bloom is a resolutely lower-middle-class everyman. Largely absent from both, however, are the lives and histories of the working classes. Scouring literature of the nineteenth and twentieth centuries for traces of domestic and menial staff within the hotel crystallises the extent to which such voices are sidelined, appearing fleetingly if at all, and only then filtered through the (frequently critical) perspective of their employers or the hotel guests. Reading the back areas of the hotel in literature thus lays bare the patterns of exclusion and marginalisation that cut deeply across the critical categories of modernism and the middlebrow.

REFERENCES

Ahmed, Sara. 2006. *Queer Phenomenology: Orientations, Objects, Others*. Durham: Duke University Press.

Anon. 1846. Continental Inns. *Chambers's Edinburgh Journal*, 142, 189–190, September 19.

———. 1866. Monster Hotels. *The London Reader of Literature, Science, Art and General Information*, 7.181, 689.

———. 1871. Manchester Hotels. *The Sphinx*, 4.131, 43–44, February 11.

———. 1882. Editorial. *The Hotel World*, 1.12, 4, March 22.

———. 1895. The Hotel Cecil. *The Hotel & Restaurant World*, 1, 31–34, December.

———. 1907. Hotel Planning. *The British Architect*, 259, April 12.

———. 1929. Keeping House for Him. *Wife and Home*, 35, October 1.

Assael, Brenda. 2018. *The London Restaurant, 1840–1914*. Oxford: Oxford University Press.

de Beauvoir, Simone. 2010 [1949]. *The Second Sex*. Translated by Constance Borde and Sheila Malovany-Chevalier. London: Vintage.

Bennett, Arnold. 1969 [1930]. *Imperial Palace*. London: Cassel & Co.

Berger, Molly W. 2011. *Hotel Dreams: Luxury, Technology, and Urban Ambition in America, 1829–1929*. Baltimore: The Johns Hopkins University Press.

Bowen, Elizabeth. 1987 [1932]. *To the North*. London: Penguin.

———. 1998 [1935]. *The House in Paris*. London: Vintage.

———. 2003 [1927]. *The Hotel*. London: Vintage.

Bristow, Joseph. 2016. The Blackmailer and the Sodomite: Oscar Wilde on Trial. *Feminist Theory* 17 (1): 41–62.

Conrad, Joseph. 2004 [1907]. *The Secret Agent*. Oxford: Oxford University Press.

Eliot, T.S. 1971 [1922]. *The Waste Land, and Other Poems*. London: Faber & Faber.

F.A. 1872. English Hotel Life. *London Society: An Illustrated Magazine of Light and Amusing Literature for the Hours of Relaxation*, 22.129, 256–261, September.

Gray, Dorothy. 1945. *Hotel Receptionist: A Balanced But Entertaining Account of Hotel Life as Seen by the Staff*. London: George Allen Unwin.

Grosz, Elizabeth. 1994. *Volatile Bodies: Toward a Corporeal Feminism*. Bloomington: Indiana University Press.

Gurney, Peter J. 2012. Co-Operation and the 'New Consumerism' in Interwar England. *Business History* 54 (6): 905–924.

Higgins, Richard. 2008. Feeling Like a Clerk in H.G. Wells. *Victorian Studies* 50 (3): 457–475.

Johnson, Paul. 2010. *Making the Market: Victorian Origins of Corporate Capitalism*. Cambridge: Cambridge University Press.

Joyce, James. 2008 [1922]. *Ulysses*. Edited by Jeri Johnson. Oxford: Oxford University Press.

Leppington, C.H. d'E. 1892. Work and Wages in Hotels and Restaurants. *Good Words* 33 (Jan.): 754–758.

Light, Alison. 2008. *Mrs Woolf and the Servants: An Intimate History of Domestic Life in Bloomsbury*. New York: Bloomsbury.

Marx, Karl. 1909 [1867]. *Capital: A Critique of Political Economy*, vol. I. Chicago: Charles H. Kerr & Co.

Micklethwait, John, and Adrian Wooldridge. 2005. *The Company: A Short History of a Revolutionary Idea*. London: Phoenix.

Moore, Robbie. 2012. Henry James, Hotels, and the Invention of Disposable Space. *Modernist Cultures* 7 (2): 254–278.

Palmer, Mary E. 1908. *Guide to Hotel Housekeeping*. Charleston, WV: Tribune Printing Company.

Rhys, Jean. 1969 [1939]. *Good Morning, Midnight*. London: Penguin.

Sandoval-Strausz, A.K. 2007. *Hotel: An American History*. New Haven: Yale University Press.

Sinclair, May. 1908. *Kitty Tailleur*. London: Archibald Constable & Co.

Smith, Albert. 1858 [1855]. *The English Hotel Nuisance*. 2nd ed. London: Bradbury & Evans.

Taylor, Derek. 1977. *Fortune, Fame, & Folly: British Hotels and Catering from 1878 to 1978*. Andover: Chapel River Press.

Taylor, Derek, and David Bush. 1974. *The Golden Age of British Hotels*. London: Northwood.

Wells, H.G. 1902. *Anticipations of the Reaction of Mechanical and Scientific Progress Upon Human Life and Thought*. London: Chapman & Hall.

———. 2005 [1905]. *Kipps*. Edited by Simon J. James. London: Penguin.

Woolf, Virginia. 1984. Diary Entry: 10 October 1940. In *The Diary of Virginia Woolf*, ed. Anne Olivier Bell and Andrew McNeillie, 5 vols., V. London: Hogarth Press.

———. 2009 [1915]. *The Voyage Out*. Oxford: Oxford University Press.

CHAPTER 7

Afterword

In what is now a largely forgotten article in *The Pall Mall Magazine* in August 1909, Arnold Bennett, that great chronicler of hotels, offered an in-depth rumination on the architecture and physiognomy of the hotel. According to Bennett, the splendour of grand hotels had, in the late nineteenth and early twentieth centuries, been continually overlooked and 'unseen', shrouded in 'the mists and distortions which prejudice has created' (Bennett 1909, p. 220). This lack of appreciation was, Bennett suggested, due to 'the shackles of utility, in which the architecture of hotels has to evolve' (1909, p. 223), and was an attitude of which he himself, as he admits, had previously been guilty, regarding the hotel in a manner 'as abusive and violent as Ruskin's towards railways' (Bennett 1909, p. 220). While this seemingly brief allusion to John Ruskin may appear to merely delineate Bennett's own former ignorance concerning the beauty and design of hotel architecture, it is perhaps worth pausing here to unpack the significance of Ruskin in this context.

Ruskin was, of course, famously opposed to the development of the railways, and was, Jeffrey Richards notes, a vociferous proponent of 'the anti-railway tendency in the nineteenth century' (1995, p. 123).[1] Ruskin attacked the railways on a number of fronts, and not least in terms of the

---

[1] Ruskin was, for example, a key member of the Lake District Defence Society that was established in 1883, and which included among its ranks figures such as William Morris, Matthew Arnold, Octavia Hill, Alfred Lord Tennyson, and Robert Browning. The concerted

© The Author(s) 2019
E. Short, *Mobility and the Hotel in Modern Literature*,
Studies in Mobilities, Literature, and Culture,
https://doi.org/10.1007/978-3-030-22129-4_7

deleterious effect that, he maintained, travelling by rail had on the moral fibre of British society. As Richards points out, for Ruskin, the railway 'interfered with the process of detailed observation, it encouraged mental torpor, and it destroyed the very scenery that the traveller should be observing' (1995, p. 135). The railway was, according to Ruskin, 'a mere passing fever, half-speculative, half-childish', and he maintained:

> No changing of place at a hundred miles an hour, nor making of stuffs a thousand yards a minute, will make us one whit stronger, happier, or wiser. There was always more in the world than men could see, walked they ever so slowly; they will see it no better for going fast. [...] A fool always wants to shorten space and time: a wise man wants to lengthen both. A fool wants to kill space and time: a wise man, first to gain them, then to animate them. Your railroad, when you come to understand it, is only a device for making the world smaller. (Ruskin 1904 [1856], pp. 380–1)

The mobility afforded by the railway, that very same mobility with which, as noted in the Introduction to this book, the hotel was so heavily bound up in the nineteenth and early twentieth centuries, was regarded by Ruskin as corroding the integrity and the intelligence of those who used it. The ability to properly view and appreciate the landscape was, according to Ruskin, lost to the newfound speed of travel, and with it the potential for self-improvement and enrichment through interacting with the natural world. In an article that stresses the importance of pausing to view the grand hotel in the natural landscape in order to fully appreciate its design, Bennett's reference to Ruskin thus takes on an added significance.

By drawing on Ruskin's well-known opposition to the railways, Bennett plays upon the curious tension between mobility and stasis that, as has been observed at several points throughout this book, characterises the hotel in modernity. Bennett understood more than most the inherent transience of the hotel existence. From the international intrigue of *The Grand Babylon Hotel* (1902) to the relentless activity of hotel employees, and their movements within the staff hierarchy detailed in *Imperial Palace* (1930), Bennett—like so many authors in this period—constructed the hotel in his novels as first and foremost a space of mobility. Perhaps more crucially, however, Bennett's allusion to Ruskin here evokes late nineteenth-century anxieties concerning the effect of increased mobility upon morality.

conservation efforts of the Society were instrumental in preventing any further development of the railway into the Lake District after 1887. See Richards (1995, p. 130).

The pervasive cultural associations of the hotel with illicit sexuality, discussed at length in Chap. 5 of this book, were arguably in no small part down to such anxieties. The hotel's very mobility was that which, for many, called its morality into question. But Bennett argued that viewing the grand hotel 'grandiosely—that is to say, [...] with a large sweep of the eye, and from a distance', enabled a fuller appreciation of the hotel's 'moral significance', which was itself, he maintained, intrinsically linked to the 'form' and structure of the building (1909, p. 220). For Bennett, the morality of the hotel is to be found in its primary purpose: to provide shelter and accommodation for its guests. Summarising the process of hotel construction as 'an unaffected human activity' that 'endeavour[s] to achieve an honest utilitarian end' (Bennett 1909, p. 222), Bennett highlights further 'the democratic quality' of the hotel, which

> necessitates an external monotony of detail. In general, all the rooms on each floor must resemble each other, possessing the same advantages. [...] The beholder, before abruptly condemning that uniformity of feature which is the chief characteristic of the hotel [...] must reflect that this is the natural outer expression of the spirit and needs of the hotel, and that it neither can nor ought to be disguised. It is of the very essence of the building. (1909, p. 224)

Bennett here demonstrates an in-depth awareness of 'the social microcosm of a hotel' (1909, p. 224), an awareness which underpins his writing. More importantly, however, Bennett offers an implicit rebuttal to commentators such as Ruskin who aligned technologies of transport, and the increased mobility they afforded, with moral degeneration. Through the space of the hotel, Bennett emphasises a morality of a different, less exclusionary kind, one that, in its 'uniformity of feature', is predicated upon ensuring that all guests have access to the same kinds of spaces.[2] Bennett's reading of the hotel locates this both as a space of mobility and as one of inherent equality, effectively forging a link between the two and thereby countering the conservative and essentially elitist attitudes of those such as Ruskin that sought to restrict the mobility of

---

[2] Of course, as this book has shown at various points, the hotel, and particularly the grand hotel to which Bennett refers here, can hardly be understood as truly democratic in the sense that accommodation within it is only available to those who can afford it, and that the staff hierarchy is rarely traversable for those employed in the more menial, domestic work of the hotel.

the wider population. For Bennett, and for writers as diverse as Virginia Woolf and May Sinclair, Jean Rhys and H.G. Wells, Elizabeth Bowen and Henry Green, Dorothy Richardson and James Joyce, the hotel provides a unique and invaluable space through which to interrogate mobility, and more broadly the social and cultural conditions of modernity, particularly in terms of class, gender, sexuality, and nationality.

I argued in the Introduction to this book that it is through the space of the hotel that we can come to redistribute cultural value that has previously been so unevenly assigned. The critical boundaries of modernism, middlebrow, and popular literature have, until very recently, been structured according to a hierarchy of literary value that prioritises modernist fiction, and which all too often positions middlebrow and popular fiction as modernism's 'other'. My approach in this book has not been to break down or dismantle these boundaries, but to question and reassess the foundations upon which they are constructed through an analysis of the ways in which modernist, middlebrow, and popular literature explore similar themes, questions, and concepts. For example, as I have demonstrated throughout this book, reading the hotel in literature of the late nineteenth and early twentieth centuries reveals a preoccupation with the phenomenological relationship between the body and space to be widespread. The dialogic relationship between the embodied subject and space is articulated and explored in the work of Rhys, Bowen, and Richardson, while the powerfully affective capacity of the various spaces within the hotel is made plain in the excruciating shame of Wells's Kipps in the hotel dining room, as well as of that of Bennett's Gracie Savott in the hotel kitchens. While writers such as Bowen and Winifred Holtby position the hotel as a space away from the restrictive morality of the home in which women are able to explore their sexual desires, others such as Rhys and Wells complicate this through an exploration of the coercive capacity of the hotel bedroom. As I demonstrated in my discussion of the hotel narrative in Chaps. 2 and 3, while modernist writers such as Woolf and Ford Madox Ford were engaged in experiments with narrative form, so too were middlebrow writers like Bennett who used the space of the hotel to shape and structure their narratives. As a unique space of mobility, and in its resistance to being confined within definitions of public or private, the hotel offers crucial insight into the shifting tensions and ideologies of modernity.

REFERENCES

Bennett, Arnold. 1909. The Hotel on the Landscape. *The Pall Mall Magazine* 44 (196): 219–225.

Richards, Jeffrey. 1995. The Role of the Railways. In *Ruskin and Environment: The Storm-Cloud of the Nineteenth Century*, ed. Michael Wheeler, 123–143. Manchester: Manchester University Press.

Ruskin, John. 1904 [1856]. Modern Painters III. In *The Works of John Ruskin: Library Edition*, ed. E.T. Cook and Alexander Wedderburn. London: George Allen.

INDEX[1]

---

[1] Note: Page numbers followed by 'n' refer to notes.

219

CPI Antony Rowe
Eastbourne, UK
December 02, 2019